Wellington and the Pyrenees Campaign

VOLUME I

Wellington and the Pyrenees Campaign

VOLUME I
From Vitoria to the Bidassoa

F. C. Beatson

*Wellington and the Pyrenees Campaign Volume I:
from Vitoria to the Bidassoa*
by F. C. Beatson

Published by Leonaur Ltd

Content original to this edition and the presentation of the text in this formcopyright © 2007 Leonaur Ltd

First published 1914

ISBN: 978-1-84677-263-4 (hardcover)
ISBN: 978-1-84677-264-1 (softcover)

http://www.leonaur.com

Publisher's Note

The opinions expressed in this book are those of the author and are not necessarily those of the publisher.

Contents

Preface	7
Introductory	9
The French Retreat After Vitoria	13
France at Bay	26
The Western Pyrenees	32
The French Prepare to Defend France	39
The Distribution of the Allies	44
Soult's Plan of Campaign	57
The French Advance	71
Soult's Advance on Pamplona	76
The Fight at the Maya Pass	91
Retreat of Sir L. Cole	110
Events of July 27	121
The First Battle of Sorauren	137
A Long Drawing of Breath	149
Second Battle Of Sorauren	160
The Retreat of the French	180
The Retreat of the French	191
Soult's Failure	207
Appendices	225
Maps	253

Preface

The story of the operations in the western Pyrenees is perhaps not so generally well known as are some other phases of the Peninsular War.

It is, however, full of interest as well for the general reader who finds pleasure in history as for the soldier. Never were the stubborn valour of the British soldier of all ranks of that old army and the quickness and decision of its great commander more signally displayed than in those nine days of desperate and almost continuous fighting amongst the ridges and valleys of those mountains.

Success in war is said to depend more on moral than on physical qualities. That men clothed, armed, and accoutred as were the British soldiers of those times, could march and fight as they did in such a country proves their possession in a high degree of those latter qualities. But perhaps no better evidence of the truth of the above statement could be found than is furnished by these operations. For no one who reads the accounts of men who took part in them can fail to be struck by the spirit which animated the allied army then at the height of its efficiency.

Officers and men considered it a matter of course that, given reasonably equal terms, they would beat the French wherever and whenever they met them. This absolute confidence in themselves had its foundation in an equal confidence in their leader.

Though the operations took place over a hundred years ago, there would still seem to be lessons for soldiers in them. The employment of a covering force is still not an infrequent necessity in war. For its working to be successful requires in the main the same general arrangements and the same qualities now as then from commander and his troops.

It has been the writer's aim to record the facts as accurately as they can be ascertained rather than to comment on the operations. Such criticisms and attempted explanations as are given are put forward with diffidence.

In one respect especially it is thought the story will be of interest to British officers, for in the Pyrenees the British Army had its first experience on a large scale in one of those hill campaigns in which both it and the Indian army have since so often taken part. Though opposed to an enemy of a different class, it would seem that not a few of the lessons learnt from fighting on and beyond the north-west frontier of India are foreshadowed by the experiences of these earlier operations.

I am indebted to Mr. Hilaire Belloc for permission to quote from his interesting book, *The Pyrenees*; as also to the publishers, Messrs. Methuen and Co.; to the Committee of the Royal Artillery Institution for allowing me to give extracts from the Dickson Manuscripts edited by Major J. H. Leslie; also to the Chief of the General Staff of the French army for permission to examine the records of the campaign in the Archives Historiques of the Ministry of War, and to Captain Vidal de la Blache for leave to quote from his articles, *"La bataille de Sorauren,"* in the *Revue d'Histoire,* September to December 1912. To all the above, as well as to living authors of other works quoted from, I tender my grateful acknowledgments.

F. C. Beatson

Note: In the district of the operations the time of sunrise towards end of July is about thirty minutes later than at Greenwich and sunset about the same time earlier.

CHAPTER 1

Introductory

There were sad, angry, and some despairing hearts in Britain when the news came of the retreat of Wellington's allied army from Burgos in October 1812. Despite brilliant successes gained, the campaign had ended with yet another retreat to Portugal, and with Spain still in the grip of the French armies. Hope deferred was having its usual result; and it might have been that both the ministry at home and the war in the Peninsula would in consequence have collapsed, had not the intelligence of Napoleon's disastrous retreat from Moscow arrived in the very nick of time. The news gave fresh impetus and strength to the determination to see the war through, which happily filled the majority of Britons of that day. Had the French been victorious in Russia, they could have maintained the war in Spain for years. Perhaps Napoleon himself might have gone there; and if he had, who shall say what the result might have been?

But now in 1813 the war in the Peninsula was, in its turn, to influence affairs on the Continent, "No reflex of fortune dims the glory of Vitoria." The victory of June 21 not only freed all but the north-east corner of Spain from French dominion but was to have a wider and more important result in its effect on the negotiations for peace then in progress between Napoleon and the Great Powers.

Defeated by Napoleon at Lutzen and Bautzen in May 1813, the allied armies of Russia and Prussia had retreated into Silesia. Both sides now desired a suspension of hostilities. The allied forces were in much confusion, and there was friction between the Russian and Prussian commanders. Napoleon wanted time to complete the reorganization of his cavalry, and also to find out what Austria intended to do. An armistice from June 4 to July 20 was signed at Poischwitz. Austria was playing a waiting game and negotiating with both sides. The outcome was the assembly of a Congress at Prague to discuss terms of a general peace.

Probably none of the Powers were very sincere in their desire for it. Napoleon, knowing the hard terms on which alone he was likely to obtain it, certainly was not. He wanted time, and took advantage of the negotiations regarding the Congress to get the armistice extended to August 10. On the very night (June 30) this was agreed to, he received the first report of the battle of Vitoria. Napoleon did all he could to suppress the news, but effective steps had been taken in London to inform the Powers and make it generally known on the Continent.[1] On July 12 it reached the allied monarchs at Trachenburg, and its effect was immediate and powerful. The news stiffened the allies in their resolution to continue hostilities, and Austria declared for war unless all her demands were conceded.[2]

But Napoleon would have none of them. At midnight on August 10 when the armistice expired, the beacon fires on

---

1. Lord Liverpool to Wellington, July 3, 1813. J. W. Croker to Wellington. "We are dispatching your Gazette in French, Dutch, and German to all corners of Europe." In the Archives de Guerre in Paris is a printed copy which a British cruiser obliged French fishermen off the coast of Fecamp to take on July 8, 1813.
2. Count Nugent to Wellington, Prague, July 27, 1813. "The action (Vitoria) is acknowledged by every one to be the most glorious of the whole twenty years war, and besides its importance relative to Spain, it is far more so by its influence on the state of affairs here. The account of the state of affairs in Spain and your plans, in short everything you desired me to say, had the greatest effect and contributed very much to the division of the Austrian Government, and the battle of Vitoria, I think, finished the matter." Wellington, Suppy. Dispatches.

the heights of Riesengebirge flashed forth the news to the allied camps in Silesia that the march of their columns into Bohemia might begin. So commenced the campaign which was to end with Napoleon's first abdication on April 6, 1814.

The operations, the story of which I propose to tell, are those connected with the gallant but unsuccessful attempt of a brave and able soldier to retrieve the defeat of the French army at Vitoria. The primary cause of that defeat and all that led up to it, was undoubtedly the inefficiency of the higher command. No one knew this better than Napoleon. He had already had many proofs of the inefficiency as a military commander of *"ce pauvre Joseph, dont les plans les mesures et les combinaisons n'étaient pas de notre temps."*[1] Now that Spain was all but lost to him it was time to act, and give his army a new commander. Napoleon chose Soult, Duke of Dalmatia.

Born, as was Wellington, in 1769, Soult was then forty-four years of age, and had been a Marshal of France since 1804. A hard and proud man, he was an able soldier of great activity and much administrative capacity. Until his recall from Spain in March 1813, on account of grave friction between him and King Joseph, he had served there during the whole of the war. He was, therefore, no stranger to the army he was to command, and that army had unbounded confidence in him. Nor was he unacquainted with Wellington's methods and his army. Under the circumstances a better appointment could not perhaps have been made, and he was not an unworthy opponent to pit against the British General.

Appointed to the command and nominated Lieutenant-General of the Emperor by decree of July 1, 1813, Soult left Dresden the same day and arrived at Bayonne on the 12th. His instructions were to reorganize the army and its services,

---

1. *Mémoires de Sainte-Hélène.*
2. *Correspondance de Napoleon I*, Dresden, July 1, 1813. No. 20,208. "You will take all necessary measures to re-establish my affairs in Spain and to relieve Pamplona and San Sebastian. To avoid all difficulties, I have nominated you my Lieutenant-General."

to take the offensive and relieve Pamplona and San Sebastian.[2] On July 5 Napoleon wrote as follows to the Count de Cessac, Minister of War Administrations:[1]

> I have given the Duke of Dalmatia full authority to re-organize the army. I have forbidden the King of Spain to interfere in my affairs, and I suppose that the Duke of Dalmatia will also cause Marshal Jourdan to withdraw from the army. Unless the losses are much greater than I know at present, I hope that 100,000 men will soon be assembled on the Bidassoa and before the pass of Jaca, and that as soon as you can provide him with artillery and transport, the Duke of Dalmatia will advance to relieve Pamplona and drive the English beyond the Ebro.

Under the circumstances, the task given to Marshal Soult was an extraordinarily difficult one, nay, almost an impossible one, yet we shall see how near he came, if not to actual success, at any rate to such a measure of it as might have materially modified the course of Wellington's subsequent operations. Moreover, a severe check to the allied armies at this time would have had effects extending far beyond the purely local ones.

Before proceeding to consider the operations connected with Soult's attempt to relieve Pamplona, it is necessary to follow in some detail the movements of both armies after the battle of Vitoria. This is specially necessary in the case of the allied army, as its distribution when the French again advanced was naturally based to a great extent on the dispositions originally made to follow up the French to the frontier, and for the investment of the fortresses commanding the two main lines of advance into France.

---

1. *Correspondance de Napoleon I*, Dresden, July 1, 1813. No. 20,220, Dresden, July 5, 1813.

Chapter 2
The French Retreat After Vitoria

On June 21, 1813, the French army under Joseph Bonaparte, King of Spain, was defeated at Vitoria by the allied army, British, Portuguese, and Spaniards, under command of the Marquess of Wellington.

Stoutly opposed by two divisions of the army of Portugal under General Reille, Wellington's left column under Sir Thomas Graham had to fight long and hard before possession could be gained of the bridges over the upper Zadora in rear of Vitoria. But, as the main battle surged nearer and nearer to the town, Reille's left flank became uncovered and his defence slackening, Graham gained the crossings and the ground beyond. Thus was the French army cut off from the "great road" from Vitoria by Montdragon, Vergara, and Tolosa to Iran and Bayonne, which had been so long its main line of communication with France, and was forced to take that leading to the fortress of Pamplona in order to gain the frontier.

The allies pursued till night fell, when the cavalry and the leading divisions halted about five miles east of Vitoria. The French continued their retreat during the night, and by 5 a.m. on June 22 the whole army had reached Salvatierra. But no man had aught save his arms and what he stood up in. All the artillery, except two pieces, the ammunition, treasure, baggage, and transport of the army, besides many private conveyances laden with the spoils of Spain, had been perforce abandoned and fell into the hands of the victors.

Such artillery teams as had survived the battle were with the two guns alone carried off.

After a short halt at Salvatierra, the retreat was resumed and on the 23rd the French reached Irurzun. From there Reille, with his two divisions, 600 cavalry and the gunners and teams of the army of Portugal, proceeded by San Estevan to Iran. The remainder of the French army moved towards Pamplona, where it arrived on June 24. Such provisions as could be hastily gathered in from the country were added to its magazines and the garrison reinforced to 3000 men. On the night of June 24/25, Gazan with the army of the south (four infantry and three cavalry divisions) marched towards France by the pass of Roncevaux, and D'Erlon with that of the centre (two infantry and one cavalry division) by the passes of Velate and Maya.

For long the French line of communication through the northern provinces of Spain had been subject to much interruption owing to attacks by Spanish guerrilla bands. These, receiving assistance in arms, ammunition and supplies from British ships of war on the coast, were especially active previous to and during the campaign of 1813. It was part of Wellington's plan that they should be. The more insecure the French line of communication became, the larger the number of troops required to hold it, involving under the circumstances a corresponding reduction in the strength of the field army. So harassed did the line become that the French garrisons were practically confined to the fortified towns and posts, convoys and officers with dispatches could not proceed except with large escorts. The inconveniences and delays became at length so great that Napoleon himself intervened. By his orders, Clausel was in February 1813 placed in command of the army of the north and given discretionary power to draw as many more troops as he considered necessary from the army of Portugal. When the campaign opened, Clausel had six divisions under his command including four from the army of Portugal. Previous to the French retreat behind the

Ebro, Joseph had sent orders to Clausel to join him; but one division only had reached the army when the battle of Vitoria was fought. Foy's and the Italian divisions were in Biscay and Guipuscoa, whilst Clausel with the rest of his force was marching towards Vitoria from the south. On June 22 Clausel was within a day's march of the town when his cavalry sent in news of the result of the battle. He at once fell back towards Logroño in the Ebro valley.

Two large convoys had left Vitoria for France previous to the battle. The first on June 19, and the second, escorted by Maucune's division, at 6 a.m. on the 21st. As soon as intelligence of the battle reached Foy, he ordered the convoys to move night and day towards the frontier, the Italian division to march to Vergara, and the garrisons of all the other posts to concentrate at Tolosa. To cover these movements, Foy, on the 22nd, with such troops of his own division as were with him and Maucune's division, took up a position at Montdragon on the great road.

The allied pursuit of the French was not characterized by the boldness and tenacity the occasion required. After the halt on the evening of June 21, the march was not resumed until midday on the 22nd. The British divisions moving towards Pamplona, whilst the Spaniards under Giron and Longa marched by the great road in order to, if possible, capture the convoy which had left Vitoria on the morning of the 21st. From Salvatierra Graham with the 1st division, two independent Portuguese brigades and Anson's Light cavalry brigade moved by the pass of St. Adrian towards Villafranca on the great road. The instructions Graham received[1] were "to act against any part of the enemy's troops or convoys which may be moving by the great road," also "against the force of the enemy which is understood to be retiring from Bilbao." Graham was also directed to get into communication with Giron and give him "such instructions as may seem most ex-

---

1. Q.M.G. to Graham, Salvatierra, June 22 1813.

pedient." This movement was suggested to Wellington by Sir George Murray, the Quartermaster-General, in a note written from Vitoria early on the 22nd. Unfortunately the officer sent with it, after having given it to Wellington and received it back endorsed with his approval, carried it back to Murray instead of taking it direct to Graham. By the time it reached the latter, his troops had passed the branch road leading to the pass and the column did not move in that direction till the morning of the 23rd, and arrived on the great road on the 24th just too late to intercept Foy's corps.

The 6th division, left behind at Medina del Pomar before the battle to cover the supplies and stores of the army, moved up to Vitoria, where a large general hospital was established.

Leaving the 5th division at Salvatierra, Wellington with the rest of the army followed the French towards Pamplona. Very wet weather had now set in and the road was a bad one. Larpent thus describes the route[1]: "It is one continued pass or valley from Vitoria to this place, the road infamous, villages every mile, but much damaged by the French." The advanced cavalry supported by the Light division, overtook the French rearguard early on the 23rd, hung on to them all day, and on the 24th captured one of the two guns saved from Vitoria. On the 25th the army was concentrated round Pamplona. The next day Wellington, leaving Hill with the 2nd and Portuguese divisions and Morillo's Spanish division to invest the fortress, moved with the 3rd, 4th, 7th, and Light divisions towards Tafalia with a view to intercepting Clausel at Tudela in the Ebro valley. The 5th and 6th divisions marched on the same day from Salvatierra and Vitoria towards Lagrono.

Clausel, who had with him about 14,000 men, reached Tudela on June 27, having marched sixty miles in forty hours. There he obtained information of Wellington's movement; and, being necessarily obliged to relinquish his intention of regaining France by way of Tafalla and Pamplona, moved rap-

---

1. Larpent's *Diary*, chap. ix.

idly towards Zaragoza. Wellington, whose movements were retarded by the badness of the roads[1] made a corresponding march to Caseda on the 28th, so as to be able to cut Clausel off from the road by Jaca into France. But here he gave up the pursuit, fearing, if he pressed Clausel too strongly, the latter would retreat still farther south and join Suchet. The partisan chief Mina alone pursued Clausel, who, believing he was followed by the allied army, destroyed some of his artillery, left the remainder with a garrison in Zaragoza, and then crossed the mountains into France by the pass of Jaca. Wellington and the army returned to Pamplona. After it was known that Clausel had passed Logroño, the 5th division was ordered to join Graham.

It is now time to return to the movements of the Spaniards and Graham's column in pursuit of the French in Guipuscoa. The great road from Vitoria to Irun (sixty-four miles) passes through the tangled mass of hills, in height from 2000 to 3500 ft. Which connect the western end of the Pyrenees proper with the Cantabrian Mountains. After leaving the valley of the Zadora, the route crosses by the pass of Arlaban (2000 ft.) into that of the river Deva which it traverses as far as Vergara. Thence it follows the course of the river Oria to within about five miles north of Tolosa. Throughout its length, therefore, it presents exceptional opportunities for delaying action by a retreating force. On June 22, Giron and Longa attacked Foy at Montdragon; greatly outnumbered the French fell back fighting to Vergara. The next day Foy moved to Villareal, and on the 24th to Villafranca, just escaping Graham's column as it descended from the pass of St. Adrian. Graham with the troops he had up—Anson's cavalry brigade,[2] the King's German Legion brigade of the 1st division, and two Portuguese brigades—pursued and attacked Foy, who held Villafranca

---

1. Verner, *A British Rifle Man* (Simmons' Diary, June 28): "The road became exceedingly bad, resembling a goat-track."
2. On Anson leaving for England early in July, command of this brigade was taken over by Major-General Vandeleur.

and a village nearly opposite the town on the south bank of the river Oria. The position was a strong one and, although the defenders were early driven out of Villafranca, the French would not give way till Graham's manoeuvres threatened both their flanks, then Foy retired to Tolosa. At Villafranca the Spanish 4th army troops under Giron and Longa joined Graham. A Spanish division of the same army under Mendizabel, which had been investing Santona, a fortified town on the coast twenty miles east of Santander, arrived at Azpatia on the river Urola, nine miles north-north-west of Villafranca.

On the 25th Foy again turned to fight at Tolosa and there was a stiff engagement. Though turned on both flanks by the Spaniards the French clung hard to the town, which had been strongly entrenched, and they were not driven out of it until one of the gates had been blown in by Graham's guns. The British and Portuguese lost over 400 killed and wounded on June 24 and 25, and Sir T. Graham was amongst the latter.

The allies halted on the 26th and 27th to get news of the main army. Foy, whose strength had now risen to over 10,000 men and ten guns by the arrival of the smaller garrisons, now halted between Tolosa and Hernani, covering the roads to San Sebastian and Irun. His position was a strong one and his numbers being reported as 18,000 men, Graham judged it too risky to attack him.[1] On the 28th the convoys having now reached France, Foy threw a reinforcement of 2600 good troops into San Sebastian and continued his retreat. On July 1 he crossed the Bidassoa into France, being followed to the river, where Reille's divisions had already arrived, by some of Giron's Spaniards.

On July 1 the French garrisons in the forts defending the defile of Pancorbo on the great road between Burgos and Vitoria, surrendered to the Andalusian army of Reserve under the Conde de la Bispal, which had been following the army. La Bispal was then ordered to move to Pamplona, as was also Don Carlos' division of the 4th Spanish army from Miranda.

---

1. Larpent's *Diary*, p. 170.

After Vitoria Wellington decided he would not immediately follow up his victory by invading France. He had several reasons for coming to this decision. The army required some rest after its march from cantonments in Portugal to the French frontier, and its wants were numerous;[1] the organization of the newly established base depots on the coast of Biscay and their communications with the army needed to be assured. Moreover, the French forces under Suchet in Aragon and Catalonia were a standing menace to such a move, and especially so at the moment owing to Sir J. Murray's failure before Tarragona, which Wellington expected would be followed by "Suchet throwing his army on our right flank."[2] But chief reason of all probably was uncertainty as to what would be the result of the negotiations then going on between Napoleon and the Powers; and as he himself said:[3] "I wait to see what turn affairs take in Germany, before I determine on my line."

Meanwhile the position already won had to be consolidated and provision made for a future advance. To establish a regular and speedy system of supply was of primary importance and was not an easy matter owing to the extended position of the army, the distances of the sea bases behind its left flank and the difficult intervening country with its indifferent communications.

Napoleon has said that though fortresses will not in themselves arrest an army, "they are an excellent means of retarding, embarrassing, weakening and annoying a victorious army." The correctness of his opinion was now about to be shown in the cases of the two fortresses, San Sebastian

---

1. After the battle of Vitoria the supply of musket ammunition had become so short that the French ammunition captured (some two million rounds) had to be issued to the allied infantry notwithstanding that the calibre of the French musket was smaller than that of the British. The men were also badly off for shoes. Convoys from Lisbon and Corunna had been delayed for want of naval escort.
2. Wellington to Sir J. Murray, Huarte, July 1, 1813.
3. Wellington to Lord W. Bentinck, Irurita, July 8, 1813.

and Pamplona, held by the French on or in close proximity to the roads by which the allied army must advance to gain the French frontier. They had either to be captured or masked in sufficient strength if there was to be security on the communications of the army. It had been Wellington's original intention to besiege them both.[1] But on reconsideration, he judged his means insufficient for two sieges. To obtain possession of San Sebastian he decided was of the greater importance. For though Santander had, since the passage of the Ebro, become the base depot of the army and Bilbao had also become available after its evacuation by the French before the battle of Vitoria, both were now at a considerable distance from the army, and nearer harbours were very desirable to facilitate its supply. Those of San Sebastian and Passages though small were suitable for the supply and ordnance ships of those days.

Passages was available as its garrison had surrendered to Longa; but, situated as it is between San Sebastian and the French frontier distant only seven miles, the port could not be a really safe one for the landing and storage of ammunition and supplies as long as the fortress remained in possession of the French; its entrance too is narrow and rocky and difficult to make in a foul wind. Moreover, the coast of Biscay is an exceedingly dangerous one for sailing-ships in bad weather; the autumn was approaching and time was precious. Wellington determined therefore to besiege San Sebastian, using Graham's corps for the purpose, and to blockade Pamplona, designing ultimately to employ there La Bispal's Spaniards then moving up from Pancorbo as well as Don Carlo's division of the 4th army. The remainder of the allied army would thus be available to watch the frontier and cover the operations.

In accordance with this decision, Hill was ordered to move one British, one Portuguese brigade, and Morillo's Spanish

---

1. Dickson MSS., Series C, chap. vii.

division under the command of Major-General Byng by the route along which the enemy's army retired from Pamplona towards France, believed to be by the pass of Roncevaux. "The objects of this movement," the order said, are "first to ascertain with certainty the direction of the enemy's march, and whether he has continued it beyond the frontier, evacuating entirely the Spanish territory. Secondly, to watch and oppose his movements if he should attempt to return or to send any parties in the direction of Pamplona."[1] Byng was to be informed there was no objection to his pushing his advanced detachments beyond the frontier, if he could do so without meeting much opposition or having to force any strong post. He was, however, to direct his attention chiefly to acting on the defensive. Hill was also instructed to obtain as perfect a knowledge as possible of the country towards the frontier by sending out officers to reconnoitre and report on it; and to establish certain and expeditious communication with Byng. In compliance with these instructions Byng with his own brigade (2nd) of the 2nd division and Morillo's Spaniards, marched towards Roncevaux.

When Wellington and the divisions with him returned to Pamplona, the 3rd, 4th, and Light divisions took over the blockade from Hill's corps. On July 3 Hill, with the three brigades of the 2nd division and the 14th Light Dragoons, moved up the Ulzama valley to occupy the Baztan valley, which the French under General Gazan had re-entered. The Portuguese division followed a day's march in rear—Campbell's brigade moving by Zubiri and Eugui to the Aldudes—it was accompanied by its two brigades of Portuguese artillery; but the British artillery of the 2nd division remained at Berrioplano.[2] Wellington and the headquarters of the army followed Hill, Lord Dalhousie taking over the command of the troops around Pamplona.

On July 4, the 7th division with the 1st Hussars, King's German Legion, marched by Marcalain to Lizaso. Its ar-

---

1. Q.M.G. to Hill, Tafalla, June 27, 1813.
2. It was subsequently moved up to Lanz.

tillery did not accompany it, but also remained at Berrioplano. On the 5th, the 6th division relieved the Light in the blockade, and the latter division followed Hill's corps up the valley road. The 2nd division reached Almandoz at about 1 p.m. on July 4 and afterwards proceeded to turn the French out of a position they occupied about the village of Berroeta, two miles beyond Almandoz. But the French developed unexpected strength and Hill broke off the action. The next day about noon, Wellington having then arrived, Hill, detaching the 1st brigade to turn the French left and pushing the rest of his force against their centre and right, drove Gazan back as far as the little town of Elizondo. Here the French rear-guard made a stout resistance, but was at length driven out. Gazan then retired with his main body to the Maya ridge, which closes the valley to the north, keeping his rearguard in the upper part of the valley. On the 6th the French held the Alcorrunz peak on the right with their centre and left across the pass and along the ridge to the east of it. Wellington and Hill reconnoitred the position and on July 7 the allied troops attacked it. There was a sharp fight, for Gazan was loth to give up the advantages of the position where he had one foot in France and the other in Spain.[1] But Hill's 3rd brigade drove the French from the Alcorrunz peak after a stubborn resistance, then the 1st brigade and the Portuguese attacked the French front. It was not till towards evening, however, that the allies gained possession of the pass when a fog came on and put an end to the fighting, both sides passing the night almost in contact. Very early on July 8 Gazan made another attempt to regain possession of the Alcorrunz; but it failed. He then under cover of the fog withdrew and marched down into France.

Meanwhile, the 7th and Light divisions had followed Hill's corps—although they took no part in the fighting—and were

---

1. Wellington to Graham, July 8, 1813, 4 p.m. The enemy appeared particularly anxious to keep hold of this fine valley of the Baztan, and Gazan has disputed every position in it.

located, the 7th at Elizondo, in direct support of Hill; and the Light, with its artillery, at San Estevan, an important road junction at the south-western end of the Baztan. On July 11, Wellington went across the hills to Graham's corps and established his headquarters at Hernani. On the way there he received information that the whole of the French army of the south was in Hill's front about Urdax and Ainhoa,[1] and, judging further reinforcement to the troops holding the Baztan necessary, ordered the 6th division to move up towards the valley on the 12th. Before Pamplona, the troops, aided by labour parties of the inhabitants of the district, had been busy strengthening the investment line; redoubts were constructed and some of the captured French guns sent up from Vitoria to arm them. La Bispal's corps having arrived took over the blockade on July 17, when the 4th division marched to Linzoain as a support to the troops under Byng in the Roncevaux passes, the 3rd division to Olague, and Dalhousie resumed command of the 7th division. The greater part of the cavalry was now quartered towards the Ebro valley about Tafalla on the Pamplona-Zaragoza road. Long's and Fane's brigades had been with the blockading divisions. The former had only the 13th Light Dragoons with him as the 14th was with Hill; the 13th was now sent into the Arga valley to keep up the communication on this side of the army. Fane's brigade and the 4th Portuguese cavalry moved to Monreal and Sanguessa with orders to watch all the valleys coming down from the main chain of the Pyrenees in that direction.

Meanwhile Graham's corps had arrived near San Sebastian on July 9 and took over the investment of the fortress from the Spanish troops, who, with the exception of part of Mendizabel's division which proceeded to reinforce the blockade of Santona, moved on the 13th to join the remainder of the 4th army on the line of the Bidassoa. The land side of the low sandy isthmus which then connected San Sebastian with

---

1. Wellington to Hill, Zubieta, July 11, 1813.

the mainland, is closed by the heights of San Bartolomeo, on which the French had constructed field works and entrenched the convent buildings. Before the close siege of the place could be undertaken, it was necessary to gain possession of these heights; therefore on July 17 the French entrenchments and the convent were assaulted and carried after sharp fighting. The formal siege operations were then immediately commenced; the troops allotted to the siege being the 5th division and the two independent Portuguese brigades; the 1st division being moved up towards Irun as a support to the Spaniards and Graham's headquarters established at Oyarzun.

To cover the right flank of the Spaniards and prevent any interruption of the siege from Reille's troops which held Vera and the heights above Echelar, Wellington on July 14 moved up the Light and 7th divisions from San Estevan and Elizondo, replacing the former by the 6th division less its artillery, which remained at Ostiz. The next day the French were driven from the Santa Barbara heights opposite Vera by the Light division and from the pass of Echelar by the 7th. These divisions then occupied the ground taken, and Longa's division held Lesaca and the heights on the left bank of the Bidassoa, his left connecting with Giron's troops on the San Marcial heights. On July 17 Wellington established his headquarters at Lesaca.

On the extreme right of the army Byng with his British brigade and part of Morillo's division held the heights of Altobiscar beyond the pass of Roncevaux, the remainder of the Spaniards held the Linduz and the Val Carlos to the north of the pass, and Campbell's brigade was in the Aldudes valley connecting with Hill's corps in the Baztan. In rear of Byng, the 4th division was about Linzoain, the 3rd at Olague, whence it could move either towards the 4th by Eugui and Zubiri, or into the Baztan by the pass of Velate. Hill's corps was distributed, the 1st brigade of the 2nd division on the Maya ridge near the pass, the 3rd brigade near the village of Maya with outposts on the ridge, the 4th Ashworth's Portuguese brigade at Errazu in support of Da Costa's brigade of the Portuguese division which guarded the principal passes of the Hausa range, the boundary of the Baztan on the east. The 6th division was at San Estevan, the 7th at Echelar, and the Light on the Santa Barbara heights.

The army was now based on the ports of the coast of Biscay, the chief of which were Santander and Bilbao. Santander was the main depot for supplies of all sorts, and all reinforcements were landed there. When San Sebastian was invested, the siege train was landed at Passages, and this port became the main depot for ordnance stores. Later on food supplies were also landed there. From the depots at the ports supplies of all kinds were sent up to the army by convoys of country carts and pack-mules. The general hospitals were at Santander, Bilbao, and Vitoria.

CHAPTER 3

France at Bay

The effect of the victory of Vitoria had been to sweep almost the whole of the French beyond the northern frontier of Spain. Of the host of French soldiers which had for so long held Spain in subjection, there remained only the beleaguered or besieged garrisons of Pamplona, Santona, and San Sebastian, and the forces under Marshal Suchet in the north-eastern provinces of Spain, about 66,000 men.[1] A glance at the map at the back of this book will show the possible influence these forces could have on Wellington's situation both before and during the operations about to be described. A brief account of what was happening in this theatre of the war seems therefore necessary to a complete understanding of the general situation.

At the opening of the campaign of 1813, Suchet, with the armies of Aragon and Catalonia, held these provinces and Valencia. Napoleon, in the instructions and remonstrances he addressed to his brother in the early months of that year concerning his conduct of military affairs, repeatedly warned him of the danger of leaving Suchet's forces outside the scope of his own operations, and ordered him to estab-

---

1. Strength on July 16, 1813, was:

	Present under arms	Detached	Hospital	Total
Army of Aragon	32,363	3,621	3,201	39,184
Army of Catalonia	25,910	168	1,379	27,454
Totals	58,273	3,789	4,580	66,688

lish a shorter and more secure line of communication with the Marshal. The King did neither. On the other hand, Wellington, with as clear an insight into the general situation as the Emperor, saw that for the success of his own operations Suchet must, by all possible means, be prevented from combining with Joseph. As Napier says: "his (Wellington's) wings were spread for a long flight," and he had no wish to find the King's armies reinforced by Suchet's troops, or these later threatening his right flank from the Ebro valley. Therefore Suchet must be kept fully occupied in his own area and tied if possible to the Eastern coast. To effect this the means at Wellington's disposal were an Anglo-Sicilian force of about 11,000 men, of whom 9,000 were British, and two bodies of Spanish troops paid and equipped by Britain and commanded by British officers. The whole, numbering about 17,000 men under the command of Sir John Murray, was about Alicante when Wellington's campaign opened. The second Spanish army under Elio, about 20,000 strong, was in Murcia, and behind it in the Sierra Morena was the third army of 12,000 men under Del Parque. Separated from these by the French army was the first army of about 6,000 men under Copons in Catalonia. At this time Suchet with about 15,000 men was in an entrenched position on the river Jucar, some thirty miles south of Valencia.

The territory occupied by the French was a large one; to keep hold of it the garrisons were necessarily numerous, especially as the Spanish partisan bands were many and active; the number of French troops available for field operations was therefore comparatively small and probably did not exceed 25,000 men. Without going into any detail, Wellington's general plan was that the French should be gradually drawn northwards by operations against their communications—power to do which was with the allies, as they had command of the sea, Murray having a flotilla of transports and the full support of the British Mediterranean fleet—and eventually by the gradual move of the Spanish armies round the northern flank of the French, opposed in front by Murray, to push them across the Ebro, prevent any communication with the King's army and confine them to the northeastern corner of Spain.

As a first step, in order to draw Suchet from Valencia, Murray was directed to embark at least 10,000 men and lay siege to Tarragona, a fortress on the coast between the mouth of the Ebro and Barcelona. Murray with about 14,000 men landed there on June 2, 1813, and invested the place. He had carried with him everything necessary for the siege, and on the 8th a practicable breach was made in one of the principal outworks, but no assault was ordered. Suchet, rightly judging that the aim of the expedition was a landing on the Catalonian coast, marched north as soon as he knew the flotilla had passed Cape Nao going north. Leaving Harispe with 7000 men to hold the Jucar, Suchet reached Tortosa on June 12 with 12,000 men. Though by the coast road Tortosa is only fifty miles from Tarragona this road was blocked to him, as a detachment from Murray's force aided by the navy had seized the fort of San Phillipe de Balaguer, which commands the road where it passes through a deep gorge. Suchet was therefore obliged to take an inland road over hilly country in bad order and impracticable for artillery. He could be reinforced by 7000 men under Mathieu from Barcelona and later by about the same number under Decaen. Meanwhile Copons with the first Spanish army had reached Reuss about twelve miles from Tarragona.

But Murray, who would give his confidence to no one, not even to his second in command, his chief staff officer, or to the admiral, now lost all confidence in himself. After several times changing his plans and orders he finally determined to raise the siege and re-embark his force; which he did on the night of June 12/13, when the French columns, which had not yet joined hands, were over thirty miles distant. The siege train—"the guns that shook the bloody ramparts of Badajoz"—much small arm ammunition and siege stores were left behind, and the army to its mortification and disgust saw them carried into the fortress by its garrison. The flotilla and its escorting division of the fleet sailed to Balaguer, where the force again disembarked on June 15 Some movements were made, but Murray had no settled plan. A few days later a council of war was held and it was decided to re-embark the troops. Hardly, however, had the decision been come to than the main division of the fleet arrived, and with it, to the delight of all, came Lord William Bentinck to resume command of the troops. Murray departed to England to be tried by court-martial twenty months later. Though, as regards its immediate object, the expedition had miserably failed, bringing discredit on British arms, the desired result had been at least partially obtained, for the French forces had been kept fully occupied. Suchet returned to Tortosa whilst Mathieu pursued Copons, who, however, escaped to the mountains.

The guns and most of the siege stores having been lost, it was impossible to at once renew the attack on Tarragona. Bentinck therefore returned to Alicante, where the force disembarked on June 27. No operations could be at once undertaken as Murray had discharged nearly all the land transport of the army before sailing for Tarragona. To procure the necessary transport for the army was therefore Bentinck's first care.

Now, however, the news of the allied victory at Vitoria reached both commanders, and the situation became entirely changed. Suchet, who knew that Clausel was at Zaragoza, determined to move there in order to secure a point where the army of Aragon could join that of the King if the latter could re-enter Spain. But to do so with the bulk of his forces meant the abandonment of the fortresses in Valencia and Catalonia, and exposed his main line of communication with France by Perpignan to seizure by the Anglo-Spanish forces, supported as they were by the British fleet; moreover, the abandonment of further territory in Spain could not but have a bad effect on the negotiations then going on during the armistice in Germany. Suchet allowed himself to be influenced by considerations such as these and determined to maintain the garrisons, thereby, of course, reducing the strength of his field force. He fixed Caspe, a town in the Ebro valley some sixty miles south-east of Zaragoza, as the concentration point for his army, and destroying the bridges over the Jucar, left his position there and marched to Tortosa. Musnier's division from Requeña marched towards Caspe, picking up some smaller garrisons *en route*. By July 12 Suchet's force was distributed along the Ebro from Caspe to Tortosa. Now, however, came the news that Clausel had abandoned Zaragoza and that Mina and all the partisan bands were closing on the city. Suchet ordered General Paris, commanding the garrison, to retreat to Caspe and gave up his intention of moving on Zaragoza.[1] It was a fateful decision, for there was no one except Mina and the partisans about Zaragoza. As he could not feed his army in the country round Tortosa, Suchet crossed the Ebro on July 15, and moving by Tarragona took up a strong position about Villafranca. The allied forces had slowly followed the French. Bentinck entered Valencia on July 9, but did not leave the city till the 16th, when Suchet was already over the Ebro. On July 20 the Anglo-Sicilian force reached the neighbourhood by the river at Vinaros, remained there till the 26th, when Bentinck threw a flying bridge over the Ebro between Tortosa and the sea, and passing the river on July 27 seized the Col de Balaguer and occupied the hilly country beyond the Ebro. Bentinck's force did not exceed 10,000 men, as Del Parque's army was several marches in rear, and Elio was at Valencia. On July 30 he invested Tarragona with about 6,000 men; and having been joined by Del Parque with 13,000 on August 3 took up a covering position beyond the river Jaya. Suchet, who had been joined by Decaen, determined to attack and moved towards Tarragona.

---

1. Paris had, however, evacuated Zaragoza on the night of July 10-11, leaving a garrison of 500 men in the citadel. Being pursued by Mina, he lost many men, together with all his artillery and baggage, in the defiles of the Sierra de Alcubierre, but gained the fortified town of Huesca; thence he moved to Jaca, where he arrived on July 14.

It is unnecessary to carry any farther this brief summary of the operations in the eastern provinces of Spain. Though but feebly carried by both the commanders on the allied side—the inadequacy of their means must not, however, be overlooked—the object aimed at had so far been attained in that Suchet was not in a position to cooperate with Soult in the operations the latter was about to begin. That events proceeded as they did was the fault of Suchet alone. Though, in the earlier stages especially, his decisions and movements had been prompt and rapid, he, like the good generals in Europe his master, when General Bonaparte, had spoken of years before, "who see too many things at once," failed to see the one thing for which alone Napoleon always looked, the enemy's main body, and to realize that in Wellington's army lay the greatest danger to French power in Spain, that if this could be defeated and driven back all the secondary matters—of which his hold on the eastern provinces was one—would then settle themselves. He accordingly failed to play the great game. Had he been content to abandon territory for the time being and concentrated all his available forces, there is little doubt he could have smashed the allies so effectually as to have been able to move into Aragon without hindrance; and there uniting with Clausel have been on Wellington's flank with not much less than 50,000 good troops. What this would have meant towards the end of July, we shall perhaps better appreciate as the narrative proceeds.

CHAPTER 4

The Western Pyrenees

Such were the dispositions of the opposing forces about the middle of July, prior to any of the preliminary movements of the French. Before touching on the details of how Soult hoped to retrieve some at any rate of the misfortunes which had befallen French arms, it will be well to glance at the topographical aspect of the area which was about to be the scene of operations.

Its main feature is, of course, the Pyrenean range, which stretching nearly due east and west from the Mediterranean to the Atlantic, forms generally the boundary between France and Spain. We are here concerned only with that comparatively small portion of the range which abuts on the Atlantic. In reality it hardly belongs to the main range, for the true western end of the main chain of the Pyrenees may be placed about Monte Urtiaga, which lies some twenty-five miles south-east by south of the corner made by the Bay of Biscay about Iran.

Hereabouts the heights begin to decrease and the watershed of the range divides; one branch going first north and then north-west ends in the Rhune mountain close to the sea near St. Jean de Luz; the other, continuing in the general westerly direction of the main range, becomes the backbone of the Cantabrian range, which under various local names bounds the northern coast of Spain and ends in Cape Finisterre. Before leaving the area, this branch throws off in northeasterly direction a minor range which joins the mass of low hills called the plateau of the Cinco Villas and ends in the Haya mountain near Irun.

From the main watersheds spring numerous lateral off-shoots, forming between them the valleys so distinctive of the Pyrenean system. On the northern or French side the following are the main valleys, from east to west, in the area: the Val Carlos, the head of which forms the Puerto de Ibaneta or the Pass of Roncevaux (3,600 ft.); the great Vallée de Baigorry, the upper portion of which is divided by a spur into the Vallée de Hayra on the east and that of Des Aldudes on the west. From the Hayra valley the communication across the main chain is by the Col de Linduz, whence tracks lead to Burguete in the Urrobi valley and by the Puerto de Mendichuri to Espinal. From the Aldudes, it is by the pass of Sahorgain to Viscarret in the Erro valley and by the pass of Urtiaga to Eugui and thence to Zubiri in the Arga valley. Whilst nearly all the Val Carlos is Spanish territory, the entire Baigorry valley is French. These two valleys contain the head waters of the river Nive, the Val Carlos, the Nive d'Arneguy and the Aldudes the Nive des Aldudes, the two streams joining near Osses, some fifteen miles north of the main chain.

The next valley, known under the general name of the Baztan, is entirely Spanish and is formed by the northern branch of the main range and by the minor range springing from the westerly branch. It contains the head waters and much of the course of the river Bidassoa, which, at the south-western end of the Baztan, has cut its way to the sea in a narrow valley through the Cinco Villas plateau. The Baztan valley is of no great width, but is a fertile and relatively well-populated district. The communications from it northwards are by the Puerto de Maya to Ainhoa and Bayonne—a fairly good road then and as now the best in the district—by the Bidassoa valley from San Estevan and Sumbilla to Vera, thence eastwards towards Sare and the Nivelle by the pass of Vera and westwards by the Bidassoa to Irun, also by the Puerto de Echelar to Sare. Eastwards, by several passes over the Hausa mountain into the Baigorry and the Aldudes, the chief of which are from north to south the passes of Arieta, Ispeguy, Elhorrieta, and Berdaritz. The communications by these passes are all merely mountain tracks. To the south by the road from Irurita over the Puerto de Velate and the Ulzama valley to Pamplona, from San Estevan by the passes of Arriaz, Loyondi, and Eradi—sometimes called the passes of Dona Maria—to Lizaso, whence tracks led to Lanz and Olague in the Ulzama valley to join the Pamplona road, also by Marcalain and Oricain to Pamplona, and also to Berrioplano and Irurzun on the Pamplona-Tolosa-Irun road. To the westward the only exits from the Baztan were by what was then a mule track from San Estevan by Zubieta and the pass of Leiza to the Pamplona-Irun road near Lecumberri, and another difficult one from Zubieta by Goyzueta into the same road near Hernani.

On the Spanish side of the Pyrenees there are the following valleys from east to west: the valley of the Irati, with the village and ironworks of Orbaizeta near its head; the valley of the Urrobi, traversed by the old Roman road over the pass of Roncevaux. These two valleys merge into one about fourteen miles-south of Roncevaux, and there is lateral communication between their upper portions by a track from the foundry of Orbaizeta to Burguete by the pass of Navala; and some two miles south of this by a track from Arrive to Burguete. This latter is now a good carriage road. The valley of the Erro, divided from that of the Urrobi by the Sierra de Labia. The valley of the Arga, through the lower part of which runs the most direct communication between Roncevaux and Pamplona by Espinal, Erro, and Zubiri. This in 1813 was probably little better than a mule track: to-day it is a well-made carriage road, though its grades on the divide between the Erro and the Arga valleys are long and rather steep. The valley of the Ulzama or Lanz, through which descends the road from the Col de Velate, which passing over the Col de Maya and through the upper Baztan is the most direct line of communication between Bayonne and Pamplona. A track from Olague to Eugui, not practicable for artillery, also gave lateral communication with the upper Arga valley.

These are the principal valleys on both sides of the range in the area; but an important difference, sometimes slight, sometimes very marked, exists between the northern and southern slopes of the range. It cannot be better expressed than in the following extract from *The Pyrenees*, by Hilaire Belloc:

> The northern slope of the Pyrenees is narrow and precipitous. The plains are for the greater part of its length clearly separated from the mountains, the easy country in Home places is not twenty miles as the crow flies from the highest peaks.
> On the Spanish side, on the contrary, the mountainous district will run from two to three times that distance . . . . and is nowhere less than two good days' journey on foot from the summits to the plains.
> This differentiation between the northern and southern slopes is not merely one of width, it is due to profound differences in the contours which make the Spanish side of the system a different type of mountain group from the French. For, on the French side, the Pyrenees consist in a series of great ribs or buttresses running up from the plains perpendicularly to the main heights of the range, and it is between these ribs or buttresses that the separate and highly distinct valleys, which are the characteristic habitations of the French Basques and Béarnais, lie. On the Spanish side the main structure is in folds *parallel* to the watershed; the lateral valleys descending from the watershed run southward for but a very short distance, they come, within a few miles, upon high east and west ridges which sometimes rival the main range itself in height and which succeed each other like waves down to the plains of the Ebro . . . . a

man looking at the Pyrenees from the French towns at their base sees in one complete view a belt of steep rising slopes and a fairly even line of summits against the sky. A man looking at the range from the Spanish plains can only in a few rare places so much as catch a sight of the main range . . . . If you follow a French valley—on the western part of the Pyrenees at least—you will find it running fairly north and south to the point where it debouches upon the plain. A Spanish valley will at first appear to have the same character, but just when you think you are in sight of the plains, you see—beyond the first lines of flat country and barring the view like a great wall—another high range.

Pamplona again is situated at the mouth of a true Pyrenean valley (that of the Arga) not very different from the valleys of the north. It stands also on a plain, but immediately in front of it runs another range of hills, and if you climb these, you find yet another, strictly parallel and straight, standing before you and masking the approach to the Ebro . . . . a further consequence of this formation is that communications are very difficult to the south of the Pyrenees. The traveller naturally ascribes the lack of communications to the character of the Spanish Government. It is not wholly due to a moral but partly to a material cause.[1]

As in the Himalayas, the southern slopes of the Pyrenees, looking as they do in the face of the sun, are more burnt and bare of wood than the northern, nor is water everywhere so plentiful. But there is in most of the valleys on the Spanish side a considerable amount of wood, fine forests of beech, chestnut and oak in many places, for instance, below the passes of Roncevaux and Velate.

Owing to its proximity to the Atlantic the western portion of the Pyrenees has a heavier rainfall than the rest of

---

1. Belloc, *The Pyrenees*, chap. iv.

the range. Storms at all seasons are frequent and, even in the height of summer, there is often much cloud over the high ground and mist in the valleys.

The writer already quoted admirably describes the existing communications in the Pyrenees as follows: "There are two kinds of platforms for travel in the Pyrenees, mule tracks and great highly-engineered modern roads. No others exist." In 1813 the "highly-engineered modern roads" had not been thought of, much less made. In addition to the coast road from Bayonne by Irun, Tolosa, Vitoria towards Madrid—called in the orders and writing of that day " the great road "—two other main lines of communication between France and Spain passed through Pamplona and followed the general line of the modern highways: that on the east by the Roncevaux gap, already described, and a central one by the Baztan and the Velate pass. In both trace and construction they were doubtless far inferior to the present highways. Larpent, writing from Lanz, thus describes the road from Pamplona and the villages in that valley:

> The first league (from Ostiz) of this *camina real* (royal road) was a narrow lane of large loose stones, nearly the size of my head, with all the interstices filled with good Brentford slop half a foot deep .... The villages are nearly all alike in general shape and accommodation; scarcely any cottages but farmhouses, and I suppose the great tables and benches they contain have been in better times used for the workmen to dine. This has been the character of all the villages for the last ten or twelve miles, and they lie very thick, four in sight here and probably ten within a league. The hills around are covered with wood; the valley almost knee deep with grass for hay and abounding in corn; the climate very cold for England in July and wet, the verdure like Ireland.[1]

---

1. Larpent, *Diary*, Lanz, July 5, 1813.

Except for the new roads in some of them, these Basque valleys have probably changed less in the last hundred years than most other places in Europe. And the same perhaps may be said of the inhabitants, a race of fine upstanding courteous people; but their dogs have not the same good quality! Most of the traffic of the district is still carried on pack mules, though on the main roads one often meets the long narrow carts of the district, generally carrying wine-casks, and drawn by a string of five or six fine mules, the wheelers often near sixteen hands in height.

A point to be borne in mind when following the movements of the campaign is that, owing to the mountainous nature of the country and the very inferior communications then existing, distances bear a different relation to the times taken to traverse them than is the case in a more level open country with good roads.

Chapter 5
The French Prepare to Defend France

The army which re-entered France after Vitoria had lost practically all the *matériel* necessary to a fighting force. Officers and men had little but their arms and what they stood up in. There was no ammunition except what was left in the soldiers' pouches after a great battle. Every gun had been lost, such artillery teams as had survived the battle alone were saved. The baggage and the transport of the army had fallen into the enemy's hands. Before the army could take the field again it had to be almost completely re-equipped. Fortunately the means were at hand. Bayonne had been for years the base depot of the French armies in Spain. In its arsenal were large supplies of clothing, boots, equipment, and other stores, from which issues to the troops were made.

Ammunition for the infantry was the first necessity, and on June 26 General Lhuillier, Commandant of Bayonne, dispatched half a million rounds to St. Jean de Luz, Sarre, Ainhoa, and St. Jean Pied de Port to meet the army. Sixty-two guns had reached Bayonne with the convoy sent from Vitoria under General Mancune on the morning of the battle. These formed the nucleus of the rearmament of the artillery, other guns and stores were received from Rochefort, Bordeaux, and Toulouse, and the Bayonne arsenal furnished four hundred ammunition wagons.[1]

---

1. Commandant Clerc, *Campagne du Maréchal Soult dans les Pyrénées occidentales en 1813-1814.*

Previous to Soult's arrival the Chamber of Commerce of Bayonne had advanced to King Joseph the sum of 500,000 francs to meet necessary expenses connected with the army, and the Emperor sanctioned the expenditure of a million francs for the same purpose.[1]

Soult arrived at Bayonne on July 12. As ordered by the Emperor, he had halted in Paris to consult with the Minister of War. The latter assured him he would find the army in possession of 50 guns horsed and ready for service, and that from 120 to 150 would be ready within a month. The Minister of War Administration also guaranteed that a month's supplies for the army would be ready "for its return into Spain." After his arrival, however, Soult soon found that the state of readiness of the army was far from being what had been represented to him; and he sharply informed the Minister that he appeared to have given him hopes rather "than facts."[2]

Determined to carry out his instructions and take the offensive with as little delay as possible, Soult set himself energetically to get his army ready.[3] He inspected the troops and outposts, and one of his first orders was to Clausel to march at once to St. Jean Pied de Port. The fortress of Bayonne, a bulwark of France and the base of his army, had been neglected; to arm and put it in a proper state of defence was also one of his first cares. A bridge head to cover the crossing of the river Nivelle at St. Jean de Luz was also thrown up.

Bakeries capable of turning out 100,000 bread rations daily were ordered to be established at Bayonne and other points close behind the army.[4] Hospital accommodation was inadequate. By means of a camp of huts and tents the accommodation at Bayonne was increased by 6,000 beds, and hospitals

---

1. Correspondance de Napoleon 1er, No. 20,234, to General Clarke, Minister of War, Dresden, July 6, 1813.
2. Soult to Clarke, Bayonne, July 14.
3. Baltazar to Clarke, Bayonne, July 17: «*Il (Soult) s'occupe Nuns relâche de reconstituer l'armée.*» Major Baltazar was the Minister's aide-de-camp detached to the army.
4. Clerc, p. 24.

were established at St. Jean de Luz, Cambo, and St. Jean Pied de Port, also a convalescent depot at Dax.

There was a shortage of horses for the artillery and also of transport; but Soult's greatest difficulty was probably in connexion with supplies. The south-west corner of France, where his army was now assembled, is mainly a pastoral country. Little corn is grown, maize is the principal cereal, and not much of this. The district is even now comparatively sparsely inhabited and Bayonne is the only large town. To the north along the coast almost to Bordeaux and for miles inland stretches the sandy waste of the Landes, producing nothing but heather and fir-trees. Excellent cattle abound and large flocks of sheep are pastured on the hills; but grain for men and animals must be brought from a distance, a lengthier process then than now.

To provide for the supply of the army at this crisis, Napoleon issued a decree to the Minister of the Treasury Unit requisitions for the supply of the army were to be made on the departments of the south, payments being made by treasury bills.[1] But, considering the time necessary for the decree to reach Paris, the necessary arrangements to be made and set at work in the Departments concerned, it is evident that it can have produced little or no results by the date of Soult's concentration of his army. It is on record that when he advanced on July 25, Soult considered that he had not more than four days' supplies in hand.[2]

Moreover, it is extremely probable that taking the army as a whole he had considerably less; and certainly little or nothing, except perhaps meat, was to be obtained in the mountainous district where the operations were about to be carried on, which had already been traversed by his army in its retreat and was now in possession of the enemy. Also, had supplies been forthcoming in greater abundance, he lacked the means of carrying them.

---

1. Napoleon to Count Mollien, No. 20,235, Dresden, July 6.
2. Soult to Minister of War, July 29: «Je suis a mon dernier jour de subsistences.»

Until Soult's arrival the French army had retained the organization in which it had fought at Vitoria, namely, the armies of the south, the centre, of Portugal and Clausel's army of the north. But, when giving it a new commander, the Emperor decided that these now out-of-date higher units should cease, that there should be one army only, that of Spain organized on a divisional basis. There were to be no *corps d'armée,* but he left it to Soult to place such number of divisions as considered suitable under the command of each of the Lieutenant-Generals, the former army commanders. The strength of the divisions was to be about 6,000 men.[1]

There were then fourteen divisions in the four armies, four were broken up and distributed amongst the remainder which were numbered from one to nine, the tenth being designated the reserve division.[2]

This latter, the command of which was given to General Villatte, had a special organization. In it were incorporated all the foreign troops serving with the French army, namely, one brigade of Spaniards, one of Italians, and one of Germans, to which was added one strong brigade of six French battalions; its effective strength in infantry was about 11,600 men. The other divisions had each two brigades, the number of battalions in which varied from three to five. These divisions were grouped in three bodies, each of three divisions; the right wing commanded by Lieut.-General Count Reille, the centre under Lieut.-General Count D'Erlon, and the left wing under Lieut.-General Baron Clausel. Lieut.-General Count Gazan became Chief of the staff.

Four cavalry divisions were recalled by the Emperor into France, and two only now remained with the army of Spain, namely, Treilhard's dragoon division of two brigades and a

---

1. Napoleon to Duc de Feltre, Minister of War, No. 20,236, Dresden, July 6, 1813.
2. The divisions retained their former numbers, and regiments which had previously served together were kept in same brigade. Lapène, *Campagnes de 1813 et de 1814 sur l'Ebro les Pyrénées et la Garonne.*

mixed division of three brigades under Pierre Soult, a brother of the Marshal. Some light cavalry regiments were attached to the reserve division.

When the forward movement of the army took place it had about 100 field and mountain guns, of which 66 accompanied it, the remainder being left with Villatte's division or in reserve.

But reorganization and new equipment were not all the army needed. Its discipline had slackened severely since the retreat from Vitoria. To re-establish it was a primary necessity, and Soult set about doing so sternly. A permanent court-martial was established. The numerous soldiers out of the ranks under various pretexts were hunted out and sent back to their regiments. The camps were cleared of the crowds of hangers-on, including many Spanish women, who had attached themselves to the army before and during the retreat.[1] A month's pay was issued to the army, but it now ceased to receive any of the allowances hitherto given in Spain. In a characteristic letter to the Minister of War,[2] Napoleon had ordered all these to be stopped. "You will take care," he said, "to inform the Generals that table money and other allowances sanctioned in the enemy's country are not to be drawn in France. Pay no attention to any appeals. Refuse all demands for indemnification on account of losses of equipment. They have sustained these losses after a battle and by their own fault."

The composition and strength of the French army on July 16, 1813, is given in Appendix B.

---

1. Clerc, 25.
2. No. 20,236, Dresden, July 6, 1813.

CHAPTER 6

The Distribution of the Allies

The distribution of the allied army as given in Chapter 2 remained without change until the operations about to be described commenced. Designed to cover two operations running concurrently, the siege of San Sebastian and the blockade of Pamplona, the front was necessarily a long one. From about Roncevaux to the mouth of the Bidassoa measured along the watershed is nearly sixty miles. Within this distance the passages over the mountains are many.[1] Then as now, however, the lines suitable for the advance of large forces through the area are limited to the "great road" from France into Spain, which running by the coast crosses the Bidassoa near Irun, the road from Bayonne to Pamplona by the pass of Maya, the Raztan valley, and the Col de Velate, and that from St. Jean Pied de Port by the pass of Roncevaux, Burguete, and Zubiri to Pamplona.

The river crossings and the passes on these roads, together with a few others in their neighbourhood by which they could be turned, alone were held by advanced detachments. In rear of these stronger bodies were placed either to give direct support to the advanced troops or to cover communication along the line. Behind these as general reserve were two intact divisions, the 3rd at Olague, and the 6th at San Estevan.

---

1. Wellington to Earl of Liverpool, Lesaca, July 25, 1813: "There are not fewer than seventy passes through the mountains, and the communication, so far as I have been able to learn hitherto, is on the side of the enemy."

The distribution thus falls into three main groups. The left, consisting of the troops engaged in and those covering the siege of San Sebastian; the centre, those holding the Baztan valley; and the right, the forces covering the lines of advance from St. Jean Pied de Port.

General headquarters were placed at Lesaca, probably from Wellington's desire to be within easy reach of the siege operations as well as with the port of Passages and the great road into Spain, whence his correspondence with England, Spain, and Portugal came and went.

Communication with general headquarters and along the line was kept up by cavalry relay posts—letter parties as they were then termed—established along the chief roads and tracks, and in such other directions as circumstances required. Vandeleur's cavalry brigade was responsible for the communications of the left of the army, and Long's brigade with the 1st Hussars K.G. Legion for the centre and right.

From the topographical description of the district, it will have been recognized that owing to the conformation of the mountains communication on the Spanish side of the range was more difficult and tedious than on the northern, where within a comparatively short distance of the crest the French had easier country and better roads. But no other line was possible in a military sense, and it was politically important to allow as little Spanish territory as possible to remain in French occupation. An advantage the allied line had was that from much of it there was good command of view over French territory.

Till the beleaguered fortresses fell, Wellington contemplated nothing further than the passive defence of his covering line. As must always happen when it is sought to defend a long mountain line, the strategical advantage lies with the assailant. By observing suitable precautions he can mass against any part of the line, cross at an unguarded pass, or by weight of numbers force an occupied one before it can be adequately supported, thus piercing the line which involves the retreat of the detachments holding other passages. As has been already shown, the shape of the country in this instance favoured the French and hindered mutual support and communication on the allied side. Given troops of approximately equal value, the chances of the defender being able to concentrate in rear in sufficient time to meet his adversary on at least equal terms depend on the appropriateness of the distribution of his troops to the particular situation, the excellence of his intelligence system, the watchfulness of his advanced detachments, the promptness and reliability of their reports and the tenacity with which they resist the enemy's advance, the quickness of the commander when action becomes necessary, and the soundness of the organization of the communication service.

The following brief discussion of the possibilities of the allied distribution in the event of a French advance on each of the three most likely lines may assist the reader in forming an opinion regarding its suitability or otherwise and be of use later on when following the actual operations.

First case. Attack on the allied left with the object of raising the siege of San Sebastian with or without the intention of a further advance southwards.

For success such a movement entailed on the part of the French the concentration of the greater part of their strength to the right, the crossing of the lower Bidassoa, and of the seizing of the strong positions on its left bank held by the allies. There was at that time no bridge over the Bidassoa below Vera, as the wooden road bridge at Behobie had been destroyed by Reille after he had crossed it on July 1, 1813. There were a considerable number of fords in this portion of the course of the river; owing, however, to the tide, which rises 16 ft. at Hendaye and makes itself felt almost as far as Biriatou, the fords from Behobie down stream are practicable only at low water. The front of attack was therefore likely to be limited to the space between Biriatou and Vera. Beyond the river here are the formidable heights of San Marcial, rising to nearly 1,000 ft., and the rugged slopes of the Haya mountain, whose rocky summit is 3,000 ft. above the sea. To meet such an attack there were immediately available that portion of Graham's corps not engaged on the siege, Longa's Spanish division, the 7th and Light divisions, a total of about 32,000 men, of whom 18,000 were Spaniards. Within from five to six hours after receipt of orders the 6th division could arrive from San Estevan, and, if the siege operations were temporarily suspended, two or three brigades from the siege troops would also be available, raising the allied force to over 42,000 men. On August 31, 1813, when the second assault on San Sebastian was actually taking place and the general positions of the opposing forces were very similar to what they had been about the middle of July—though Wellington had rather a larger number of men immediately available—Soult concentrated about 45,000 men on his right, attacked this front and failed, although a considerable portion of the allied strength never came into action.

Second case. Attack on allied centre and advance to relieve Pamplona.

In this case it was necessary for the French to cross two ranges of heights and to leave from 15,000 to 20,000 men on the lower Bidassoa to contain Graham's corps. Moreover, from no part of the allied front was a better view to be obtained over French territory than from the Maya ridge and its neighbourhood.

It will be noticed that in the case already dealt with the allied troops, who would have to meet the French attack, were practically already concentrated and the superior commander and his staff were on the spot. In the second and third cases, however, conditions were different; considerable distances and indifferent communications separated the several bodies to be assembled both from the point of concentration and from general headquarters. The speedy concentration of troops, especially in such country as we are here concerned with, depends largely on the successful combinations of many factors concerning the then working of several of which detailed information cannot now be obtained. It is hardly possible therefore to frame a reliable estimate of the time required for concentration in any particular instance under conditions as they then existed. As, however, our purpose here is merely to test the distribution of the allied army in a general manner, it may suffice if we take the conditions in each case to be favourable and assume, for instance, that early and reliable information of the enemy's intentions and movements had reached allied headquarters, that divisions had been warned to be ready to move at short notice, that reports and orders were promptly dispatched and carried as expeditiously as circumstances permitted, and that orders were conveyed and divisions moved for the most part by daylight, the weather being fair.

Under the existing allied distribution it would seem inadvisable to attempt to meet a French advance in great strength in a position so far forward as the Maya ridge, but rather to concentrate towards the strong position on the slopes south of Irurita, which covers the Col de Velate road and indirectly that from Elizondo to San Estevan. Under the conditions already assumed, Hill's force (four brigades) less his rear-guard, the 6th and 7th divisions, a total of about 15,500 men and eighteen guns, could be assembled in this position in eight hours from the time of dispatch of orders from headquarters at Lesaca. By the eleventh hour the 3rd division from Olague, together with the rearguard, would bring the total to about 22,000. It would probably be considered necessary to retain the Light division about Vera until the direction of the enemy's march from the Col de Maya was sufficiently pronounced to show he did not intend to move westwards from there against the flank of Graham's corps; also to keep Campbell's brigade for the present in the Aldudes, he had a safe line of retreat by the pass of Urtiaga into the Arga valley. If, however, both these units were moved they could arrive by the eleventh hour, as could also the British battery of the 2nd division from Lanz, bringing the total strength to over 31,000 men, including one regiment of cavalry and twenty-four guns.[1] Under the most favourable conditions the 4th division from Linzoain could hardly reach the position under twenty hours, by which time the artillery of the 6th division from Ostiz could also have arrived, bringing the strength up to about 38,000 men and thirty guns. The cavalry about Tafalla could be concentrated in the vicinity of Pamplona in about twenty-four hours after dispatch of orders from Lesaca.

Third case. Attack on allied right and advance to relieve Pamplona.

For the French this required a concentration on the left of their line, about St. Jean Pied de Port—a small fortified town connected with Bayonne by a good road—and the leaving

---

1. The speed of transmission of orders to the more distant units has been taken at six miles an hour. It is difficult to say what the usual day and night rates were owing to lack of information as to the routes by which carried, and want of exactness regarding time of receipt of the few letters and reports regarding the transmission of which there is any information. Sir Lowry Cole's report regarding the fighting about Roncevaux sent off at 1 p.m. on July 25 reached Wellington at Lesaca about 8 p.m. (Larpent). The route was probably by Linzoain-Olague-pass of Arraiz and San Estevan, which gives a rate of 6 miles an hour, mostly over hill-tracks. A letter from Wellington to Graham, sent off from the field of Sorauren at 3.30 p.m. on July 28, reached Graham at Oyarzun that evening "when Generals Giron and Howard were at dinner with me." The usual dinner-hour at Wellington's headquarters was 6 p.m., and Graham, who entertained largely, probably had the same hour. If the time of arrival of the letter is put at 8 p.m., it travelled at nearly 11 miles an hour; if at 9 p.m., at about 8¾, over a fair road throughout. A message sent by the Q.M.G. to Graham from Lizaso about 11 a.m. July 31 did not reach the latter till "the middle of last night" (July 31-August 1). If this is put at 1 a.m. on August 1, it gives a rate of 3¾ miles an hour only along a fair road partly by day and partly by night. A message from the Col de Maya by the track over the hills to Echalar would probably take about two and a half hours to reach Lesaca by day and considerably longer by night. It is equally difficult to ascertain what the usual rate of marching was during these operations. From the little data available the rate for a division by day seems to have been a little over two miles an hour, including halts long and short.

of sufficient troops to contain Graham's corps and also cover the road from the Baztan valley by the Col de Maya, which is the shortest line from the frontier to Bayonne, and from which the road between that fortress and St. Jean can be directly threatened. For this reason an advance from St. Jean would probably be combined with one from Ainhoa so as to cover the communications and permit the French to bring the greatest possible strength into action.

For the allies this was the most difficult of the three cases to meet. Not only were the distances between the divisions and between general headquarters and the advanced detachments longer, but the country was more difficult, whilst an advance on this line was for the enemy the shortest route to Pamplona. Owing to the distances to be traversed as well as the proximity of the French at St. Jean Pied de Port an attempt to concentrate towards Byng's advanced position would be exceedingly hazardous; moreover, any position on the Altobiscar can be turned on its left by the Linduz, and on the right towards Orbaizeta. The next suitable position—and indeed the only possible one until quite close to Pamplona—in which to meet the French in strength is on the high ground which separates the valleys of the Erro and Arga streams, and is crossed by the direct route from St. Jean to Pamplona.

Byng's force, Campbell's brigade, and the 4th division, in all about 14,000 men, of whom about 4,000 were Spaniards, were the troops immediately available to meet the French advance. On their resisting power depended the possibility of concentrating in the Erro position in their rear a sufficient force to deal with the French advance. The 3rd division having been placed at Olague as a support to 4th, would move up without further orders as soon as information of the French advance in strength reached it. The fighting portion of the division could then reach the position in about six hours. The movement of other troops outside the group would have to be ordered from general headquarters. It would be necessary for those under Hill in the Baztan to retain their positions until it was certain that the French were not going to attempt to advance into the Baztan, also because Hill's position covered the shortest routes by which troops could be drawn from the left to reinforce the right as well as the communications with headquarters.

The 6th division was designated as the first reinforcement for Picton.[1] Under the most favourable circumstances, that is having been already warned and having many hours of daylight for its march, the division could reach the position in about fifteen hours after receipt of orders. If, however, the movement was not ordered until information of the enemy's advance in strength reached general headquarters, allowance must be made for the time required for reports to reach Lesaca, for orders to be issued and to be conveyed to San Estevan, which could hardly be less than from ten to eleven hours. Under such circumstances the division could not arrive on the position until about twenty-six hours after the dispatch of the report from the front. If the enemy's advance could be delayed for this period,[2] the arrival of the 6th division would bring the allied strength up to about 25,000 men.

Under like conditions the 7th and Light divisions could arrive in about thirty-four hours; it is unlikely, however, that both could be moved until the situation in the centre had been further cleared up. In about the same time a Spanish reinforcement from the corps blockading Pamplona could also have arrived, as well as the artillery "brigades" of the 3rd and 7th divisions from Huarte and Berrioplano, with such cavalry as was considered necessary. If the position could be held until the arrival of the 7th division, the artillery and say 4,000 Spaniards, the allied force would be increased to over 35,000

---

1. Wellington to Hill, San Estevan, July 14, 1813.
2. On July 26, 1813, the French under Soult did not arrive in front of the position till about 5 p.m., thirty-five hours after Byng was first attacked. Besides the stubborn resistance put up by the allies, the French advance was also delayed by a fog which covered the mountains on the afternoon of July 25 and did not clear off till late on the morning of the 26th.

men. As soon as it became evident that the French were not also advancing into the Baztan, Hill's troops and the Light division, amounting to about 12,500 men, would be available.

The fact that the position near Erro was within twenty-four miles of St. Jean Pied de Port, whilst the nearest support outside the group (6th division) was twenty-five miles distant and general headquarters nearly fifty miles from Byng's advanced position, shows that with the then existing means of communication there was little margin of time in which to effect sufficient concentration to meet a French advance in force. It will also be noticed that in both this and the second case much time would have been gained had general headquarters been placed in a more central position.[1]

Of what the British portion of the allied army was at this period it is perhaps unnecessary to say much here. Veterans for the most part of many years of war, in a high state of physical training, full of confidence in themselves and in their commander, and led by gallant and experienced superior officers, it may safely be said that at no time during the war was the *moral* of the army higher or its efficiency in all respects greater.[2] The campaign just ended had shown what that army could do; by its deeds it may be known.

But perhaps so much may not be known of the army whose officers and men had stood shoulder to shoulder with the British in all the later phases of the war. A brief reference, therefore, to the organization and military qualities of the Portuguese army of this period may be of interest. The more so as its regeneration is an instance of that capacity for organizing and leading men of other races of which British officers both of former times and of today have given many signal proofs.

---

1. "Ask me for whatever you please except *time;* that is the only thing beyond my power " (Napoleon).
2. "I have always thought that I could have gone anywhere and done anything with that army. It was impossible to have a machine more highly mounted and in better order."—Wellington, evidence before Commission on Military Punishments.

Early in 1809 General Beresford was appointed to command and reorganize the Portuguese army with the rank of Marshal and a staff of British and Portuguese officers. When Wellington arrived at Lisbon on April 22, 1809, to assume command of the British army the forces of Portugal were, as he expressed it,[1] "but in their infancy in respect to organization, discipline, and equipment," and were quite unfit in his opinion to be pitted against "the veteran and disciplined troops of France."[2]

On July 6, 1809, Wellington was appointed Marshal-General of the Portuguese forces. The army was raised and organized on a territorial basis, each province or district finding a certain number of units. The establishment in 1813 consisted of twenty-four infantry regiments of two battalions, twelve caçador (light infantry) battalions, twelve cavalry regiments, and four regiments of artillery. The established strength of the infantry regiments was 1,501, exclusive of officers, of the cavalry regiments 590. In July 1813 there were serving with Wellington's army twenty-one line regiments and eleven caçador battalions, five regiments of cavalry, and three batteries of field artillery. In every division of that army except the 1st and the Light, there was a Portuguese brigade composed of two line regiments and a caçador battalion. The 1st division (Guards and King's German Legion Infantry) had no Portuguese troops; in the Light the Portuguese troops were brigaded with the British, the 17th regiment in the 1st brigade, and the 1st and 3rd caçadores in the 2nd. There was also a Portuguese division of two brigades which always worked with the 2nd division and two unattached brigades. Four of the Portuguese cavalry regiments formed one brigade, the fifth regiment was unattached.

Beresford's task was no light one, but steady progress in rendering the army efficient for war was made. As by the

---

1. Wellington to the Junta of Estremadura, Lisbon, April 28, 1809.
2. Wellington to Earl of Liverpool, Badajoz, November 14, 1809.

ancient laws of the kingdom every man had to serve either in the army or militia, conscription was available to fill the ranks. For years the officers of the Portuguese army had done little or no duty, many were old and most of them inefficient. A wholesale riddance was made of these, their places being filled by Portuguese gentlemen of higher class, and four or five British officers were appointed to each regiment; one either commanded a battalion or was second in command to a Portuguese lieut.-colonel, and the others generally captains. When a Portuguese officer commanded a brigade the colonels of the regiments were British. The pay of the officers, hitherto miserably small, was raised and all were forced to do their duty. Wellington, writing to Beresford, thus expressed his ideas of what the Portuguese army wanted:[1]

> We are mistaken if we believe that what these Portuguese and Spanish armies require is discipline properly so-called. They want the habits and spirits of soldiers—the habits of command on one side and of obedience on the other; mutual confidence between officers and men; and above all, a determination in the superiors to obey the spirit of the orders they receive, let what will be the consequence, and the spirit to tell the true cause if they do not.

It is to the lasting credit of the men of both nations concerned that in the end the result desired was largely attained.

A potent factor in the success obtained was the general good-will the people of Portugal had for the British nation and for the British army in particular.

Constant and serious as were Wellington's difficulties with the Portuguese Government and officials, by whom, as he said, "the British army had been so unworthily treated," he has repeatedly put on record his appreciation of the "respect and affection the people of Portugal had for the British na-

---

1. Wellington to Beresford, Badajoz, September 8, 1809.

tion and particularly for the military qualities of the soldier," and how well they got on with the latter. Therefore, when in 1810 the Portuguese army was by the brigading system already mentioned practically absorbed in that of Great Britain, there was nothing but good fellowship between the men of both nations. "I have never known an instance," wrote Wellington to Lord Liverpool in 1810, "of the most trifling disagreement among the soldiers and officers of both nations. The Portuguese soldiers eat the same food"—perhaps for the moment his thoughts turned to India and its sepoys— "and as military men, adopt the same habits as our soldiers."[1]

And the fusion was equally successful in the field. "We do what we please now with the Portuguese troops, and manoeuvre them under fire equally with our men and have some dependence on them;"[1] and already in 1811 Simmons declared, "The Portuguese deserve every praise; they fight like lions." From good they went, to better, and in 1813 the praise of the good qualities of the Portuguese soldiers was in all men's mouths. Wellington called them "the fighting-cocks of the army,"[2] and Picton writing to one friend said: "The Portuguese brigade attached to the 3rd division was the admiration of the whole army;" and to another, "The Portuguese brigade, if possible, exceeded the British in gallantry."[3]

It was a splendid result. "I believe we owe their merits more to the care we have taken of their pockets and bellies, than to the instruction we have given them," was Wellington's opinion as to how it had been attained.

On July 16, 1813,[4] the total number of Portuguese serving with the allied army was 35,300 officers and other ranks,

---

1. Wellington to H. Wellesley, Elvas, May 22, 1811.
2. Wellington to Lord Liverpool, Lesaca, July 25, 1813.
3. Robinson, *Life of Picton*, letters to Colonel Pleydell and Mr. Marryat, July 1 and 7, 1813.
4. From the morning state of that date. The states do not give the strength of the artillery and engineers, as these corps were then under the Master-General of the Ordinance. Napier estimates they numbered 4,000.

of whom 23,417 were present and effective. The effective strength of battalions varied very considerably. In the Portuguese brigades of the 3rd and 7th divisions the average strength was only about 350 officers and men. In other divisions it was generally from 450 to 550. That of the cavalry regiments was a little over 300 officers and men.

On this date the effective strength of the British army present in the field was:

	Officers	Other ranks
Cavalry	361	6,336
Infantry	1,606	31,490
Total	1,967	37,825
Total all ranks		39,792
Artillery and Engineers		4,000
Total		43,792

The total effective strength of the Anglo-Portuguese army on July 16, 1813, was therefore 79,092 officers and men.[3]

---

3. See Appendix A.

CHAPTER 7

Soult's Plan of Campaign

As we have already seen the news of the defeat of the French army at Vitoria and its retreat into France reached Napoleon at Dresden at a very inopportune moment. Such a disaster and the possibility that France herself might soon be invaded, drove a wedge into the bold front he was maintaining against his foes in central Europe. To do something at once in the south which should be a set-back to the hopes raised by Vitoria, was no doubt Napoleon's eager desire, and accounts for the despatch of Soult at a few hours' notice and the pressing instructions sent to the War Minister to see that the offensive was taken with the least possible delay. He was most anxious that Soult's arrival before Pamplona should coincide with the opening of the Congress of Prague, and his envoy there, Caulaincourt, was directed[1] to regulate his conduct of the negotiations accordingly.

A recent writer[2] has remarked that, "it is well to remember the mental peculiarity which had long led him (Napoleon) to exaggerate his own fighting force and under-estimate that of his enemy;" and he adds, "Napoleon's dispatches relating to the war in Spain reveal a strange inability to grasp the difficulties of his marshals and the tenacious character of the British and Spanish defence."

---

1. Napoleon to Caulaincourt, No. 20,317, Mayence, July 29.
2. Dr. Rose, *Pitt and Napoleon: Essays and Letters*, Napoleon's conception of the battle of Waterloo.

That vast power of imagination with which Napoleon, "the spoilt child of victory," was endowed had now "degenerated into wilful self-deception."[1] The slave of hard facts, as he had earlier declared himself to be, had become "an apostate from his old belief in facts and began to believe in things which had no reality,"[2] and, as Count Yorck says, "events were to be as he wished them to be; and, if they were not so, he declared the hard fact to be simply untrue, thinking such a declaration sufficient to attain what was impossible and to undo what had been done."

It is perhaps on some such assumptions as these that Napoleon's insistence on the speedy assumption of the offensive can best be explained. At a period of much stress, when he was playing a great game and fully occupied with all his vast interests, he seems to have given too little consideration to the Spanish problem and come to hasty conclusions on insufficient data. Indeed after Soult's departure, when writing to Count de Cessac[3] on July 5, he says he "is still in ignorance of events and does not fully know what has actually happened." Yet the next day he informs the War Minister[4] that these events "fix two objects of the first importance—1st, that a position is taken up to cover San Sebastian; 2nd, to manoeuvre in order to relieve Pamplona before its supplies are exhausted."

Great master of both the practice and theory of war and a supreme organizer, Napoleon, had he looked at even the facts he had squarely and honestly, must have realized in what state his army of Spain was, how little fit it was to take the field immediately, and the risks he ran by at once committing it to an attack on the allied army flushed with victory. He either took this risk deliberately, impelled thereto by circumstances, or else would not see things as they really were.

---

1. Count Yorck v. Wartenburg, *Napoleon as a General*.
2. Carlyle, *On Heroes*.
3. Napoleon to de Cessac, No. 20,229, Dresden, July 5, 1813.
4. Napoleon to Clarke, No. 20,237, Dresden, July 6.

The Emperor was zealously seconded by his Minister of War. No sooner had the tidings of Vitoria reached Paris, than Clarke, Duke de Feltre, Minister of War, hastened to impress on King Joseph the necessity of a speedy assumption of the offensive.[1] "The offensive," he said, "alone befits the circumstances and the honour of the imperial arms. It is urgent that no time be lost before an advance is made to relieve Pamplona." Joseph replied,[2] that the minister had gravely overestimated the available strength of his forces for such a movement and under-estimated those of the enemy, that his generals agreed with him that to at once re-enter Spain would be to gain nothing and perhaps to lose the French army. Nevertheless, fortified by the Emperor's instructions, the minister continued to press at first on Joseph and then on Soult the necessity for speedy action. It has been said,[3] that this line of action both on his part and on that of other ministers in Paris was prompted less by anxiety for the honour of the imperial arms than by the desire to get the army once more out of French territory, where it remained a charge on the State.

Soult arrived on the scene, determined to assume the offensive, to prove to France, "to Europe, to the enemy likewise, that there was still a French army on the Pyrenean frontier."[4] He had indeed the Minister of War's instructions to do so; but he owed besides a debt of spite to his predecessor, who had been the cause of his recall from Spain in the previous January.

Halting at Paris on his journey from Dresden to Bayonne, Soult had there received his final instructions, and with them the minister had given him a copy of an appreciation of the situation submitted to Joseph on July 5, by Marshal Jourdan, the chief of his staff. This is an important document, as on it Hoult undoubtedly based his plan of action.

---

1. Clarke to Joseph, July 2.
2. Joseph to Clarke, July 6.
3. *Revue d'Histoire—»La Bataille de Sorauren,»* No. 142.
4. Soult to Clarke, October 26.

The following précis of it is taken from the *Revue d"Histoire* for September 1912: *"La bataille de Sorauren."* Basing his proposals on the information he then possessed regarding the enemy, namely that Wellington was about to besiege Pamplona under cover of a corps placed in observation in the passes leading into Navarre and Aragon, that a British detachment had moved towards Zaragoza in pursuit of Clausel and that only Spanish troops supported by a British corps faced Reille's troops at Iran, Jourdan offered the King the choice of three lines of action.

> *First.* To attack the enemy opposite Reille *(i.e.* on the lower Bidassoa) and push them back beyond Tolosa. Then, either to leave a corps of 15,000 men at Tolosa and march with the remainder on Pamplona, or else to advance with the whole army towards Vitoria or even so far as the Ebro so as to oblige Wellington to evacuate Navarre, to concentrate and fight a battle. In either case the task assigned to Clausel would be to re-enter Navarre, raise the siege of Pamplona and join the King's army.
> *Second.* To leave a corps of 15,000 men in observation on the Bidassoa, the rest of the army to move by Roncevaux on Pamplona. By such a movement junction with Clausel would be better assured than in the first proposal.
> *Third.* To move the army by the Somport pass and Jaca into Aragon, effect a junction there with Clausel and also with Suchet, so as to form a mass capable of dealing with the enemy's army wherever it might be. In this case also a corps of 15,000 men was to be left on the Bidassoa.

The first proposal had, Jourdan considered, the advantages of at once freeing the frontier from the enemy and relieving San Sebastian.

The army would also have had a good road fit for artillery and train for its movement. But Wellington, placed as he was between the army and Clausel, would be able to attack one or the other with the bulk of his forces. If the movement was made on Pamplona by the Tolosa road, which is a long defile as far as Irurzun, the security of the army would depend on the corps of 15,000 men left at Tolosa, without which it ran the risk of being attacked in front and rear and of losing its artillery, if compelled to retreat along mountain paths. If on the other hand the army moved directly on Vitoria, it left behind it the Pamplona-Tolosa road by which Wellington could issue, and the farther it advanced the weaker its fighting strength would become, owing to the number of detachments necessarily left *en route* to guard the line of communication. This proposal was favoured by the Minister of War, but all the generals of the army were against it.

The second alternative would give the army the shortest route to Pamplona, and it would directly cover its line of communication with St. Jean Pied de Port. But it was, Jourdan said, by no means certain that artillery could cross the pass of Roncevaux until considerable work had been done to the road. The necessity of leaving 15,000 men on the Bidassoa would reduce the strength available to enter Navarre to about 80,000, whilst the 12,000 infantry with Clausel about Jaca could not be counted on to reinforce it. When issuing from the mountains there was always the possibility of meeting the British army ready to offer battle at its full strength.

Both first and second proposals possessed other disadvantages in common. In neither Navarre, Guipuzcoa, nor Biscay was there any hope of obtaining supplies, even at harvest time, already traversed as they all had been by French and allies in turn. Moreover, the Spanish troops were at their best in mountain warfare.

The third alternative had the advantage of concentrating in Aragon a force of 42,000 men without taking into account Suchet's weak army of Aragon or any troops he could detach from Catalonia.

The country there was open and favourable for movement and the crops more abundant than in the mountains of Navarre. It was doubtful, however, if artillery could cross the

Somport pass, nor was it certain that it could be replaced from Zaragoza or even that the army would reach that depot.

The movement would take a considerable time, and meanwhile its objective, Pamplona, might have fallen. Moreover, success was only possible if Wellington, deceived by demonstrations, held his troops concentrated in Navarre.

Jourdan expressed himself in favour of the third project[1] and concluded by stating that he felt himself unequal to undertaking the execution of any of the plans. On the margin of the document, Joseph wrote, "Give a copy to Soult."

The senior generals had all along pressed for some definite plan of action for the army. As Reille expressed it in a letter to the War Minister, "We want a plan of operations, not movements made only in consequence of those of the enemy."[2]

Now it was for Soult to decide what this was to be. By the information at his disposal regarding the distribution of Wellington's army, he was led to conclude that the larger part of it was in the Baztan Valley, that the pass of Roncevaux was held by Spanish troops only, and that Cole's and Picton's divisions were still around Pamplona.[3]

Owing to this conclusion probably, as well as to grave doubt whether Pamplona could make any long resistance, Soult had early expressed his preference for the second of Jourdan's alternatives—a concentration of the army towards its left about St. Jean Pied de Port and movement thence on Pamplona. But he hesitated for some while before finally deciding, mainly owing to the War Minister's strongly pressed views that he should advance towards San Sebastian and relieve that fortress.

Having, however, been assured by the aide-de-camp of General Rey, governor of San Sebastian, who had come in by sea on July 18, that the place could hold out for at least fifteen days longer, Soult finally decided to move on Pamplona.

---

1. Clerc, p. 46.
2. Reille to Clarke, Irun, June 20.
3. Soult to Clarke, Bayonne, July 18.

On July 18, the army of Spain was distributed as follows:

Right wing under Reille, holding the right bank of the Bidassoa from the sea to the Bayonnette Mountain. Villatte's reserve division, about Sare.

Centre, under D'Erlon. Maransin's and Abbé's divisions about Ainhoa, the former finding posts at Zugarramurdi and Urdax. Darmagnac's division, about Espelette.

Left wing. Clausel moving up from Jaca in accordance with Soult's orders with Vandermaesen's and Taupin's divisions had arrived at St. Jean Pied de Port on July 15 and 16, when Conroux's division also came under his command. The latter was at St. Etienne de Baigorry with detachments in the Aldudes watching the passes thence into the Baztan valley, and one of two regiments at the Adarca peak.

Vandermaesen's division had a post of 500 men at Château Pignon on the Roncevaux road. A reconnaissance made from this detachment on July 17 came in contact with the outposts of Byng's troops, and in consequence Clausel moved up the whole of this division to the Orisson heights behind the advanced detachment, fearing lest the British should interrupt the work of repairing the road which was then going on. Later on he also moved Taupin's division up to the plateau, less one regiment placed at Arnéguy in the Val Carlos.

Headquarters of the army were at Bayonne.

The movement of Reille's right wing towards St. Jean Pied de Port was ordered to commence on July 20.

To lessen the chance of information of the movement reaching the enemy, the French outposts took men from all the frontier villages and held them as hostages. On July 18 and 19, Villatte's reserve division took over the outposts along the right bank of the Bidassoa from Reille's troops. In order to prevent the allied outposts suspecting that anything special was taking place, the reserve division took up exactly the same posts, and there was thus no change in the appearance of the line. Where British and French outposts were opposite each other, the French brigade took the posts and the foreign brigades those in front of the Spanish outposts. After relief, Reille's divisions were concentrated behind the hills on the right bank of the river, and the reserve division held the line from the sea at Hendaye as far as Sare. Covered by this division and by those of D'Erlon, which maintained their positions at Ainhoa and Espelette, Reille's wing, accompanied by several horse artillery batteries, commenced its movement on July 20. General headquarters left Bayonne on the same day and were established at the Château of Olhonce near St. Jean Pied de Port on the 21st. The two cavalry divisions were also ordered up to join the army.

Heavy rain fell on the 19th and 20th, and the indifferent cross country roads, by which Reille's divisions moved from St. Jean de Luz by Ascain, St. Peé and Cambo to gain the main road from Bayonne to St. Jean Pied de Port, were consequently in a very bad state—the soil of the district generally is a deep stiff clay—and the march of the columns was retarded. Moreover, the advice of inhabitants of the district, that the artillery should be sent round by the great road through Bayonne, was apparently disregarded, and the guns accompanied the infantry.[1] The two leading divisions arrived in their cantonments about St. Jean Pied de Port on the evening of the 22nd, but many men had fallen out and, owing to the bridge over the Nive at Cambo having been washed away by the rise of the river, the main body of Lamartinière's division did not arrive until July 24. Already the troops had suffered considerable fatigue and privation owing to the weather, the state of the roads, the lack of transport, and faulty supply arrangements. There had been no biscuit ready for Reille's wing when the movement commenced, flour was issued instead, and as there was no transport it had to be carried in the men's haversacks, where it soon became wet. Nor were supply measures any better at St. Jean Pied de Port; arrangements were bad and confusion reigned. Meat, flour and grain were all insufficient for the needs of the assembled troops, the bakeries could not turn out the bread and biscuit required, and matters came to such a pass that the oxen collected to drag the guns up the pass had to be guarded against the hungry soldiers, as well as the houses of the villagers, whose men folk were away in the mountains doing their duty as national guards.[1] It was ordered that when the troops advanced they were to be in possession of four days' rations—they had to be carried by the men as transport could not be provided—it is doubtful if even the most lucky units received more than two days.[1] Some few cattle perhaps might be obtained as the army advanced, but nothing else could be expected seeing that both French and allies had already traversed the valleys in which few crops are grown.

Soult dared much in that, however great success he looked for in his military operations, the raid carried with it the germ of failure in his defective arrangements for feeding his force.

The troops now assembled about St. Jean Pied de Port and Ainhoa numbered over 60,000 men, exclusive of national guards, and after making a fairly liberal deduction for casualties during the concentration. About 7,000 were cavalry, and there were sixty-six guns.

On July 23, Soult issued his final orders for the advance on the 25th. His order (see Appendix C) prescribed the preparatory arrangements to be made on the 24th and the tasks of the different columns on the 25th.

On the 24th, the army was to take up preparatory positions as follows:

Clausel's wing in two columns, on the plateau of Orisson, on the then main road to Pamplona, about five miles in front of St. Jean Pied de Port and some 2,300 feet above it, and on the heights above Arnéguy.

The artillery, except eight mountain guns which were to accompany Reille's column, was to be dragged up the steep mountain road by means of 300 pairs of oxen collected for

---

1. *Revue d'Histoire*, No. 141.

the purpose, the horses following. On reaching the plateau a few guns were to be placed in action and the rest parked behind the infantry. Clausel was also to send out a detachment under a selected officer to his left towards the plateau of Iropil, where it was to join the national guards of the district and manoeuvre so as to threaten the right of the allies.

Reille's right wing, having relieved the post at Adarca by its own troops and placed national guards in those in the Baigorry valley found by Conroux's division, was to be concentrated in a concealed position behind the Adarca mountain. It was to be accompanied by eight mountain guns and by a party of sappers for work on the mountain path along which the column was to advance on the 25th.

D'Erlon was to place the divisions of the centre so as to be ready to attack and carry the pass of Maya on the 25th. On his left the national guards of the Baigorry and the Aldudes, were on the night 24th-25th to occupy the Hausa range, which bounds the Baztan valley on the east.

Information was to be sent to Villatte that the army would attack the enemy's positions on the 25th. He was then to act according to the special instructions he had already received. These were to the effect that if in consequence of Soult's operations the enemy in his front retired, he was to relieve San Sebastian and follow them up; if, on the contrary, he was attacked and obliged to relinquish his position on the Bidassoa, he was to fall back on Bayonne, disputing the passage of the Nivelle at St. Jean de Luz, and also making a stand on the heights of Bidart beyond that town.

The orders for the 25th were that there was to be a general and simultaneous advance of all the columns at 4 a.m. Clausel was to attack the allied position on the Altobiscar, and having seized it, to pursue the enemy vigorously, pushing on by Ibaneta and Roncevaux to Burguete. He was also to send a detachment into the Val Carlos which was to drive back the enemy's troops in the valley and move towards the pass of Ibaneta. His left flank detachment and the national guards on the Iropil were to light fires on the mountain before daybreak and then make demonstrations, so as to induce the enemy to believe there was a large force in this direction. The advance of this column was to be directed towards Orbaizeta, thus threatening the enemy's retreat on Burguete if he held on too long in the Altobiscar position. Clausel was to get into communication with Reille's column as early as possible.

Reille's orders were to advance and seize the Linduz, moving by a track which runs close below the crest of the Hayra spur on its western slopes. This ridge bounds the Val Carlos ravine on the west. Having seized the Linduz, he was to take up a position there and send advanced guards in the directions of Ibaneta, Roncevaux and Espinal, also towards the passes of Atalosi and Sahorgain, in order to gain possession of them or at least deny their use to the enemy. Detachments were also to be sent to threaten the passes of Urtiaga, Ernazabal and Velate. Reille was also to order the national guards on the Hausa Mountain to light fires after 5 a.m., to spread themselves out along the mountain and demonstrate so as to make the enemy believe a large body of troops were assembled there. They were if possible to seize the pass of Berdaritz, and when the enemy retired they were to move by the crest of the mountains towards the pass of Velate, sending a detachment to meet the first division of D'Erlon's troops which crossed the pass of Maya to give the General information and provide him with guides.

The artillery was to follow Clausel's advance and was to be preceded by all the available sappers who were to improve the road. The commandant of the artillery was ordered to bring as many guns as possible into action as soon as Clausel's attack commenced.

Each column of attack had one or more light cavalry regiments attached to it. The two cavalry divisions were ordered to concentrate behind St. Jean Pied de Port and be ready to advance on receipt of orders. P. Soult's division was directed to send a detachment into the Baigorry valley to open up communication with D'Erlon and also to watch the pass of Ispeguy.

D'Erlon was to vigorously attack the allied troops holding the pass of Maya. Having seized it, he was to move on Elizondo and thence according to the line of the enemy's retreat either towards the pass of Velate or that of Urtiaga. *But he was never to lose sight of the fact that it was to be his duty to join the rest of the army as soon as possible and gain communication with Reille.*

The Marshal concluded his orders by stating, "that the aim of the prescribed movements was to force back the right of the enemy's line, to seize the position of Altobiscar and to give us command of the principal routes leading towards Pamplona as well as of those passes by which the enemy's troops in the Baztan could retire in that direction. When. these results have been obtained, the divisions of the right and left wings will manoeuvre in the direction of Zubiri," also that the Commander-in-Chief would move with Clausel's column, to which all reports were to be sent.

With this order, Soult issued a stirring proclamation,[1] which was to be read at the head of every company. After telling the army how matters stood in Germany, he compared them with what had happened in Spain, where they, the soldiers who had formed "a veteran army, small indeed in numbers, but great in all that constitutes military character, which had fought, bled and triumphed in every province of Spain," had been hustled out of the country "with tarnished laurels" owing to the incompetence of a commander unworthy of his troops. Then paying a just compliment to the skill of the allied commander and "the valour and steadiness of his troops," he concluded:

> Soldiers! I partake of your chagrin, your grief and your indignation. I know that the blame of the present situation is imputable to others; be the merit of repairing it yours. I have borne testimony to the Emperor of your bravery and zeal. His instructions are to drive the enemy from those lofty heights which enable him to proudly survey our fertile valleys, and chase them across

---

1. Wellington's Dispatches.

the Ebro. It is on Spanish soil your tents must next be pitched, and from thence your resources drawn. No difficulties can be insurmountable to your valour and devotion.... Extensive but combined movements for the relief of the fortresses are upon the eve of taking place. They will be completed in a few days. Let the account of our success be dated from Vitoria, and the birthday of the Emperor celebrated in that city; so shall we render memorable a date deservedly dear to all Frenchmen.

Words and sentiments well calculated to rekindle ardour in the hearts of officers and men, those veterans of the Peninsula who, though their army had been overthrown at Vitoria, knew it was not they but their leaders who had been beaten. "Never was an army more hardly used by its commander, for the soldiers were not half beaten."[1] Witness the testimony of Tomkinson, who with his squadron of the 16th Light Dragoons was pressing their rear-guard. The enemy, "seeing the rest of the Brigade coming up, retired through the defile, leaving a square of Grenadiers in its mouth. We came close upon them without perceiving they were there.....I rode up within a yard of the enemy's infantry, they had their arms at the port, and were as steady as possible, not a man attempting to fire till we began to retire. I never saw men more steady or exact to the word of command."[2] The *moral* of the army was still good, and officers and men had complete confidence in their new commander.[3] The resolute bravery and skill with which they fought in this short campaign, often despite fatigue and hunger, is ample evidence that the fighting value had not abated of that redoubtable imperial infantry, which, till it met the British soldier, had failed to find its match in Europe.

It is hard to say what the Marshal's real opinion now was as

---
1. Napier, *History of the Peninsular War.*
2. *Diary of a Cavalry Officer*, Lieut.-Col. Tomkinson, 16th Lancers. Available in a Leonaur edition under the title *With Wellington's Light Cavalry.*
3. Soult to Clarke, July 19, 1813: "*L'armée a repris confiance, elle ne parle pas de les derniers revers que pour manifester la résolution de les venger d'une manière éclatante.*"

regards the probability of the successful issue of his operations. He was of course bound to speak and write as if confident of success. Though he subsequently used somewhat different language, he now wrote on July 23 to the War Minister, outlining his plan as given in his orders and added, "The results of this movement ought to be that San Sebastian will be relieved and, unless I fail in my attempt, several of the enemy's corps will be compromised. When I have fulfilled the task indicated in my letter I shall manoeuvre so as to get into line with the army of Aragon."

CHAPTER 8

The French Advance

The news that the assault on San Sebastian had failed reached Lesaca at 11 a.m. on July 25. Wellington immediately ordered his horse and soon afterwards rode off to Graham's headquarters. During the afternoon, distant firing in the Maya direction had been heard in the British camps about Vera and Echelar, and it was said at headquarters that D'Erlon, after pushing a strong reconnaissance against Stewart at the Maya, "made a show but gave way again."[1] The Quartermaster-General, who had not accompanied Wellington, now considered it necessary to warn both the 7th and Light divisions to be ready to move[2]—the 7th, possibly that evening, towards San Estevan if the enemy had any decided success in the upper part of the Baztan Valley, and the Light at short notice. Lord Dalhousie was also asked for early intelligence of what had happened at the Maya, and Alten requested to warn Ross's troop of horse artillery, attached to light division and camped about three miles up the Bidassoa from Lesaca, to be also ready to move.

Later, about 7 p.m., Ross was ordered to march that night to Sumbilla,[3] and thence next morning towards Berroeta, in

---

1. Larpent, Diary, p. 202.
2. Q.M.G. to Dalhousie and Alten, Lesaca, July 25.
3. Larpent, *Diary*. Having dined with the officers of the troop, he left to return to Lesaca, and met the messenger carrying the order to Ross shortly after 7 p.m.

71

order to clear the river road by Sumbilla, and because the only possible exit for the troop from the Baztan valley being over the col de Velate, it was necessary to get it away early in the event of the retirement of the army.

Wellington returned to Lesaca about 8 p.m.; on his way back he had heard of the firing at Maya, and just as he arrived a report came in from Cole, sent off at 1 p.m. on 25th, that he and Byng were engaged at the Roncevaux with strong French forces. There was as yet no reliable news of what had happened at the Maya. It was still believed at headquarters that D'Erlon's attack had been but a feint and that he had retired. This, together with the attack on Roncevaux, might be regarded as corroborative of Wellington's opinion concerning Soult's move. Always patient, he decided that further news from the front must be awaited before putting the army in motion. Writing at 10 p.m. that night to Graham, he gave him such information as had reached him and added:

> It is impossible to judge of Soult's plan yet, particularly till I know the results of his operations of this day. I understand the enemy were driven off the Puerto de Maya. One can hardly believe that with 80,000 men he proposes to force himself through the passes of the mountains. The remainder of his force, one would think, must come into operation either to-morrow or the day after, and it is desirable you should be prepared.[1]

He also suggested it would be well to prepare to embark all the siege material not absolutely necessary, to return the borrowed guns to H.M.S. *Surveillante* and to remove all others from the batteries except a few left to keep up a fire on the breach.

The general lines of the action it would be necessary to take if Soult really did attempt to advance by Roncevaux towards Pamplona had evidently been settled between Wellington and Murray some days previously, and are foreshadowed in the latter's instructions to Cole and Picton of July 23 and 24, and in

---
1. Wellington to Graham, Lesaca, July 25, 1813, 10 p.m.

his letter to Hill of the 25th. Cole and Picton must hold the French whilst the rest of the army makes such movements as will bring them assistance whilst covering both Pamplona and San Sebastian, and it was intended that the 6th division from San Estevan should be the first reinforcement for Picton.[1]

During the night, a messenger arrived at headquarters with a verbal message from Stewart at the Achiola; and now Wellington learnt what had really happened at the Maya and that Hill was falling back on Irurita.[2] The presence of a large French force on the col de Maya was a new and complicating factor in the situation, especially as no further news had come in from the Roncevaux. To keep communication with Cole, Picton and Pamplona, and in order to be able to concentrate the whole or part of the covering army south of the main chain of the mountains, it was necessary to hold the southern exits from the Baztan Valley, namely the road by the col de Velate, which would be covered by Hill when his concentration to the rear on the heights above Irurita was completed, and the important road junction near San Estevan, where tracks led over the passes of Arraiz and Loyondi (passes of Doña Maria) into the Lanz valley and to Lizaso, and also westwards by Zubieta into the Pamplona-Tolosa road near Leiza. Moreover, the French strength on the Maya was such that it was equally necessary to have the means of promptly supporting Hill if D'Erlon advanced directly against him. The 6th division at San Estevan was well placed to do this; if moved, however, it must be replaced there at once. The simplest way to do this would be to move the 7th division—Barnes's brigade, and the 82nd regiment were now with Hill—to about Sumbilla. But now that Stewart was evacuating the Achiola, it was also open to D'Erlon to make a move against the lower Bidassoa valley by Echalar or Vera, whence he could move by tracks over the Haya mountain towards Oyarzun, thus turning the

---
1. Wellington to Hill, St. Estevan, July 14, 1813.
2. Wellington to Graham, Lesaca, July 26, 4 a.m.: "I had a verbal message from General Stewart at 10 p.m., when Hill had ordered him to retire."

flank of Giron's Spaniards holding the lower part of the river. And it was especially necessary to guard against any interruption from this side whilst the embarkation of the siege guns and stores was going on. Therefore both Vera and Echalar must continue to be held, and it would be inadvisable to make the movements preliminary to a concentration towards Pamplona, till there were more definite indications of the line D'Erlon would take.

Wellington, who was in no sense anxious about Cole and Picton's divisions, as from the first he considered them strong enough to be in no danger from Soult's 80,000 infantry in such a country as they were working in,[1] determined to proceed very early on the 26th to Hill's corps and see for himself what the actual situation was before issuing orders for a general movement of the army. But in order that all might be prepared and know what they had to do, Murray drew up an instruction to divisional commanders to be acted on "in the event of its becoming necessary to assemble a force to oppose the advance of the enemy towards Pamplona by the Roncevaux road,"[2] and this was issued early on July 26.

There were, however, other movements not affected by the considerations mentioned, which Wellington decided to order at once. In the existing distribution of the army the 6th division was regarded as first reinforcement for the troops on the Roncevaux, and Picton had been so informed; under present circumstances, however, the division was not so available, therefore Wellington that night wrote to La Bispal[3] directing him, whether or no Don Carlos' division had reached Pamplona, to send half his force towards Zubiri in support of Cole and Picton. La Bispal was also requested to inform Mina at Zaragoza of the present state of affairs and order him

---

1. When the 3rd division joined the 4th, Picton would be in command of nearly 20,000 men, which included Byng's and Campbell's brigades, Morillo's Spaniards, the 18th Light Dragoons, and one battery of artillery.
2. Arrangements for July 26, Lesaca, July 26, 1818.
3. Wellington to La Bispal, Lesaca, July 25, 10.30 p.m.

to move with half his infantry towards Pamplona, leaving the remainder to blockade the citadel. The Quartermaster-General also dispatched orders to Sir S. Cotton, commanding the cavalry to move up to the neighbourhood of Pamplona with as little delay as possible with Ponsonby's and the Hussar brigades which were to be followed by the brigade of Household cavalry and D'Urban's Portuguese. Fane's brigade only was to remain about Monreal, keeping a detachment at Sanguessa, and was to watch all the roads coming from the north down the Salazai, Irati and Erro valleys. Cotton was also instructed to place an officer's party of cavalry at Villaba, which was to post a letter party at Ostiz and also a party at Lizaso, to keep communication by dispatch riders with San Estevan over the Doña Maria pass.[1]

Wellington himself wrote to Graham at 4 a.m. on July 26, probably just before he started for San Estevan, telling him how he proposed to cover his flank about Lesaca and Vera, and now definitely ordered the embarkation of the siege guns and stores suggested in his letter of the night before. The siege of San Sebastian was therefore for the time being turned into a blockade.

This would in any case have been inevitable, as, owing to the non-arrival of ordnance transports from England, gun ammunition was almost exhausted and siege operations could not be resumed till a fresh supply was received.

---

1. Q.M.G. to Cotton, Lesaca, July 25, 1813.

CHAPTER 9

Soult's Advance on Pamplona

On the evening of July 23, Wellington was in possession of information that Soult had moved the greater part of his force towards St. Jean Pied de Port.[1] He judged the object of the movement was to draw his attention from the side of Iran towards the right and to induce him to make a counter movement, whereby Soult might gain an opportunity to cross the Bidassoa and make a dash to relieve San Sebastian. Wellington's usually accurate insight into his opponent's intentions was in this case at fault. He seems to have been a good deal influenced in forming this opinion by the fact that Soult had a bridge equipment ready at Urrugne behind the Bidassoa, and that it remained there. But, perhaps more so by the stage which the siege of San Sebastian had now reached. The assault on the fortress originally fixed for July 23 had been postponed till the next day; and again, on account of a fire round the breach, till the morning of the 25th. Wellington naturally was anxious about the siege operations,[2] and also that nothing should interfere with them just as the culminating-point was about to be reached. That Soult with 80,000 men would attempt to force his way through the mountains he found it

---

1. Wellington to Don P. Giron, Lesaca, July 21, 1813, 11 a.m. Wellington to Graham, Lesaca, July 21, 1813, 11.30 a.m.
2. Larpent, *Diary*: "and he (Wellington) has been as usual very anxious about the event. He was very fidgety when I went to him yesterday." Lesaca, July 25, 1813.

difficult to believe,[1] and if he did so he judged the existing distribution of the army would suffice to stop him before any serious success was gained.[2] Wellington therefore determined to make no change for the present in his dispositions.

In a letter to Sir Lowry Cole, the Quartermaster-General, on July 28, had sent him Wellington's instructions that he was to support Byng's troops as effectually as possible, and in the event of being compelled to give up the passes he was to make arrangements further back for "stopping the enemy's progress toward Pamplona." A copy of this letter was also sent to Picton with instructions "to act accordingly."

In view, however, of Soult's reported move Wellington considered a further instruction to Cole was necessary, and on the 24th Murray again wrote[3] to him that "Lord Wellington has desired I should express still more strongly how essential he considers it that the passes in front of Roncesvalles should be maintained to the utmost and every arrangement made for repelling effectually every direct attack that the enemy may make in that quarter."

It is not stated at what time this letter was written—Murray in this respect was often less careful than Wellington—but it did not reach Cole till 9 a.m. on the 25th, "just as Byng's people had driven back the enemy in their first attack."[4]

> Here you must make ready for one of the greatest sights in Europe. You are on a very high upland plain something like the glacis of a fortification. The last crest of the Pyrenees stands like a long wall of white cliffs which seem low and familiar because you are so high up on this plain. You go through a fine northern-looking wood which might be in

---

1. Wellington to Graham, Lesaca, July 25, 1813, 10 p.m.
2. Wellington to Hill, July 14. Referring to movement ordered of 4th division to Viscarret, 3rd to Olague, and 6th to Lanz, he said, "These movements when effected will render us full strong enough for anything."
3. Q.M.G. to Cole, Lesaca, July 24, 1813.
4. Cole to Q.M.G., Linzoain, July 27. In Suppy. Dispatches, vol. viii, this letter is dated July 27—evidently a mistake of either writer or printer, as Cole retired from Linzoain on the afternoon of July 26.

England, with great spacious clumps of beeches and broad glades. You pass the monastery and then go up through the hamlet of Roncevaux, quite an insignificant few hundred feet of road. You see a ruined chapel on your left, then suddenly you are at the summit and a profound trench opens sheer below you and points straight away to France miles and miles away. It is here that Roland died.[1]

Such is the approach on the Spanish side to the Pass of Roncevaux, the profound trench below is the Val Carlos, a deep wooded gorge down which is carried in many zigzags the modern road into France. Where the road crosses the col its height is about 8,600 feet and is naturally about its lowest point. But the port itself is some three miles in width, a long grassy saddle with rounded slopes, thickly wooded below the crest on the northern side and less so on the south, stretching from the Altobiscar (5,000 feet) on the east to the Linduz (4,000 feet) on the west and about a mile and a half from where the road crosses the ridge, which point was in 1813 known as the col or *puerto* de Ibaneta. At that date the existing road through the Val Carlos had not been made. From St. Jean Pied de Port to Pamplona the line of communication followed that of the old Roman road from Gaul into Spain, the route of Charlemagne's army. Ascending almost due south from the town of St. Jean Pied de Port to the plateau of Orisson, the road, known locally as the *chemin d'artillerie,* ran along towards the crest of the heights by the col de Bentarte and the Altobiscar to the col de Ibaneta, and from there descended by Roncevaux to the upland plain surrounding the village of Burguete. This is a broad expanse of pasture land, quite open, except for clumps of wood here and there, and well watered by numerous streams.

Besides the *chemin d'artillerie,* two other tracks led from St. Jean over the port. One by the Adarca peak and along the crest of the Hayra spur to the Linduz, whence the pass of Ibaneta could be reached by a track down the hillside, or the travel-

---

1. Hilaire Belloc, *The Pyrenees.*

ler could proceed direct to Espinal by the Mendichuri pass. The other led up through the Val Carlos. Both were steep, and bad going, especially the latter, which was little used. From Burguete the old road ran due south down the valley of the Urrobi until it met the Pamplona-Zaragoza road at Aoiz. Today a good modern road branches off from this about a mile south of Burguete and runs by Espinal, Viscarret, Zubiri and the Arga valley to Huarte and Pamplona. This in 1818 was probably little better than a mule track.

On the evening of July 24, the troops under Byng at the Roncevaux were posted as follows. The light companies of the brigade and the rifle company under Major Acland, 57th regiment, together with some Spaniards of Morillo's division, held a strong position across the road on the steep rocky slopes of the Leiçar-Atheca peak, with outposts pushed forward towards Château Pignon. The Buffs and 1st provisional battalion were in rear on the Altobiscar. To cover the flanks, a Spanish battalion was placed at a foundry about three miles north of the village of Orbaizeta, whence a track leads over the hills by the pass of Navala to Burguete. In the Val Carlos on the left were the rest of Morillo's division and the 57th regiment. The Spanish troops found a piquet of 100 men in a redoubt, a relic of former wars, on the summit of the Linduz. It seems probable that all or the greater part of the Spaniards in the Val Carlos were withdrawn during the night of July 24-25, towards the Altobiscar, because when General Ross rode up to the redoubt on the morning of the 25th and expostulated with the officer in command of the piquet on account of the bad look-out which was being kept, the latter excused himself by saying that two battalions of the regiment of Toledo were in his front. The narrative adds, they had gone off in the night.[1]

---

1. Smyth, *History of the 20th Regiment*, Gen. Bainbrigge's narrative, from notes by Lieut. Fall, who was A.D.C. to Gen. Ross: "From further inquiry it turned out that those two battalions had moved off during the night preceding without any intimation having been given to the piquet or to a regiment (57th) of Gen. Byng's brigade posted in a dell to their right towards Roncevaux."

Beyond Byng's left in the Aldudes, was Campbell's brigade of the Portuguese division, placed there to watch that valley and keep open the communication between Byng and Hill in the Baztan. On July 24 this brigade was in bivouac on the col de Mispira, on the eastern slopes of the valley, about five miles as the crow flies from the Linduz but some eight miles by a mountain track. Byng's nearest support was the 4th division in echelon of brigades along the Roncevaux-Pamplona road from Espinal, where the leading brigade (Ross's) was, to Linzoain, where the divisional artillery remained owing to the state of the road. At Espinal, Ross was two and a half miles from the Mendichuri pass by a mountain track, and about five miles from the Linduz. At Espinal, he was five miles from the col of Ibaneta and nearly ten from Byng's forward position on the Leiçar-Atheca.

During the night of July 24-25, Sir Lowry Cole received a report from Byng stating that he expected to be attacked the next morning.[1] He immediately ordered Ross's brigade to move at daybreak up the Mendichuri to reinforce Byng's left and cover his communication with Campbell; Anson's and Stubbs's brigades to move to Espinal. Ross had already been warned by a Spaniard that the advanced posts would be attacked the next morning,[2] and had secured guides and made all his arrangements for moving up the mountain.

The simultaneous advance of Soult's two columns was ordered to commence at 4 a.m. on July 25. To cover his right flank and clear the Val Carlos, Clausel, whose first objective was the capture of the Altobiscar heights, sent a right flank detachment into the valley with instructions to drive the enemy out of it and gain possession of the col about the chapel of Ibaneta. His left, as we have seen, was to be flanked by a band of national

---

1. Cole to Wellington, heights before Pamplona, July 27, 1813. This report does not appear to have been sent on to Wellington's headquarters. 2. Lieut. Fall's Notes. "On arrival at Espinal the General showed me a piece of soiled paper that had been sent him by some one unknown on which was written in Spanish, 'A good Spaniard informs the officer commanding the advanced posts that he will be attacked by a very powerful force at 8.30 a.m. to-morrow.'"

guards, to whom was added a detachment of regular infantry. After demonstrating on the Iropil mountain in the early morning, this column was to move towards Orbaizeta.

In order to clear the way for his advance along the narrow crest of the ridge beyond Château Pignon, Vandermaesen, who commanded Clausel's leading division, attempted before dawn to surprise the allied outposts. His attempt was unsuccessful, and the piquets so strongly resisted his advanced guard of two regiments that it was not till about 6 a.m. that the French approached the northern slopes of the Leiçar-Atheca, where Byng's line was strongly posted under good cover amongst the rocks.[1] The French advanced guard attacked vigorously, and for four hours the fight went on. Despite all attempts against their front and flanks the allies held their position with comparatively little loss, and about 10 a.m. the French, who had lost heavily, ceased their attacks. The advance of the French divisions in rear had been slow, but now they were closing up, Vandermaesen's behind his advanced guard, which so far had done all the fighting, Taupin's along the Arnéguy heights, and Conroux's in rear of all.

The British position had been skilfully chosen. The ground in front was perfectly open, its height gave good command of view and fire and the rocky slopes excellent cover to the defenders, whilst on both flanks deep ravines to east and west narrowed the front on which the French could directly approach. Moreover, from a point about a mile to the north of it, the French advance could no longer be continued in a sort of double column, for unless Taupin's division was to move along the wooded eastern slopes of the Val Carlos with their alternating spurs and ravines, it must there fall in rear of that of Vandermaesen.

From 10 a.m. till nearly noon, the French made no further attempt to advance. Then Soult ordered Vandermaesen to again attack. This after three successive assaults, again failed; and the allies "did not yield one inch of ground."[2]

---

1. Clausel's report on operations of the left wing.
2. Byng to Cole, Linzoain, July 26, 1813.

Sir Lowry Cole, after his division was in motion, went on himself direct to Byng's position, where he arrived about 10 a.m. Finding Byng's troops contending with very superior numbers, which were being continually increased,[1] and fearing an outflanking movement by Orbaizeta in consequence of Byng's resistance, he sent back orders to Anson to move towards the foundry and reinforce the Spanish battalion there, and also to Stubbs to take position on the col de Ibaneta and send assistance to Byng's posts on the Linduz. Shortly afterwards, however, information reached Cole of the advance of Reille's strong column along the Hayra spur towards the Linduz. He immediately sent a counter order to Anson, directing him to move up immediately to Ross's assistance and proceeded himself towards the Linduz.

Ross, leaving the 23rd Fusiliers in camp near Espinal, had started at dawn (some accounts say at 2 a.m.) for the Mendichuri heights. The track winding up to the pass was narrow and difficult and much blocked by fallen trees, and the General at the head of the column did not reach the pass until 7 a.m.[2] "The whole position had then the appearance of perfect quietness; the men in Colonel Campbell's camp were undressed, as we could see with our glasses." Ross then rode on to the Spanish piquet in the old redoubt on the Linduz—where a very bad look-out was being kept—and afterwards returned to the brigade. As everything seemed so quiet, the General determined to order the 23rd up with the camp equipage and baggage, and then to camp the brigade on the plateau near a spring; but just as the pre-arranged signal was about to be made, information came that Byng, five miles away across the valley to the right, was being attacked. Ross at once ordered the 23rd to come up, bringing with them the ammunition mules and all spare mules with biscuit and rum. The parties left in camp were ordered to pack up everything ready to move, and to secure guides from the village in case they were

---

1. Cole to Wellington, heights before Pamplona, July 27, 1813.
2. Smyth, *History of 20th Regiment*.

required for Anson and Stubbs's brigades. His advanced guard, composed of the Light companies, was sent up to the Linduz, "where they remained lying down quiet spectators of the attack on General Byng on the extreme right." The 20th and 7th regiments remained below on the southern slopes of the mountain. So the forenoon passed, and as yet there was no sign of Reille's advance.

By Soult's order of July 23, the position of assembly of Reille's wing was fixed in the vicinity of the rock of Adarca. On the night of 23rd-24th, the three divisions were cantoned in the villages of Anhaux, Ancille and Alphat-Ospital.[1] The staff arrangements for the march on the 24th were bad. The divisions did not move till 1 p.m., and were led through St. Jean in order to receive an issue of two days' bread. The steep and narrow streets of the town became blocked with troops, and such delay ensued that at nightfall Foy's division, which was leading, bivouacked about four miles short of the assembly position, being joined later by that of Maucune. Lamartinière's division halted for the night on the track to the Adarca less than a mile south of Anhaux. The cavalry regiment of Reille's wing, 13th Chasseurs, and all the baggage moved by the *chemin d'artillerie* in rear of Clausel's column, and the wing was accompanied only by the eight mountain guns and 60,000 rounds of reserve ammunition on mules.

The march was resumed before daybreak on July 25, Foy's division leading, followed by Maucune and Lamartinière without any interval; in rear came the mountain guns and some sappers. From Foy's bivouac to the Linduz is about thirteen miles and an ascent of some 2000 feet. Beyond the Adarca the track mounts the Hayra spur and runs along it close to the crest on the western side; it was so narrow and the slopes so steep that the troops could only move in "Indian file."[2] At 7 a.m. the head of Foy's division passed the Adarca but did not

---

1. Anhaux and Alphat-Ospital are about three miles west and east respectively of St. Jean.
2. Colonel Michaud's report and that of Reille.

reach the Laurinaga peak, about two miles from the Linduz, till 1.30 p.m., when the rear of the column was just about passing the Adarca.

It was probably just about this time that a sergeant of the Brunswick Oels' company reported to General Ross that dust could be seen rising among the forest trees below,[1] and not long after French skirmishers could be seen working their way among the trees towards the Linduz. Ross moved up the 20th Regiment and, leaving the right wing in position across the crest below the Linduz peak, he moved forward with the left wing (three companies) and the Brunswick rifle company, towards a rise on the spur beyond. On reaching it they suddenly came under a heavy fire from French skirmishers. Ross called out for a company to clear them off, and Captain Tovey doubled out his company and drove the skirmishers out of the wooded hollow beneath.

On reaching the edge of the wood, Tovey came face to face with the 6th French Light at the head of Foy's division. Calling on his company to charge, Tovey dashed headlong into the French with the bayonet. "Brave men fell by that weapon on both sides,"[2] and Foy was momentarily checked. Twenty-four men of Tovey's company fell, but with the remainder he was able to rejoin the other companies, which now, by Ross's order, fell back, followed by the French, towards the right wing of the 20th formed across a narrow part of the ridge in front of the Linduz peak with "a dense thicket on each side," as well as the almost precipitous slopes of the Val Carlos and the Heyra valley.

When the General and the advanced companies had passed through, the right wing of the 20th opened "a deliberate and deadly fire" which brought the French to a halt. Again and again did Foy attack with drums beating and the French officers leading with great gallantry, "but this furious bravery was of no avail, the 20th stood firm and unshaken;

---

1. Gen. Bainbrigge's Narrative.
2. Napier.

the French were met with withering volleys, and any who reached our ranks were bayoneted. No prisoners were taken during this day's fight."[1]

Despite all his efforts Foy could not win his way to the Linduz, for the rest of the brigade had now come up, and as the companies in first line ran out of ammunition they were replaced by others from the rear, and finally the 7th Fusiliers took the place of the 20th. Moreover, other reinforcements were approaching. Anson's brigade was moving up from the col of Ibaneta, and on the left Campbell's Portuguese brigade appeared about 4 p.m. on the further side of the Val de Hayra. Again the narrow steep-sided mountain crest had come to the aid of the British. For Reille, probably uncertain as to the strength of the force opposing him, and seeing that Clausel's column was not making way towards the col of Ibaneta, waited till he had developed greater strength before making another frontal attack. But his troops in rear made slow progress along the steep mountain side, and it was not till near 5 p.m. that Foy and Maucune's divisions were all up; then a thick fog rolled up from the valley and covered the crest, and Reille determined to advance no further that day. At 7 p.m. the two divisions and the leading brigade of Lamartinière's—the other being still in rear—went into bivouac where they stood.

Meanwhile on the right, Byng having repulsed Clausel's attacks about mid-day, maintained his position on the Leiçar-Atheca. But about 8 p.m., as his ammunition was nearly expended and seeing that the 4th division was heavily engaged at the Linduz, he fell back to another position—probably across the Northern end of the Altobiscar—which still covered the col of Ibaneta and brought him closer to the 4th division, but the track to Orbaizeta was now open to the enemy. "The movement was made in good order without losing a single prisoner, and I brought off all my wounded except about thirty, whose lives would have been endangered by immediate

---

1. Smyth, *History of 20th Regiment.*

removal."[1] The French followed slowly, but never attempted to renew the attack, and at 5 p.m. fog covered the mountains and hid their movements. As the track to Orbaizeta was now open to the French, Byng felt his position was insecure and determined to retire.[2] His troops had already commenced to march covered by the light companies, when orders to retreat sent by Cole reached him. The latter General, already in possession of a report from Campbell that Reille's column was at least 15,000 strong, realized as soon as he heard that Byng had been obliged to quit his first position that a general retreat was inevitable.[3] But it was very necessary to hold on to the passes as long as possible. If Byng and other allied troops about the Ibaneta were forced off the col and down into the open level country about Burguete during daylight, they would be exposed to grave risk in face of the overwhelming superiority of the enemy, and it was above all necessary to keep the Linduz, the shortest line into the Pamplona road, lest Byng and others falling back by Burguete should be cut off from it altogether. So the coming up of the fog when it did was a piece of good fortune for the allies.

On the Linduz there was no further resumption of hostilities and both sides settled down in close contact. The British lighted fires, such of the wounded as could be moved were sent down the hill towards Espinal, and Ross's brigade got an issue of biscuit and rum. But as soon as it was dark enough to screen the movement from the French sentries, Cole ordered the retreat to commence. Piquets were left on the positions occupied, with instructions to keep men moving about in front of the fires, so as to be seen by the enemy's sentries, and in silence Ross's brigade moved off. It was found impossible to carry off all the wounded; "they were therefore placed near the camp fires, a card being attached to each recommending them to the mercy and aid

---

1. Byng to Cole, Linzoain, July 26.
2. Cole to Wellington, heights before Pamplona, July 27.
3. Bainbrigge's *Narrative*.

of the French, who, to their honour, treated ours as they did their own."[1] Sergeant Cooper, 7th Fusiliers,[2] thus describes his experience during the night march.

> The order to retire came along the line of skirmishers in a whisper. While making this movement we came to an open space in a wood, where a number of our badly wounded men were lying wrapped in their blankets. They heard the rustle of our feet and one of them asked, 'What regiment is that?'
> 'The 7th,' we answered, and passed on, for the retreat was so suddenly and quietly ordered that we were obliged to leave them on the ground.
> This night's march was horrible, for our path lay amongst rocks and bushes, and was so narrow only one man could pass at a time, consequently our progress was exceedingly tedious. This was made worse by the pitchy darkness. Many were swearing, grumbling, stumbling and tumbling; no wonder we were worn out with fatigue and ravenous with hunger. However I kept up, though my garter strap and all of my shoe ties were broken. I called the roll of the company when I halted, and was surprised to find every man present.

It was not till a little before daylight that the brigade reached the Pamplona road. There, "we had well nigh fallen into a scrape with a cavalry piquet of Byng's column also in full retreat." Having reached the road, the brigade halted to enable the piquets and stragglers to come in and then followed the rest of the division except Anson's brigade, which had been left as a general rearguard on the col of Ibaneta. The Spanish battalion at the Orbaizeta foundry had during the day repulsed two attacks by the French flank detachment. In the evening it fell back by the pass of Navala and during the night joined Mo-

---

1. Bainbrigge's Narrative.
2. Sergeant Cooper, *Rough Notes of Seven Campaigns*. Available in a Leonaur edition under the title *Fusilier Cooper*.

rillo near Espinal. Campbell's Portuguese brigade had not been engaged at the Linduz, Napier implies, because no supplies for the brigade or transport for his sick could be guaranteed on the Roncevaux-Pamplona line, a very inadequate reason in face of the great numerical superiority of the French.

As Campbell did not arrive in the neighbourhood of the action till 4 p.m., when Ross's brigade was well holding its own, it is probable Cole did not order him up because he had already determined to retreat during the night, and, the reinforcement not being urgently required at the moment, did not wish to increase the numbers of retreating troops on the narrow Pamplona track. Campbell, moreover, had a line of retreat by which he could join later on by the Urtiaga pass on Eugui. For the time being it was an advantage to have him on the flank off the road. Campbell marched during the night and arrived at Eugui on the morning of July 26. Anson's brigade remained on the col during the night, and early next morning moved down towards Burguete unmolested by the French.

So when night fell on July 25, the progress of the French during the day, alike at Roncevaux and at the Maya, had fallen far short of what Soult had hoped it would be. He was still twenty-nine miles from Pamplona. Fortune indeed had been against him in that the long summer day had been shortened by several hours owing to the fog. The position of the enemy had been skilfully chosen and defended with steadfast valour by both British and Spaniards. But that fortune was fickle must not be used as an excuse to cover faults both of leading and of arrangement.

When, as at daybreak on July 25, but three miles separated the head of Clausel's main column from Byng's advanced position, it is hardly reasonable to (doubt, after making all allowance for the difficulties of the country, that if Soult had put in all his strength, men and guns, he must have swept the allies, who had no artillery, from the Leiçar-Atheca long before three o'clock in the afternoon. Instead of this, he allowed his advanced guard to dash themselves for nearly four hours against a strong position held by at least equal numbers, a period far too long for any purposes of reconnaissance. Then nearly two more hours were wasted before another frontal attack was delivered, which was again insufficient to force Byng from his position.

In his general order Soult had predicted that the enemy on the Altobiscar would put up but a feeble defence when he saw himself being turned by Reille's divisions moving on the Linduz. When the latter move did not take place as expected and Byng remained firm, Soult seems for a time to have been at a loss what to do, and to have forgotten that as his chief hope of ultimate success lay in rapidity of movement, if it could not be secured in the way first arranged it behoved him to try other means at once. This also illustrates the danger of attempting to forecast in orders the probable course of events in combined operation.

It is probable that Soult overrated the strength of the force opposed to him; but he was on that day in a better position to err on the side of rashness than he would be on any subsequent occasion.

That Reille's divisions did not reach the appointed assembly position on the evening of July 24, and that in consequence of this and of the difficulties of their route they did not arrive near the Linduz on the 25th till much later than the Marshal expected, is plainly due to faulty supply and staff arrangements.

To the confusion with regard to the former we have already alluded, but both the headquarters and Reille's staffs should have been aware of the difficulties the Hayra track presented to the march of such a large body of troops and arranged accordingly.

The result of the day shows how stoutly the allied troops fought and how well they shot. It was just a day of dogged resolution both at the Altobiscar and on the Linduz, and Byng's simple words of praise seem just to fit the case. "I can truly say that I witnessed the most earnest desire on the part of every officer and man to obey the orders I gave." He mentions no corps or individual save only General Morillo, "whose conduct was everything that was praise-worthy."[1] In the History of the 66th Regiment, it is mentioned that the Spaniards fought with "determination and their leader Morillo exhibited great personal courage." Sir Lowry Cole mentions the 20th Regiment, and says the conduct of the three leading companies and the Brunswick company "was particularly distinguished."[2]

---

1. Byng to Cole, Linzoain, July 26.
2. Cole to Wellington, heights in front of Pamplona, July 27.

Chapter 10

The Fight at the Maya Pass

The northern end of the Baztan valley may be likened in shape to a blunt-headed angle whose sides are formed by the Gorramendi heights on the east and the Achiola mountain on the west, the head being a narrow connecting ridge, about two miles in length, running from east-north-east to west-south-west.

This ridge, known as the col de Maya, is quite open, and is covered with grass and patches of heather and gorse. Its northern slopes are steep at first, then the ground falls more gently, running out into long spurs. On the south the fall is steep into the valley, where the streams from the surrounding hillsides, forming the head waters of the Bidassoa, unite and flow past the village of Maya, distant about three miles from the ridge. The lower slopes on this side are fairly well-wooded.

The main road of the valley ascends to the col along the eastern slopes of the Achiola mountain, and, crossing it at a height of about 2000 feet above the sea, descends by a long spur which runs northwards towards France. To-day this is an excellent and well-graded road. In 1813 it was probably a much inferior one in all respects. From the col de Maya by the valley road, and then over the col de Velate, the distance to Pamplona is thirty-six miles. From Maya village various paths lead up to the col and the adjacent heights. Close to the point where the main road crosses the ridge, a mule track leaves it and runs along its southern slopes close below the crest, and from its eastern end is continued along a divide, which running northwards connects the Gorramendi with the Mondar-rain, passing along the latter range it joins the road from Ainhoa to Espelette and Cambo on the Nive. This track is also continued from the western end of the col along the Achiola mountain towards Sumbilla and San Estevan with a branch to Echalar. It is known as the "English road"; but why so-called I do not know, as it was already in existence in 1813, though probably much improved then.

Byng's brigade of the 2nd division having been detached to Roncevaux and Campbell's Portuguese brigade into the Aldudes, Sir R. Hill had but two British and two Portuguese brigades with which to defend the valley. On his right, Campbell's brigade covered his communication with Byng at Roncevaux and the 4th division at Espinal, practically a two-days march for troops by the passes of Ispeguy or Berdaritz and Atalosi, though the distance from Elizondo to the Roncevaux pass hardly exceeds sixteen miles. To the left the nearest troops were those of the 7th division around Echalar, about seven miles away across the mountains. But this division had detached the 82nd Foot of Inglis's Brigade to maintain communication with the 2nd division, and the regiment was on the Achiola mountain above the Elizondo road about two miles behind the ridge. At the other end of the valley the 6th division was at San Estevan, nine miles from Elizondo and sixteen from the col.

Sir R. Hill's headquarters were at Elizondo, and those of General Stewart, commanding the 2nd division, in the village of Maya.

The 1st British Brigade, temporarily commanded by Lieut.-Colonel Cameron of the 92nd Highlanders, was camped at the western end of the col; the 92nd about two hundred yards to the west of the road where the Alcorrunz peak rises from the pass; the 71st was some three hundred yards to the left of the 92nd, and the 82nd of the 7th division about a mile up the mountain to the left of the 71st. The 50th regiment was to the east of the road about half a mile from the 92nd down the slope on the Spanish side.¹ The 3rd Brigade, under General Pringle, who had only taken over command of it a few days previously, was encamped in the valley a little to the north of the village of Maya. This brigade found a piquet of eighty men beyond the eastern end of the col, to watch the track from the Mondarrain. This duty was taken by each battalion of the brigade for a week at a time, and the battalion finding the piquet camped further to the north of Maya village than the rest of the brigade.² Between this advanced battalion and the piquet, the light companies of the brigade were placed on the southern slopes of the ridge about a mile in rear of the piquet post to keep up communication and as first reinforcement for the piquet.

On Sunday, July 25, the 2nd battalion 34th was the advanced battalion, and at 7 a.m. Captain Sherer of that regiment with his company relieved the ridge piquet.³ It was a fine bright summer morning and so the weather continued to be throughout the day. Surgeon Henry, in his account, mentions "the singular clearness of the weather," and that "the day was still as well as clear,"⁴ and other accounts corroborate this. The captain of the relieved piquet told Sherer that at dawn he had seen "a group of horse and a column of troops pass along the face of a distant hill and then disappear." The latter requested him to report this as soon as he reached camp, which the officer did. Not long afterwards Major Thome, an officer of the Quartermaster-General's department, visited the piquet and, having been told either by Sherer or the relieved piquet commander that the movement of French troops had been seen, rode out to a hill beyond to reconnoitre. On his return he told Sherer that he had indeed observed a small column

1. Hope, *Military Memoirs of an Infantry Officer*.
2. Major-General Sir G. Bell, *Rough Notes of an Old Soldier*, 34th Regiment. General Bell's Peninsular War experiences can be read about in the Leonaur book *Ensign Bell in the Peninsular War*.
3. Colonel Sherer, *Recollections of the Peninsula*.
4. Dr. Henry, *Events of a Military Life*.

in a valley about three miles off, but that the movement did not seem of any consequence and was probably only a change of French bivouacs. Sherer was not at all satisfied with this explanation, and perhaps the staff officer may also have had misgivings, because on his way back to camp about 9 a.m. he ordered the light companies to move up and reinforce the piquet. No other precautionary measures appear to have been taken. Meanwhile, the demonstration was in progress which Soult had ordered the national guards of the Baigorry valley to make towards the long ridge of the Hausa mountain which separates that valley from the Baztan. The passes over this range were held by the two Portuguese brigades of Hill's force under Ashworth and Da Costa. Nothing more than a skirmish appears to have taken place, and the national guards finding the passes held, retired again into their valley and remained there. But the demonstration nevertheless had full effect. It caused both Hill and Stewart to concentrate their attention on the passes on the right flank, and no orders were given to the British brigades responsible for the defence of the front at the col de Maya. Receiving information of the enemy's appearance on the Hausa, Stewart had ridden off early to Elizondo to report and confer with Sir R. Hill; after which, says Dr. Henry, "both generals and several of the staff rode to the right towards les Aldudes, and the day being fine and clear almost everybody in Maya followed in the same direction, so that by twelve o'clock I found myself the only commissioned officer in the village."[1]

The movement seen in the early morning from the Aretesque piquet was probably that of Abbé's division towards the position of assembly for D'Erlon's main attack on the Maya, which was fixed at the foot of the northern end of the Mondarrain mountain out of sight from the British position. Darmagnac and Abbé's divisions having assembled there were to move, the former leading, by the *chemin des*

---

1. Henry, *Events of a Military Life.*

anglais, and seize the Aretesque hill and the eastern end of the col. Maransin's division in bivouac behind the village of Urdax was to attack the western end where the main road crosses the ridge; but was to keep its bivouac fires alight and make no movement until the advanced guard of the main column had become engaged with the enemy. Urdax lies in the bottom of a valley and is not visible from the ridge, but troops moving southwards from it along the road would be seen soon after they had passed the village. Darmagnac's division moved from Espelette at 1 a.m. on 25th,[1] but Abbé's division, delayed by an issue of rations, did not start from Ainhoa until daybreak, and only reached the concentration point at 9 a.m.

At 10.30 a.m. the advance of the French main attack, which was under D'Erlon's personal command, commenced. It was headed by an advanced guard of all the light companies of Darmagnac's division—the men without their knapsacks—under the command of *un officier de sang-froid* (Commandant Duzer, 28th of the Line) who was ordered to push on and seize the Aratesque rock before its defenders could be reinforced.

Meanwhile on the ridge the quietness of the bright summer day was undisturbed. The regiments of Cameron's brigade were preparing for divine service, and had sent their mules and batmen down into the valley for forage.[2] There the regiments of Pringle's brigade were cooking and the usual camp life going on. It was the calm before a storm about to burst.

Suddenly heavy firing began on the east of the ridge beyond the Aretesque rock. Patrols sent out from the piquet and light companies had met the leading sections of the French advanced guard towards the southern end of the Mondarrain. After a short but sharp resistance they had to fall back towards the piquet, closely followed by the enemy. It was now about half-past eleven, and the alarm guns were

---
1. Report of Darmagnac's division, July 20 to August 10, 1813.
2. Henry.

fired by Major Cunha's battery of Portuguese artillery, four guns of which had been placed on the high ground to the west of the main road where it crosses the ridge.

Now all was haste and bustle in the camps. Quickly getting themselves ready for parade, the men fell in, and soon Cameron's brigade was formed up on the hill to the east of the road. In the valley, as soon as the companies of the various regiments were formed, they were hurried off towards the ridge in support of the piquet and light companies. The 34th being the battalion on duty, was the first to get off and was followed by the 39th and 28th regiments.

The full brunt of the rush of the French advanced guard fell on Sherer's piquet; fighting desperately, it was swept back on to the light companies who were now holding the Aretesque hill. The French voltigeurs came on with great dash and ardour, but were stopped by the British fire from the hill. On the arrival of the 16th Light, the leading battalion of Darmagnac's division, the French, led by General Chassé commanding the leading brigade, again attacked and were again driven back with heavy loss. And now the defenders were joined by the leading parties of the 34th; but Darmagnac's division was rapidly arriving. "The enemy's numbers now, however, increased every moment; they covered the country immediately in front of us and around us. The sinuosities of the mountains, the ravines, the water courses were filled with them in overwhelming force."[1] For Darmagnac was determined to have the hill and that quickly. Throwing his division into several columns preceded by swarms of skirmishers he again assailed the front of the hill and turned its flanks. Despite their reinforcement the gallant defenders of the hill could not stand against such odds, already their losses had been heavy, and they were pushed off the hill on to the ridge and into the small valley below. And now a confused but stubborn fight took place; as the remainder of the 84th arrived

---

1. Sherer, *Recollections of the Peninsula*.

followed by the 89th and 28th, the companies, breathless from their haste and the steep ascent, were thrown into the fight as they came up and a line became formed, I think, across the ridge and on along the hill covered with large rocks which forms the southern side of the ravine behind the Aretesque hill—Hills B and C on the plan—and now a welcome reinforcement reached the defenders. Cameron, seeing the fierce struggle going on about the Aratesque hill, and the rapidly increasing strength of the French, sent off the 50th regiment to the assistance of Pringle's brigade. That "fierce and formidable old regiment" rapidly advanced, and meeting the head of Darmagnac's right flank column, charged and drove it dean out of the col de la Zúrrela and along the northern slopes and then joined the 34th.[1] The British probably then stood, the 50th and 34th on the left across the main ridge, the 28th and 39th on the right to the east of the track leading to the Mondarrain; regiments and probably even companies were much mixed up. There was charge and counter charge,[2] and for a time the heavy fire of the British checked the French advance. A volley from the 28th "nearly annihilated the leading regiment" of one of the French columns "and checked the advance of the remainder."[3] Ten days later, when the position was reoccupied, the unburied dead showed that their opponents had been the French 28th of the line. It was now probably about 2 p.m.

In accordance with his instructions Maransin had not moved beyond Urdax until he knew that D'Erlon was engaged. Then he put his division in motion towards the col de Maya, sending the main body straight towards the pass by the road which then passed through the village—the modern road is to the east of it along the slopes on the other side of the valley—and a right flank detachment by a ra-

---

1. Fyler, *History of the 50th Regiment*.
2. Bell, 34th: ". . . . for the men were desperately enraged, and renewed all their exertions to be at them with the bayonet."
3. Cadell, *Narrative of Campaigns of 28th Regiment*.

vine more to the west, with the object of turning the left flank of Cameron's brigade towards the Achiola mountain. His advance would be seen by the piquets of the 1st brigade probably about noon. Cameron reinforced these with the left wings of the 71st and 92nd Highlanders, and then moved with the right wing of the 92nd, about 400 strong, under Major McPherson, to give further support to Pringle's brigade. The right wing of 71st remained as support to its left wing and that of the 92nd, now soon to become engaged with Maransin's division. The right wing of the 92nd moved at the double towards Pringle's line. But Abbé's division was now arriving and D'Erlon was no longer to be denied. Pushing the whole of Darmagnac's division, less one battalion only kept in reserve, in several columns covered by skirmishers against the front and flanks of the British line, he drove it back. Once the centre was pierced the shape of the ground forced the retreat of the brigade into divergent lines; the 50th and greater part of the 34th along the ridge towards the pass; whilst the 28th and 39th—though some portions of these regiments went back with the 50th and 34th—fighting stoutly with the left of Darmagnac's advance, were pushed along the spur running southwards from the ridge and then down into the valley below, though they do not appear to have been followed very far in this direction. Meanwhile the 92nd had arrived—I think about hill D—and the retreating 50th and 34th came towards them closely followed by the French.

> The Highlanders were a good deal blown, having advanced over a mile at a hurried pace. The situation of their friends was such that they formed line without a moment's delay and at once advanced. The enemy seeing their intention to charge, halted and thereby afforded the 34th and 50th an opportunity of retiring to reform their ranks. Enraged at his failure to capture these two regiments, the French general now turned his fury

against the Highlanders and sought to annihilate them by showers of musketry. Perceiving that the enemy was acting cautiously, Cameron, wishing to draw him on to ground where he could charge, retired the Highlanders, when the French General, mistaking the reason for the retrograde movement, pushed forward over 3000 troops, who advanced making the air ring with their shouts of *Vive l'Empereur*. Conceiving that the enemy had made up his mind to meet the steel, Cameron ordered his men to halt front and prepare to charge. On seeing them halt, the French did the same and instantly opened a terrific fire of musketry. At this time the space between the combatants was not more than a hundred and twenty paces, while the French numbered about eight to one against us. From the 92nd to the French front line the ground was almost level, but in rear of their foremost troops was a narrow ravine, behind which rose abruptly a considerable eminence, from the face of which the French fired over the heads of their comrades on the small body of the Highlanders. These did not, however, return it, but directed the whole of their fire on that part of the enemy's force on the brow of the ravine nearest to themselves, and so coolly and admirably was it given that in less than ten minutes the French dead lay literally in heaps. The slaughter was so appalling, that the utmost efforts of their officers failed to make their men advance beyond the slain.[1]

Aided by the 34th on their right and the 50th on their left, who again twice charged the enemy,[2] "this sanguinary combat was sustained for over twenty minutes," but in all the regiments the losses had been terrible. More than half the men of the 92nd wing had been killed or wounded, and all

---

1. Hope *Military Memoirs*. Lieut. Hope was one of the two unwounded officers of the right wing of the 92nd and brought it out of action.
2. Fyler, *History of 50th Regiment*.

the officers except two lieutenants. No help was in sight and a heavy fight had broken out behind them at the Maya pass, where General Stewart, who had now arrived, was engaged with Maransin's division. Retreat was inevitable and was begun by the 34th and 50th, covered by the wing of the 92nd, who in turn fell back with perfect steadiness and order. The French pursued slowly; in front of the Highlanders the bite had been taken out of their attack, and they would not close with the remnant of that redoubtable wing. Thus the British went slowly westwards along the ridge, halting from time to time to fire and "defending the ground foot by foot."[1] Soon, however, a heavy column pressed down on the 34th, who were on the southern slopes of the ridge, and pushed them down into the valley. The 50th and 92nd had now reached the eastern slopes of the hill to the right of the pass and were joined by the right wing of the 71st and part of the 28th.[2] The 28th charged the enemy's leading column, but were in turn driven back and down into the Maya valley. The Highland wings fell back towards the pass whither the 50th had already been ordered back. A stubborn fight had been going on here, but the pass was still held by the left wings of 71st and 92nd. General Stewart sent news of the fight to Lord Dalhousie at Echalar and requested help from the 7th division; he had also ordered the 82nd regiment down from the Achiola. Now, however, seeing Maransin's division gathering thick in front and Darmagnac's advance on his flank threatening his retreat and also the line by which the expected reinforcements from the 7th division would arrive, he decided to fall back from the pass. Sending the 50th and 71st right wing to take up a position a little distance in rear, with the 92nd and left wing of 71st, he opposed a front to the French advance.

There appears to have been now a pause in the action. Maransin had swung round the heads of his division to join

---

2. *Revue d'Histoire,* No. 141.
1. Hope

Darmagnac, but this latter division was now in much confusion; it had lost heavily and was running out of ammunition, and was therefore halted to reform and for the issue of ammunition,[1] and Maransin's division placed in the first line. When Darmagnac's division had been reformed, an advanced guard of three battalions from it was sent down into the valley towards Ariscun and Maya to cut off the retreat of the Portuguese troops holding the lateral passes.[1]

Meanwhile the French, after some skirmishing, again advanced, bringing forward a mass of infantry to oppose all resistance.[2] The British opened fire, but, after a few rounds, Stewart retired the advanced line through that of the 50th and right wing of 71st and placed it in rear. But the four Portuguese guns were lost. They "had been taken up the mountain in pieces and placed in situation where animals could not go; they were left firing case shot to the last moment and consequently could not be saved."[3] As soon as the front was clear, the 50th and right wing of the 71st opened a heavy fire on Maransin's column and then in their turn retired. In this manner Cameron's brigade fell slowly back, each line relieving the other "with the utmost regularity and disputing every inch of the ground." It was indeed a fine performance. But the French pressed on, and by 4.30 p.m. the camps of the brigade were in their hands. The 82nd had in the meantime come up and a stand was made; but "after a hot contest" was compelled, like the other regiments, "to retire by alternate wings,"[4] and the retreat of the whole continued.

About a mile south of where the main road descends northwards a narrow col with steep slopes on both sides joins the Maya ridge to the Achiola mountain. Above it rises an under feature which commands the main road and also

---

1. *Revue d'Histoire*, No. 141.
2. Hope.
3. Dickson MSS. Report by Lieut.-col. Tulloh, commanding the Portuguese artillery, to Lieut.-Col. Dickson, August 16, 1813.
4. Capt. Wood, *The Subaltern Officer*.

the track leading from it up the mountain. Here Stewart formed up Cameron's brigade and the 82nd for a last stand and Maransin pressed forward to the attack. The ammunition of the British was almost exhausted, some of the men were reduced to hurling down rocks on their assailants. Matters seemed so critical that Stewart was about to give orders to retire up the mountain, when about six o'clock the cheers of the tired defenders heralded the approach of General Barnes and his brigade of the seventh division. Putting himself at the head of the 6th regiment and the Brunswick Oels, that gallant officer and his men, with not a few of Cameron's brigade who were not to be denied another charge, dashed to the sound of the Highlanders' pipes full at Maransin's front and drove him back fully a mile to the pass, and the rest of Stewart's troops followed closely.

This swift and unexpected stroke was a blow to D'Erlon. The British advance was menacing and he hesitated. Instead of putting in all his men—three nearly complete divisions were now on the ridge—and driving back the weak British force, he appears to have thought more of what his position would be if greater British reinforcements arrived than what he could do by a vigorous renewal of the offensive. He ordered up one brigade of Abbé's division to reinforce Maransin, and sent messengers into the valley to recall his advanced guards to the ridge. Finally he gave up all idea of any further offensive that day, and by dark the whole of his command was concentrated and bivouacked on the ridge. But the British were still on it, and, until driven from their flanking position, forbade any further advance. D'Erlon's task for the day was not half fulfilled.

And so the long summer day wore itself out. Night fell and the bivouac fires of both sides shone out on that Pyrenean ridge which, to those who know its history, must ever be sacred ground. For there on that day hundreds of brave and gallant men of both nations had fought their last fight and take their long rest beneath its grassy slopes. The total British losses were 1,484 officers and men. On the French side Darmagnac's division lost 1,400 men and Maransin's 600.¹

But there was to be little repose for the British survivors. News of what was happening at Roncevaux and the imminence of Byng and Cole's retreat had reached Sir R. Hill.

He had probably already received a letter from Sir George Murray written that day, warning him of the probability of Soult making "an effort upon Byng and Cole on the Roncevaux road," with demonstrations elsewhere which he would be prepared to follow up if successful, in which case, Murray added, "you would have to evacuate your more advanced positions in the Baztan valley, and that the army as a whole would have to take up a more retired line."² Hill, who does not appear to have been at any time present during the Maya fight, was therefore in possession of the general views of army-headquarters as to what was necessary under the circumstances, and when he received Stewart's report on the situation he ordered the whole of his command to retire immediately on Irurita, about ten miles south of the col de Maya at the junction of the valley road and that to Pamplona by the col de Velate.

During the night, therefore, the tired and hungry men of Cameron's brigade, the 82nd and Barnes' brigade, leaving their bivouac fires burning,³ moved down the road unmolested by the French. And it was well it was so, for there was much confusion in the valley. The state of things was expressed in homely but graphic language to an officer of the 34th by an orderly dragoon who arrived from headquarters during the night with a message for Sir R. Hill.⁴

"The whole of the country is a mixed fair. The commissary, artillery, baggage and wounded all jammed on that narrow road, trying to get away," and it was not the troops only and their impedimenta which filled the roads, for the inhabitants also were

---

1. D'Erlon's report of the centre. See Appendix D for detail of British losses.
2. Q.M.G. to Sir R. Hill, Lazaca, July 25, 1813 (no time given).
1. Wood.
2. Bell.

fleeing before the expected advent of the French. It was not till after daybreak that the 82nd passed through Elizondo. Early in the day, however, the whole of Hill's force, except one Portuguese brigade left in front of Elizondo, was concentrated on the slopes of the high ground above Irurita across the road towards the col de Velate and commanding the valley road to San Estevan.

Such were the main incidents of the combat on the Maya ridge and the results. It was indeed a veritable soldier's battle. To speculate what would have happened had not Barnes' brigade arrived at the critical moment, or what Hill might have done had Byng and Cole been able to hold the Roncevaux passes, seems superfluous.

But to inquire into the causes of a repulse which, but for the stubborn gallantry of the regimental officers and men, might easily have been a great disaster, cannot be amiss. Especially as the main causes were neglect of principles just as applicable to-day as they were on that July 25, one hundred years ago. And first may be put a tendency on the part of Wellington and the higher command of the allied army to underestimate the potential value of the French army in respect both of its capabilities of assuming the offensive and of its fighting value when it did. That such feelings existed on the part of Wellington and the only other officer in the army admitted into his entire confidence, Sir George Murray, the Quartermaster-General, "the life and soul of the army next to Lord Wellington," as Larpent, a shrewd and disinterested observer, terms him,[1] seems evident from the wording of a letter [2] written by the latter to Sir Lowry Cole, instructing him as regards the support his division was to give to Byng in the defence of the Roncevaux pass; the support he said was to be as effective as possible without committing Byng and the 4th division against a force "so superior, that the advantage of the ground would not compensate for it, *making allowance also for the inferiority which may influence the enemy at present in meeting our troops.*"

---

1. Larpent, Diary.
2. Q.M.G. to Sir L. Cole, Lesaca, July 23, 1818.

A great battle had been won, and the enemy, after losing heavily in men and material, had retired rapidly to France, and such a feeling was natural. But as subsequent events proved, it was the French Commander, *ce pauvre Joseph*,[1] rather than his troops, who had been defeated, and the recuperative qualities of the French seem to have been under-rated.

This is put first as, if correct, it seems to be at the bottom of the failure to do things at the Maya which ought have been done by troops who had been on the ground for a fortnight.

No attempt was made to add in any way to the defensive strength of the ground. Not a redoubt was thrown up, trench dug, or obstacle created. For this the immediate commanders of the troops must be held responsible. But Hill—nor indeed Wellington himself, if he visited the position as it seems probable he did[2]—cannot be absolved from blame.

In a dispatch to Earl Bathurst on July 12, Wellington wrote, "I hope we shall soon have San Sebastian and, *if we get well settled in the Pyrenees,* it will take a good reinforcement to the French army to drive us thence." Owing to the operations then being carried on by the allied army, the siege of one fortress and the blockade of another, and to the character of the country, Wellington had necessarily to hold a long mountain line crossed by several passes to cover his operations. It was inevitable that the defenders of such passes as could be held must be relatively very weak as compared with the masses which the French, who had the advantage of better communications on their side, could suddenly throw against any selected crossing. To allow the troops to neglect the obvious precaution of entrenching the passes held, was hardly the way *to get settled in the Pyrenees,* and it was a precaution all the more necessary because both the nature of the operations going on

---

1. Napoleon, *Mémoires de Sainte Hélène.*
2. Larpent, *Diary,* chap, ix: "The day before yesterday (July 14) .... away he went (Wellington) over the mountains to San Estevan. He is going to see more of the mountain passes that way, he says, and will be back on the fourth day."

and that of the southern side of the mountains necessitated a system of defence in great depth demanding the longest possible resistance at the point attacked, failing which the whole system was liable to collapse.

No doubt the scale of entrenching tools with the army was such as would to-day be termed utterly inadequate, and the siege of San Sebastian and blockade of Pamplona made heavy demands on it and on the small royal engineer establishment. But with what the troops had, and what could have been got from the district, something might have been done. That this was possible and that the lesson had been learnt, is proved by the fact that when the passes were reoccupied ten days later, the troops were soon busy constructing blockhouses, breast works and other defences.[1]

On July 9, 1813, the Commander of the Forces had issued a general order, "that every military precaution must henceforth be used to obtain intelligence, and to prevent surprise."

Napier says, "General Stewart was surprised, his troops were not." The General certainly was; as regards the troops, the statement is only partially true, or as Sherer puts it, "It was a surprise and it was not a surprise." The piquets and light companies were not surprised, but it can hardly be denied that the rest of the troops were. Wellington termed it a surprise. Why was the second division surprised? Readers of the narrative will have already answered the question for themselves. Reconnaissance, that important part of outpost duty, had been neglected. "If an enemy is so continuously watched, that he can make no movement without being observed, surprise will be impossible,"[2] and the conditions for this watching were all favourable. The French were close at hand; all knew where they were; for indeed their camp at Ainhoa was plainly visible from the ridge, and reviews and other movements had been seen.[3] The day was fine and clear, and much of

---

1. Cadell.
2. Field Service Regulations, Part I, sec. 75 (5).
3. Cadell: "We could plainly see the French army in bivouac near the village of Ainhoa."

the country in front was such as to facilitate concealed approach to points whence a close watch on the French could have been maintained. Had infantry observation posts been kept out—the country is unsuitable for cavalry both as regards movement and concealment—from the time the British occupied the pass, and good arrangements made for the transmission of intelligence, surprise on July 25 would not have been possible. Moreover, no use for this purpose seems to have been made of the local inhabitants who were Spaniards.

Instead of attacking as he did, D'Erlon might have moved to his left into the Aldudes—the orders he had received from Soult to seize the col de Maya were of course unknown to Hill—and thence attempted to gain the Baztan valley by the Ispegui and other passes over the Hausa. Such a move would have meant a long detour over difficult country, and the use of the main road would have been barred till he had cleared the British from the upper valley. But it was a possible move, and perhaps it was to meet such a one that Pringle's brigade was placed in the valley about Maya so as to be ready to support the Portuguese troops holding the lateral passes. But placed as this brigade was, it was all the more necessary to ensure that it should reach the ridge in ample time in the more probable case of an attack from the front.

To mystify and mislead your enemy in every possible way is a maxim of war.

By the demonstration of the national guards towards the Hausa mountain on the early morning of the 25th, Soult signally achieved his object- Stewart was completely misled by it and so also was Hill. Both rode off early towards the Ispegui pass and were accompanied or followed by all the staff of the 2nd division. It is almost certain that Major Thorne, on his return to camp from the outposts, would report to General Pringle that he had ordered up the light companies in consequence of what he had seen. But if he did, the latter officer does not seem to have taken any action on it and certainly no orders were received from Stewart. The British brigades of the division fought till the afternoon without the divisional commander and his staff being present. Wellington's comment is perhaps sufficient, "Stewart's affair on the 25th was in fact a surprise, occasioned by the fancy people have to attend to other matters than their own concerns."

But whatever faults and omissions may be laid at the door of the higher command of the division, how nobly and at what cost the regimental officers and men strove to redeem them, we have tried to show. For over six hours and under almost every possible disadvantage did a British force, no more at the outset than six battalions numbering about 4,000 officers and men, contend against not less than 18,000 tried warriors of France. Never perhaps was the indomitable stubborn courage of the veterans of many battles, the redoubtable infantry of that old Peninsular army, put to a severer test, and it stands out perhaps in yet bolder relief as one reads what those who fought there that day say of the fight. Almost without exception they pay a generous tribute to the dash and valour of the French infantry and to the leading and devoted bravery of their officers.

Where all were brave it may be thought invidious to apportion praise. But in every narrative by officers of other regiments, unstinting admiration is expressed for the gallant conduct of the 92nd, whose "stern valour," Napier says, "would have graced Thermopylae," a regiment not as stated "principally composed of Irishmen," for nearly every officer and man was a Scot.

"They stood like a stone wall," writes one who saw them well,[1] "overmatched by twenty to one till half their blue bonnets lay as a barrier to the advancing foe. Oh! they fought well that day! I can see the line now of the killed and wounded stretched on the heather as the living retired

---

1. Sir G. Bell, 34th Regiment.

closing on the centre." And who too, whether soldier or not, can picture to himself that last retreat of the remnants of Cameron's brigade towards the Achiola mountain without his heart being stirred with pride in that triumph of battle discipline.

Verily that day one more beacon light was lit to guide the way of those who in all succeeding generations follow for King and country in the footsteps of those gallant men.

CHAPTER 11

Retreat of Sir L. Cole

Soult spent the night of July 25-26 in bivouac with Clausel's column in front of the Altobiscar, intending to resume his attack on the allied position in the morning.[1] At daybreak on the 26th, the fog still hung over the mountains and in the valleys below. But scouts had discovered Byng's retreat, and very early in the morning Clausel's column commenced its march. On reaching the col of Ibaneta, touch was gained with Reille, who had sent a detachment there. Then the column moved by Roncevaux towards Espinal, but progress was slow on account of the fog and the bad state of the road.

Reconnoitring patrols sent out from Reille's column had also ascertained that the British had left the Linduz. This column likewise was early in motion, and the report of the enemy's retreat was soon confirmed by finding his wounded who had been left on the ground. In accordance with his instructions Reille now ordered Lamartinière to hold the Linduz, the Atalosti and Mendichuri passes.

Shortly afterwards, Reille received a letter from Soult informing him that the Marshal with Clausel's divisions was moving on Espinal and directing him to follow this movement, "on the right of Clausel's troops, keeping as far as it is possible to do so on the heights."

In accordance with this order, Foy, whose division was still

---

1. Soult to Clarke, bivouac on the heights of Altobiscar, 11 p.m., July 25, 1813.

leading, was directed to move along the crest towards the pass of Sahorgain. Guides had been secured, but Basque was their only language and no one in Foy's column could understand them. On reaching the Atalosti pass, which was thickly wooded, at about 10 a.m., the head of the column, owing to the fog and to want of knowledge of the guides' language, took the wrong turning and went south instead of keeping along the crest, and found itself coming down into the valley of Espinal half a league from the column. In a message to Reille, Foy explained how the wrong direction had been taken and added, "Everything indicates the English divisions are retiring on Espinal, the road has lately been repaired, and our men have found a large number of the enemy's wounded."[1] How easily the error could be made will be recognised at once by anyone who has been caught in a fog on these or any other mountains without a compass or a good guide. It was, however, yet possible to rectify it, as one of Foy's brigades was still on the crest, but Reille allowed himself to be persuaded by his subordinate. "Not only did the track lead toward traces of the English, but also to Clausel's column, where the baggage, left behind three days ago, was,"[2] and following the lead given by Foy, the whole of his wing moved down towards Espinal and eventually joined Clausel's column on the Pamplona road in rear of the guns and cavalry.

In a message to Soult dated Linduz, 12.30 p.m., Reille informed him of his decision, and, aware he was not carrying out the instructions he had received, added that he was assured that by leaving Zubiri on his left he could move on Eugui and thence, if necessary, re-ascend on to the main ridge either by the col of Artezia or that of Velate. The information was correct, but to adopt that route would mean a further loss of valuable time, even if no count is taken of opposition by Campbell, whose presence in the neighbourhood might be expected and from whom the movement could hardly be hidden.

---

1. Foy to Reille, bivouac a'Atalosti, July 26, 1818.
2. *Revue d'Histoire*, «La Bataille de Sorauren.»

That a march along the main watershed was a possible one, must, I think, be assumed. Soult would hardly have ordered it unless he had ascertained it could be done. It would, however, have been a slow and difficult one, more so than the march on the 25th up the Hayra spur, where there was at least a used track. Not less than sixteen miles of steep hillside would have to be traversed, and with the fog in the morning it seems doubtful if the head of the column would have reached Velate by nightfall. But, if they could keep the march concealed, the pass might have been in the possession of the French early on July 27. The best exit from the Baztan to the south would then have been closed, junction with D'Erlon would have been assured, and the combined six divisions moving down the Lanz valley would have threatened Picton's retreat and reached the neighbourhood of Pamplona long before any assistance from the Baztan by the round-about way of Zubieta and the Tolosa road could have reached him. But Reille, it may be from want of knowledge of the country, had failed entirely to grasp the possibilities of his position at the Linduz.

It was about noon when Clausel's advanced guard gained contact with Cole's rear guard beyond Espinal. Driving in the point, composed of the light companies under Lt.-Colonel Wilson, 48th Regiment, and a squadron of the 13th Light Dragoons, the French briskly attacked Anson's brigade. The latter fell back on the main body, which had taken up position on a ridge over which the road ran behind the village of Linzoain. About 2 o'clock the French were up in force and Soult deployed for attack. When the enemy at 4 o'clock had gained high ground on his left flank, which Cole's strength did not allow of his occupying, he retired about a mile towards the village of Erro, and again offered battle in a strong position on the lower slopes of the high ridge which divides the Erro valley from that of the Arga. Meanwhile, Campbell's brigade, coming from Eugui, came in sight on the summit of the ridge at some distance from

Cole's left, but Soult, who estimated Cole's force at 15,000 men, probably judged that reinforcements were reaching him, and did not attack.[1]

About this time Soult received a letter from D'Erlon dispatched at 3 p.m. on the 25th, and learnt from it that his "centre" column had not been able to advance from the col de Maya because the enemy still maintained a position on its right flank.[1] He was now able to judge generally how far his operations were working out as against his plan. The enemy's right had been forced back, and the Roncevaux and Linduz seized.[2] But D'Erlon was hung up on the Maya, Reille and his three divisions were not threatening the Velate pass, but were in his rear in the Espinal valley; it was clear, therefore, that the exits from the Baztan, by which the allies could march towards Pamplona, were still open, though it could still be hoped D'Erlon was that day pressing forward to the col de Velate. Soult cannot but have realized that the time already lost was giving the enemy opportunity for concentration, that any further dispersion of his forces would be unsafe, and that success lay only in a resolute advance, trusting that D'Erlon would join him in time for the decisive battle. Yet with all his strength he allowed the long day to pass without another effort to crush the inferior allied force immediately opposed to him.

Picton, having received information of Cole's retreat from Roncevaux, marched early on the 26th from Olague by Eugui towards Zubiri. Moving on himself in advance of his division, he joined Cole as the 4th division and other troops were retreating to their second position. As he approached, a man of the 20th recognized him at a distance and exclaimed

---

1. Soult. to Clarke, Linzoain, July 26, 11 p.m.: «*Il y un petit engagement, mais je n'ai pas jugé devoir attaquer ce soir*»; and he closes his dispatch by saying, «*Je n'ai jamais vu les troupes mieux disposées ni montre plus d'ardeur.*» This dispatch reached Paris either on night July 30-31 or early on 31st, as it is the first entry in the diary of receipts for July 31.
2. See Soult's order for movement, Appendix A.

to his comrades, "Here comes old Tommy, now boys make up your minds to fight."¹ But there was to be no more fighting that day. After conferring with Cole, who was with his rear-guard, and seeing the French strength, Picton decided that the retreat towards Pamplona should be continued that night and then returned to Zubiri. As soon as it was dark, the wounded and baggage were sent off, and about midnight the troops followed, passing on the way the 3rd division which then took the rear.

As soon as it was decided to retire, Sir L. Cole dispatched an officer to Pamplona with a request for assistance from the Conde de la Bispal commanding the blockading force. This officer also carried orders to the 13th Light Dragoons—the regiment was distributed in several villages about Larrasoana—to retire beyond Huarte and clear the Zubiri valley of all transport, and to the officers commanding stations beyond Pamplona to break up hospitals and depots preparatory to retreating.²

On his return to Zubiri, Picton at 8.30 p.m. sent a report to Wellington announcing the decision come to in the following terms:

> The affair terminated with the day, and the country offering no post between this place and Pamplona where it would be safe to hazard anything like an effectual stand against such superior force, I agreed with Lieut.-General Sir Lowry Cole in opinion that it was advisable to retire, and we have in consequence ordered the baggage, &c, on the Vitoria road, where we shall take up a position at as short a distance as practicable from Pamplona. Had I known your Lordship's intentions sooner, I would have joined Sir Lowry Cole before he retired from the passes, and in that case would have endeavoured to give effect to your Lordship's wishes.³

---

1. Smyth, *History of the 20th Regiment*, General Bainbrigge's Narrative.
2. Smythies, *Historical Records of 40th Regiment*, letter written by Major Mills on August 5, 1813.
3. Picton to Wellington, Zubiri, July 26, 8.30 p.m.

Had there been at Erro that afternoon a superior officer to give definite orders that a stand was to be made on the Zubiri ridge, it is certain that no general officer in the army would have made a stouter fight of it than the gallant leader of "the fighting 3rd" division, whose courage, energy and fighting instinct were proverbial throughout the army. Now qualities of a different nature were required. On Picton alone rested the responsibility of deciding whether, with the 20,000 troops he could bring into action, he would stand and face the French, whose numbers Cole estimated at from thirty to thirty-five thousand of all arms, in order to give the rest of the army time and space in which to concentrate to cover the blockade of Pamplona.

The burden of responsibility was too heavy for him, and he failed, as many another man of proved valour and skill in the field has failed, under the stress of independent command. It has been said Picton was influenced by Cole. But as Napier has shown, this was very unlikely. His was not the nature to be led by others; self-willed and inclined to be restive under the orders and methods of his seniors, he was little likely to allow himself to be guided by the opinion of a junior officer. Moreover, it was his duty to bring to bear on the situation that broader view, which might possibly have for the time escaped the attention of a man who for thirty-six consecutive hours had been absorbed in the conduct of that most difficult operation, a clean retreat in the face of very superior numbers led by one of Napoleon's ablest Marshals; and who, having been in the saddle nearly all the time, was, as he had written to the chief of the staff a few hours previously, "somewhat fagged."[1] That Picton failed or was unable to take the larger view the situation required, and to consider what an immediate retreat might involve, seems evident from his letter already quoted,

---

1. Cole to Murray, Linzoain, July 26, 1813. The date of this letter is given in Supply Dispatches as 27th, but it was evidently written on the 26th. (See Murray to Picton, Almandoz, July 26.) "Having had no sleep for two nights and been on horseback from 4 o'clock (a.m.) to 11 at night, I am somewhat fagged and cannot be as particular just now as I could wish."

for what was likely to embarrass his chief more than his hastening "to take up a position at so short a distance as practicable from Pamplona"? In his letter to Wellington, Picton was perfectly correct in saying that there was no good position for battle "between this place (Zubiri) and Pamplona," but omits any mention of the ground between Erro and Zubiri, where the high divide between the Erro and Arga rivers gives good positions for defence, as will be admitted, I think, by anyone who has traversed it. His last paragraph is somewhat difficult to understand if he received his copy of Murray's letter to Cole of July 23. The latter undoubtedly received it.

It is now perhaps not difficult to understand why Wellington, writing to Lord Liverpool[1] about these operations, said there was nothing he disliked more than "these extended operations which I cannot direct myself." It has been often charged against him, as also against Napoleon, that failures such as this were really his own fault, because his system failed to create a school of generals fit for independent command. But perhaps those who bring the charge may be asked the question, Is war the time and place to try experiments regarding the capacity of subordinate commanders for independent command? For in those days no means existed for testing this capacity beforehand, and let the whole course of the war in the Peninsula as well as the state of public opinion at home, especially during its earlier years, be considered. Commencing with a small untrained army, outnumbered for years by the total troops, mostly veterans, which the French commanders could bring against him, Wellington by his skill, prudence, patience and not least by the confidence he was at length able to inspire in the King's Ministers, and in the public at home, had been able to keep the war going; but he knew full well that, if by any grievous mishap that confidence in him was shaken, the withdrawal of the British Army from the Peninsula was only too likely to follow. He simply could

---

1. Wellington to Liverpool, Lesaca, August 4, 1818.

not afford to take risks, certainly not those which might follow from the inexperience or incapacity of subordinate leaders about whose appointment to the army he had generally little or nothing to say. Perfectly confident in himself, he always preferred to direct personally. But like all great men he had a highly developed faculty for judging the character and capacity of those serving under him and used it accordingly. Hill and Graham were trusted with independent enterprises and fulfilled the trust, but Hill and Picton's capacities for war were very different.

In accordance with the orders issued in the early morning of 26th two brigades of the 6th division were advanced along the Bidassoa towards Hill's left. The 7th division after sending off its baggage moved to Sumbilla; the light division, moving down from the Santa Barbara heights, concentrated on the left bank of the Bidassoa near Lesaca, but left outposts on the heights, and Longa rearranged his division also on the left bank so as to guard the river from the bridge of Lesaca to the ford of Enderlaza.

Meanwhile D'Erlon remained on the col de Maya, only Darmagnac's division moved down into the valley towards Ariscun with orders to send reconnoitring parties to ascertain if the enemy still held the passes of Ispegui and Berdaritz. From the col Abbé reconnoitred towards Echalar and reported troops still there; whilst from Darmagnac came information that the passes had been evacuated and that the enemy was in camp above Irurita. Darmagnac accordingly moved his advanced guard up to Elizondo.[1]

Wellington left Lesaca very early in the morning, and passing through San Estevan proceeded to Hill's troops and thence on to Almandoz, where general headquarters were established. On his way he had seen how severe the casualties had been in the British troops of the 2nd division. It was, however, also manifest that D'Erlon was not pressing

---

1. D'Erlon's report on the operations of the centre, July 24 to August 2, 1813.

forward from the Maya. No further report from Cole or Picton had as yet come in, and all that Wellington knew of what had happened on the right was from Cole's message sent off at 1 p.m. on the 25th. He now, however, considered it necessary to provide further reinforcements for Picton, and orders[1] were therefore issued for the 6th division to march at daybreak on the 27th to Olague, and the 7th division to San Estevan, extending its right as far as the village of Oyergui, where the road from San Estevan to Álmandoz branches off from that to Elizondo, so as to cover Hill's left flank. With the information he then had, Wellington did not consider it necessary to order any other movements, because, as he said later, "I was unwilling to lose a bit more of the mountains than was absolutely necessary from the probable loss of men in recovering such ground."[2] Though a retreat from his advanced positions had become necessary, and was likely to be extended still further southwards, the resumption of the offensive was always before him. It is curious that neither he nor Murray seems to have thought at Lesaca, or afterwards, of sending a staff officer to see what was happening on the right, and to impress the Commander-in-Chief's views on the generals.

Later on in the evening the long expected report from Cole came in, and it only arrived then by what was more or less an accident. General Long, commanding the cavalry brigade responsible for the communications of the army in this area, was with Hill on the morning of the 26th, and the latter had expressed his anxiety to receive intelligence from Cole. Long had then set out for Lanz, and on his way, or on arrival there, had been shown a letter from Cole to Murray,[3] which he opened and sent a copy of it to Hill, and the original on to San Estevan, being evidently unaware that general headquarters had moved and that Wellington would

---

1. Q.M.G. to Pack and Dalhousie, Almandoz, July 26, 1813.
2. Larpent's *Diary*.
3. Cole to Murray, Espinal, July 26, 1813.

be with Hill that day. Hill sent his copy at once to Murray and it probably reached the latter about 6.30 p.m.[1]

From this letter Wellington learnt of Cole's retreat from the passes and that the latter looked forward to the likelihood of having to continue to retire upon Pamplona.

It must now have been apparent to him that the possibility of Soult's real object being the relief of Pamplona was much greater than he had hitherto imagined, and that early steps to meet it were necessary. Yet no further orders were issued that night. Wellington determined to go off himself early on the 27th to the 3rd and 4th divisions, and in the meanwhile to make another effort to induce Picton to resolutely oppose Soult's advance. In consequence Murray wrote to Picton[2] that night, informing him that as he was the senior officer with the troops between the enemy and Pamplona—

> Lord Wellington has desired me to represent to you how necessary it is that the advance of the enemy in that direction should be stopped. Reinforcements for your support are moving upon Olague from this quarter, and the Conde de la Bispal is ordered to move with a very considerable body of Spanish troops from Pamplona upon Zubiri. Lord Wellington is of opinion, therefore, considering the nature of the country and the very respectable force of good troops which will be at your disposal, that even should the enemy have already penetrated beyond Linzoain when you receive this, that he will be undoubtedly stopped between that place and Zubiri.
>
> Headquarters will be to-morrow at Olague, and Lord Wellington purposes to go on himself to join the 3rd and 4th divisions unless he should receive reports in the meantime to render that unnecessary.

---

1. Hill to Q.M.G., Berroeta, July 26, 6 p.m.
2. Q.M.G. to Picton, Almandoz, July 26, 1813.

Picton was also reminded of the necessity of sending frequent reports. The hour at which this letter was dispatched is not stated. If it ever reached Picton it could not have been till his column was well on the way towards Pamplona.

Larpent thus describes the scene at Almandoz when he arrived there that evening at about 7 p.m.:

> At Almandoz we found the effects of the battle at Maya. The wounded had just reached that place, and there those that had not been dressed had their wounds examined and all were urged on to the rear over a mountain pass to Lanz as fast as possible. The village of Almandoz was very small; the wounded lying about in all directions, till cars and mules could help them on. It was near seven o'clock and the inhabitants all in the greatest distress, beginning to pack up to desert their homes as the people in the valley of Baztan, Elizondo, etc., had done already, the French having got possession. A retreat is a most distressing scene, even when conducted with perfect order as this was. About nine o'clock that night orders came to march at daylight for Olague, a place about halfway between Lanz and Ostiz.[1]

---

1. Larpent's *Diary*.

Chapter 12
Events of July 27

Wellington left Almandoz early on the 27th with the intention of joining Picton. On reaching Ostiz he met General Long, and from him received definite information that Picton was retreating towards Huarte. The fog of war which had hitherto obscured the doings of the right of the army was lifting, and Wellington had now surer grounds on which to base his measures to meet the situation.

Soult's movement directly threatened the blockade of Pamplona. To meet it Wellington had the 3rd and 4th divisions with Byng, Campbell and Morillo, about 20,000 good troops now in retreat towards the fortress seeking a position on which to bar the French advance. Don Carlos' division of 4th Spanish army was now due at Pamplona and a large force of cavalry was assembling there. Thus strengthened, la Bispal could safely spare some six or seven thousand men to join Picton, as indeed he had already been ordered to. The 6th division was due at Olague during the day and would be there within eight miles of Villaba. It was just possible for this division to reach Pamplona by the evening of 27th, but it certainly could by the early morning of 28th if all went well there, when over 30,000 men would be available to meet Soult. No other addition to this strength could be reckoned on before the evening of the 28th.

Wellington had good information about the strength of

Soult's column, and as we know, considered that on suitable ground Picton's force should be able to hold its own against it. But the possibility of failure to check Soult before he reached Pamplona had to be reckoned with. If this happened, the event could best be dealt with if the dispositions of the army still permitted a speedy concentration out of his immediate reach and covering Graham's force about San Sebastian. An immediate rush of all the available divisions towards Pamplona might be quite an unsuitable move.

Moreover, it was possible that Soult's intention was just to induce such a movement towards the fortress, whilst he turned sharp to his right, which he could do by Eugui and Olague, in order to effect a junction with D'Erlon in that neighbourhood or later and then advance towards the Pamplona-Tolosa-Irun road, thus cutting in between Wellington and Graham and from there attempt the relief of San Sebastian in conjunction with Villate from Behobie.

There was also D'Erlon to be considered, whose intentions were as yet by no means clear. He could move to join Soult by the col de Velate as soon as that pass was uncovered or along the Bidassoa valley against Graham, either by Sumbilla or Zubieta and Leiza. Therefore the San Estevan corner of the valley must still be held, and in any case D'Erlon's junction with Soult delayed as long as possible.

Such would seem to be the principal considerations which influenced Wellington in deciding on the movements he now ordered.

Having no doubt discussed the situation with his chief of the staff and given his decision, he rode away down the valley towards Pamplona, leaving Murray at Lanz to issue the necessary orders. At 9.30 a.m. these were sent out in the form of an instruction to Sir R. Hill, directing the following movements to take place.[1] The troops under Hill's immediate command to move at 2 p.m. and fall "back to the passes between Al-

---

1. Q.M.G. to Hill, Lanz, July 27, 1813, 9 a.m.

mandoz and Lanz," the 7th division to move "at same hour by Dona Maria towards Lizaso," and Lord Dalhousie to place his infantry in the most convenient situation for enabling it to maintain the passes behind Dona Maria.

The 1st Hussars K.G.L. to fall back from Dona Maria to Lizaso as soon as the order reaches them. The Light division to move to Zubieta. The orders to it to be sent through Dalhousie, and Alten to be warned to inform himself there of the roads which lead from thence into the great road from Tolosa by Lecum-berri to Pamplona, and in the event of his retiring from Zubieta, his march will be directed into that great road.

Hill, Dalhousie and Alten were to keep in communication with each other "for the mutual conveyance of orders or of intelligence which might affect the situation of any of these corps." They were also to put themselves in communication with Lizaso, where general headquarters would be that evening. Alten was also warned to communicate all his movements to Graham.

Longa's Spanish division was to retain its present positions, the order to be communicated to him by Alten, who was also to inform him of the move of the Light division to Zubieta. In a covering letter forwarding this instruction, Hill was also requested to send off at once his own artillery and that of the Light division, Murray also informed him that Wellington would send further instructions regarding the movements of 2nd and 7th divisions from the passes.

The channel to be used for the transmission of the orders will be noticed, Hill to Dalhousie, Dalhousie to Alten, Alten to Longa. Though slower than a separate order to each, it ensured all being acquainted with the others' movements and the establishment of communication between them on the line of senior to junior.

With the orders Murray also sent a confidential letter to Hill putting him in possession of Wellington's views of what would be necessary in case Soult could not be stopped in front of Pamplona.

To Lieut.-General Sir Rowland Hill, K.B.

Lanz, July 27, 1813

If things should not go well towards Pamplona, we may in that case have to wheel the army back upon its left, placing the troops now about Pamplona near Irurzun. The centre of the army between that and Tolosa, the left, under Sir Thomas Graham, remaining nearly where it is now.

There is an artillery road from Olague to Irurzun (four leagues) and one branches from it to Lecumberri. These roads will give the means, therefore, of moving the 6th division (now at Olague) the 14th Light Dragoons, and the troops with you and in this neighbourhood, the sick and wounded, as also the 7th division and the 1st Hussars towards the line I have mentioned, should any communications arrive to render it necessary and expedient to do so.

The Light division can move from Zubieta into the same line, which being that of the great road from Tolosa towards Pamplona, our communications and lateral movements would be easy.

G. Murray
Q.M.G.

At daybreak on July 27, Soult learnt that the British had retreated towards Pamplona, and at 5 a.m. put his troops in motion. Clausel's column moved by the road on the right bank of the Arga river and was followed by the artillery and the cavalry, whilst Reille marched along the hills on the left bank.[1] The progress of the latter by narrow paths over steep slopes, through woods and thickets was difficult and slow; his column in consequence fell behind that of Clausel. The latter's advance guard had skirmished with the 3rd division rearguard from Zubiri to Zabaldica, but here it was stopped, for the high ground to the right above and beyond the village was found strongly held by the enemy.

---

1. Colonel Michaud's report on operations of right wing.

The high ground dividing the valleys of the Arga and Ulzama rivers, which on the level of Zubiri has a width of about six miles, gradually contracts as it approaches Pamplona, until at Sorauren and Zabaldica the distance between the streams is little more than a mile and a half. The slopes of the hills generally are brown and bare but the summits often wooded. There is little cultivation except on the lower slopes bordering the streams. Some two miles south of Sorauren there stretches right across the courses of both streams a high, narrow and generally bare rocky ridge running almost west to east, which seems raised as a barrier to forbid exit from the valleys and the high land between them to the upland plain of Pamplona, which stretches away to the south of it. Highest on the west, where it is known as the San Christoval heights, it falls thence and gradually sinks to the level of the surrounding country to the east of Huarte. Through this barrier both rivers have worked their way, the Ulzama at the gap of Villaba and the Arga near Huarte, and they unite behind it to flow as the Arga river round the northern and western sides of the fortress of Pamplona. The divide between the valleys is continued almost up to the barrier ridge, but beyond a line from Sorauren to Zabaldica its character has considerably changed: its elevation is considerably less and a long, deep ravine running eastwards from Sorauren almost cuts it off from the main heights, to which it remains directly connected only by a col above the village of Zabaldica. It is about here that this ground is at its highest, throwing out several rounded spurs with steep slopes towards the Arga stream; this line of high ground runs southwards for about half a mile. From its eastern end the ground falls gradually northwards towards Sorauren in the form of a long spur, the upper slopes of which terminate at a point where in 1813 there stood the little chapel of San Salvador, of which only the ruins now remain. From the chapel the ground falls pretty steeply down into the ravine on one side and towards the Villaba road and the Ulzama stream on the other. The sides of the long ravine are steep, and except at its mouth near Sorauren are covered nearly up to the crest with gorse, box-scrub and low fir trees. The western end of the high ground has a fan-shaped form with salients and re-entrants; at its south-west corner is the village of Oricain a little way up the slope. Between the salient on the slope of which this village stands and the long northern spur is a large and generally fairly gently sloping re-entrant which forms the northern side of the feature. The ground is nearly all quite open and now most of it is under cultivation as potato fields.

It was on this ground from its highest eastern point near the col and along the spur northwards that Cole, with the 4th division, Byng and Campbell's brigades, had taken up his position. To his right and lower down on a spur overlooking the Arga valley were posted two Spanish battalions, which had been previously sent out from the blockading force.

Picton had originally intended that Cole's troops should hold the western edge of the high ground on a line between Oricain and Arietta. But the latter General, "with a surer eye" having seen the greater capabilities of the ground farther forward, requested and obtained permission to occupy it. Turning his troops about, therefore, Cole moved forward to form his line along the edge of the high ground on the left of the Spaniards. As his men approached, "a compact but inconsiderable party of the French"[1] made a dash for the hill occupied by the Spaniards under cover of the fire of many skirmishers and some guns which opened from near Zabaldica. The Spaniards met them gallantly and drove the French down the hill. Though admired, this charge created some amusement in the ranks of the 20th who saw it, as the men declared that in their hurry to be at the French the Dons had forgotten to fix bayonets.[2]

The troops under Sir Lowry Cole were placed as follows:

---

1. Smythies, *History of the 40th Regiment.*
2. Smyth, *History of 20th Regiment*, General Bainbrigge's Narrative.

on the left holding the spur overlooking Sorauren and the Ulzama valley was placed Ross's brigade with the 7th Caçadores of Stubbs' brigade in its front, then came Campbell's and Stubbs' Portuguese brigades and to the right on the highest ground was Anson's brigade, the two Spanish regiments being reinforced by the 4th Portuguese from Campbell's brigade. As was the invariable custom in the Peninsular army the line was withdrawn behind the crest so as to be out of view and fire; in front were the light troops only who kept off the French skirmishers. Byng's brigade of the 2nd division was in reserve towards the southern end of the highest part of the ridge, about 500 yards behind Anson's brigade. The 4th division artillery "brigade" was placed on a low spur, forming the southern end of the high ground, whence it commanded the road from Zabaldica.

The 3rd division and Morillo's Spaniards had meanwhile passed on and taken up position, the 3rd division on the right with its left at Huarte and its right on the low hills on left bank of the Egues stream where its artillery was in action. The cavalry had arrived from Tafalla, and the Hussar brigade was placed on the right of the 3rd division, and Ponsonby's and the Household brigade behind it. Morillo held the San Miguel height between Huarte and Villaba.

Having information of Soult's approach, the governor of Pamplona had early in the morning made a vigorous sortie. The Spaniards were surprised, and there was nearly a disaster. Luckily, Don Carlos' division of the 4th Spanish army arrived at the moment and drove the garrison back. La Bispal then moved out and occupied the San Christoval heights on Morillo's left, placing a detachment to hold the tracks which cross the ridge south of the village of Azoz.

Such were the positions of the allied troops at about 10.30 a.m. Cole, who had hardly more than 10,000 men, completely commanded the exits from the Ulzama and Arga valleys, his position was a strong one in itself and his troops fitted well into it for a pure defence. But he was exposed to the full brunt of the attack of an enemy at least three times as strong, and the allied second line, to which alone he could look for aid against complete envelopment, was a mile and a half in rear behind, a serious obstacle to movement, and one which the troops holding it could leave only at the peril of uncovering the last barrier in front of the fortress Soult sought to relieve. The resolution taken to hold the front line was a bold one. As often happens, audacity brought its own reward.

In the meantime the French had been gathering thick in front. Hearing the firing about Zabaldica, Reille determined to bring down the greater part of his column into the valley. Having reached the heights above Iroz, he moved down with the divisions of Lamartinière and Maucune, while Foy continued to move along the crest as far as the village of Alzuza, where he halted.[1] Clausel, when he found the Oricain hill so strongly held, had halted his column for a short time, and then wheeled the heads of Taupin's and Vandermaesen's divisions to the right in order to seize the high ground facing that occupied by the enemy,[2] and gain possession of the village of Sorauren, and with it command of the Ulzama valley road. Conroux's division remained at Zabaldica covering the artillery and cavalry.

It was nearly eleven o'clock when Wellington, accompanied only by Lord Fitzroy Somerset, approached Sorauren. As he entered the village he saw the French on the heights above and realized at once that the Olague-Sorauren road was no longer available for the 6th division and the artillery and that they must be turned off on to the Lizaso—Marcalain road. Dismounting on the bridge of Sorauren, he wrote an order to Murray and sent it off by Somerset. Not long afterwards he thus described the incident to Larpent:

---

1. Colonel Michaud's report on operations of the right wing of the army of Spain, May 25, 1814.
2. *Rapport de l'aile gauche*, August 2, 1813.

Why, at one time it was rather alarming, certainly, and it was a close run thing. When I came to the bridge of Sorauren, I saw the French on the hills on one side and it was clear we could make a stand on the other hills in our position on the 28th, but I found we could not keep Sorauren, for it was exposed to their fire and not to ours. I determined to take the position, but was obliged to write my orders accordingly at Sorauren to be sent back instantly, for if they had not been dispatched back directly by the way I had come I must have sent four leagues round in a quarter of an hour later. I stopped, therefore, to write accordingly, people saying to me all the time, ' The French are coming! The French are coming! ' I looked pretty sharp after them, however, now and then, until I had completed my orders, and then set off and I saw them near one end of the village as I went out at the other end; and then we took our ground.[1]

Wellington was always well mounted and probably the French little knew how great a prize they had just missed! His order to Murray was as follows:

To the Quarter-master-General
At the bridge near Larrasoana[2]
July 27. 11 a.m.
Our troops are formed on the heights .on this side of Pamplona, the enemy in their front. The enemy's right is close to the road to Ostiz near this village.
The road therefore by Ostiz can no longer be used. The artillery and other carriages at Ostiz must march immediately to Olague.
As soon as the 6th division have cooked, they, and all the artillery at Olague and that now at Ostiz, are to march to Lizaso.

---

1. Larpent's Diary, August 24, 1813.
2. Evidently a mistake for Sorauren. Larrasoana is in the Arga valley south of Zubiri.

Lieut.-General Sir R. Hill should march this night, if possible, to Lanz, leaving a post at the head of the pass, which he should withdraw in the morning.

I will send orders to Lanz and Lizaso for further proceedings.

The 7th division should also march towards Lizaso.

Wellington

Having sent off this message Wellington, now alone, galloped down the road and then turned up, probably behind the chapel spur, on to the high ground where Cole was in position.

As he ascended he was recognized by a Portuguese regiment (probably the 7th Caçadores), which "raised a cry of joy, and the shrill clamour caught up by the next regiments swelled as it ran along the line into that stern and appalling shout which the British soldier is wont to give on the edge of battle and which no enemy ever heard unmoved."[1]

Wellington was dressed in the Spanish uniform he often wore, "grey frock coat, buttoned close up to the chin, with his little cocked hat covered with oilskin without a feather."[2] Moving along the line he placed himself on the highest point of the position. He wished both armies to know he was on the ground, and as Soult on the opposite hill was pointed out to him, he is said to have remarked, "Yonder is a great commander, but he is a cautious one and will delay his attack to ascertain the cause of these cheers: that will give time for the 6th division to come up and we shall beat him." He said himself later, "I had an excellent glass: I saw him spying at us—then write and send off a letter—I knew what he would be writing and gave my orders accordingly."[3]

Wellington's arrival gave the allied force just what it wanted, a fillip to its confidence in itself. For there was never a retreat made yet which did not more or less disturb the moral

---

1. Napier.
2. Smythies.
3. Stanhope, *Conversations with the Duke of Wellington*.

of even the best troops. The feeling that things are not going well upsets the balance of the weaker vessels, rumours of all sorts spread through the ranks, and perhaps most trying to all is the uncertainty surrounding the situation and the general want of knowledge of where other units of the army are, and what is happening to them.

A regimental officer who was present thus describes the effect of Wellington's arrival on the officers and men of his battalion:

> I can never forget the joy which beamed in every countenance when his lordship's presence became known. It diffused a general feeling of confidence through all ranks. From that moment we had none of those dispiriting murmurs on the awkwardness of the situation, etc., so common in our army whenever a retreat is ordered. Now we talked of driving the French over the frontier again as a matter of course.[1]

Another officer, whose remarks were written within a few days after the event, after stating that it was always the men's custom to greet the Commander-in-Chief on all occasions in the field or on the line of march "with a burst of welcome and enthusiastic cheers," adds:

> But to-day these acclamations were still more marked and hearty as he showed himself near the brigades, and I cannot adequately express the sense of confidence and assurance that was revived by his presence in the midst of a single division of his army; cheers upon cheers were vehemently raised along the whole line.[2]

It was a veritable triumph for the Commander, and with such men he might well be confident of victory. They may not have "loved" him as we hear so often nowadays, but better far in war, they had absolute confidence in him and

---

1. Smyth, *History of 20th Regiment*, General Bainbrigge's Narrative.
2. Smythies, *History of 40th Regiment*, Major Mills' letter.

knew that if they did their part—and they had never failed him yet—he would assuredly get them out of the tight place all knew they were in.

Whether or no it was the fact of Wellington's arrival which really led Soult to delay his attack or whether he so decided, hoping for D'Erlon's early appearance, or to rest his men, remains undecided. But it is certain that after the repulse from the Spaniards' Hill he made no further real attack that day.

The French army spread itself out on the hills opposite the allies' position—the divisions of Taupin and Vandermaesen on the mountain facing Cole with the right in the village of Sorauren. Maucune of Reille's wing relieved Conroux about Zabaldica with Lamartinière's division in rear about Iroz, the latter having one brigade on the left bank of the Arga in touch with Foy's division, which bivouacked on the high ground above Alzuza village. A few guns were placed in action at Zabaldica, the rest of the artillery and the cavalry remained in the Arga valley behind the infantry. The whole French front was covered by numerous skirmishers who all day kept up a bickering combat with the allied Light troops, in which the French guns about Zabaldica occasionally joined. Under cover of this, Soult reconnoitred the allied position on the Oricain hill. The only change made in its occupation was that Wellington, recognizing the importance of the Spaniards' Hill, had shortly after his arrival withdrawn the 4th Portuguese, replacing it by the 40th regiment, whose commanding officer had orders to hold the hill to the last.

Towards evening Soult ordered Foy to make a reconnaissance to ascertain how the right of the allied second line was held. Foy sent out two regiments from Alzuza. As they approached the Egues stream, the whole of the high ground beyond it as far as Huarte was manned by a line of British infantry, whilst guns opened on the French and cavalry showed on the right. Foy's detachment then retired.

During the afternoon heavy clouds had been gathering,

and at about seven o'clock[1] a terrific thunderstorm, with drenching rain, burst over the hills, which put a stop to the firing. Soaked to the skin, the tired and hungry soldiers of both armies—for supplies were short that day—lay down to get what rest they could. And with the day passed Soult's best chance of success.

The Quartermaster-General, after issuing orders at 9 a.m., left Lanz and proceeded to Ostiz, where he received Wellington's instructions written on the bridge of Sorauren. After having sent off the artillery quartered at Ostiz, towards Lizaso—it was probably Brandreth's brigade which had not accompanied the 6th division into the Baztan—Murray returned to Olague.

The 6th division arrived there about 1 p.m. and General Pack was ordered to move to Marcalain as soon as the troops had had their dinners. At 4 p.m. the 6th division moved off again, having already done about fifteen miles from San Estevan; owing, however, to the state of the roads and the storm which came on in the evening, it could only reach Lizaso, and there halted for the night. The artillery preceded the 6th division and with it went the small arm ammunition mule column, which Hill had been ordered to send to Olague.

Murray proceeded from Olague to Lanz and Lizaso, where general headquarters were established.[2] During the afternoon orders were dispatched to Hill, Dalhousie and the 1st Hussars at Dona Maria for all to continue their retreat to Lizaso. The 7th division was ordered to leave a post of observation at the Dona Maria pass with a few Hussars as orderlies, and Colonel Arentschild to send a small party of 1st Hussars under an officer to Lecumberri on the Pamplona-Tolosa road to keep up

---

1. Larpent.
2. Larpent's *Diary*. "On 27th we arrived at Lanz. We there found General Murray and several officers looking very serious and gloomy, and orders given for everything to be turned off to the right and not to go to Olague, as Cole had been pressed."

the communication between the right and left of the army, the officer being instructed to establish communication with the Light division at Zubieta as soon as possible.

During the day this division had moved from about Lesaca to the Sta. Cruz mountain above Sumbilla, where it remained, as the order of 9 a.m. to move to Zubieta did not reach General Alten.

Both Hill and Dalhousie moved off in the afternoon and evening, but neither got beyond the mountain passes. The night was a most dismal, rainy one; it was so pitch dark no object could be seen a yard off, and both divisions were obliged to halt on the mountain from sheer inability to proceed till daylight showed them where they stood.[1]

At 4 p.m., Wellington sent off to Murray his promised instructions for further proceedings. They were as follows:

> Orders for movement of the Army
> Heights of Villaba. July 27, 4 p.m.[2]
> The 6th division and all carriages and other troops now at Lizaso are to move to-morrow morning at the dawn of day from Lizaso upon Ollocarizqueta (a village a mile south of Marcalain and about three from Oricain).
> Sir Rowland Hill and Lord Dalhousie, with the troops under their command, are to move at the same time from the stations where they will be this night to Lizaso and thence, if the men be not over fatigued, to Ollocarizqueta at as early an hour as may be in their power.
> Headquarter baggage by Ollocarizqueta to Orcoyen.
> The wounded to be taken to Berrioplano.

All the above, except the intended movement of 2nd and 7th divisions towards Ollocarizqueta, had been already provided for by Murray's orders, and it only remained to inform Hill and Dalhousie accordingly.

---

1. Henry, *Events of a Military Life*.
2. Wellington *Dispatches*, vol. vi.

The scene at Lizaso when the civil staff and headquarter baggage arrived there in the afternoon is thus described by Larpent.

> All the wounded from Lanz had just arrived there, in cars, on mules, crawling on crutches and hobbling along; all those with wounds in their hands and arms, etc., walking. About six that evening the wounded were ordered to move on towards Irurzun on the Vitoria and Tolosa roads. About seven a furious thunderstorm came on, and caught all our poor wounded men on their march: they could not get to Irurzun but got to Berrioplano near Pamplona.[1]

Late in the evening, Murray received another communication from Wellington, dated at Villaba 8.30 p.m. July 27, telling him that as a body of the enemy reported as 1,200 strong had crossed the Ostiz road and the river and might go into the hills bordering the Lizaso-Marcalain road, he had ordered 2,000 Spanish infantry to Ollocarizqueta with directions to piquet the hills. Wellington also said: "the following measures must be adopted"—

> 1st. The baggage of headquarters and of the troops must march from Lizaso to Irurzun, the troops bringing with them meat and bread for two days.
> 2nd. The artillery must follow the 6th division and, if there is any difficulty in passing the road, the artillery must return and go from Lizaso to Irurzun.
> 3rd. The 6th division, if opposition should be of such a nature as to render it necessary, must quit the road and go upon the hills to the right of the valley coming from Lizaso, but they *must* arrive at their destination.
> The great reserve of musket ammunition must come with the 6th division.[2]

---

1. Larpent's *Diary*.
2. Wellington to Q.M.G., Villaba, July 27, 1813, 8.30 p.m.

When Hill quitted his position about Irurita in the afternoon, D'Erlon had taken up position for the night in front of Elizondo, and his strength in the valley was estimated at from 10 to 12,000 men.[1]

The promptitude with which Clausel on arrival at Zabaldica moved to his right and seized the hill facing Cole's position and the village of Sorauren is to be much admired. Having possession of the village and the high ground above it, he entirely blocked the Ulzama valley road, obliged Wellington's divisions coming from the Baztan to make the detour by Lizaso and Marcelain, thereby gaining many hours for his chief. Wellington's ready grasp of the situation on his arrival at Sorauren and his prompt action probably saved the allies from a serious mishap;[2] for had he delayed and sent his instructions to Murray by the roundabout way of Lizaso, the 6th division might have moved down the valley road into the trap awaiting it near Sorauren.

Soult himself does not seem to have grasped the significance of Clausel's action, else he would surely have hardened his heart and forthwith attacked. D'Erlon's inaction on the 26th and 27th is unaccountable unless it be that he was so shaken by the resistance of the British on the 25th as to have lost all confidence in himself.

---

1. Rooke (A.A.G. 2nd division) to Q.M.G., Lanz, July 28, 1813, 4 A.M.
2. «Ce movement, dont la prudence peut nous étonner, était conforme aux principes de la stratégie Napoléonienne.»—Dumas, «Neuf mois de Campagnes à la suite du Maréchal Soult.»

CHAPTER 13

The First Battle of Sorauren

On the morning of July 28 a splendid sunrise succeeded the storm of the previous evening. The allies were early under arms, but the French[1] showed no signs of attacking. Beyond some movements of troops from their left to the right, they retained for several hours their positions of the evening before; and Wellington, writing from the field to Graham, said "I have in my front Soult, with from 30 to 35,000 men, but he does not appear inclined to attack us."[2]

After his reconnaissance of the allied position during the afternoon of 27th Soult discussed the situation with his Lieutenant-Generals. The alternatives were a manoeuvre to either his right or left and a frontal attack. The latter was resolved on, despite Clausel's opposition. Soult again reconnoitred the position on the morning[3] of the 28th and the plan of attack was definitely settled as follows: The three divisions of Clausel's wing, with that of Conroux on the right moving from Sorauren were to envelop and attack the left of Cole's line, their objective being the spur on which stood the Chapel of San Salvador. This attack was to commence at 1 p.m.

1. Bainbrigge's Narrative before quoted.
2. Wellington to Graham, on heights in front of Villaba, July 28. The time of the letter is given as 10.30 a.m., but this is probably a mistake for 11.30, as he says the 6th division have just arrived. The time of their arrival is put by all authorities at about 11.30 a.m. Moreover, his letter is interrupted by the commencement of the fight.
3. Baltazar to Clarke, Bayonne, August 3, 1813.

Simultaneously Reille was to make a diversion from the Arga valley by attacking the right of the 4th division on the highest ground with Maucune's division and the Spaniards' Hill with that of Lamartinière, each division keeping one brigade in reserve. Foy, with the 13th chasseurs and P. Soult's cavalry division, was to again advance from the Alzuza heights against Picton; but was ordered not to engage himself so seriously as to be unable to regain the heights if the main attack on the Oricain hill proved unsuccessful.

During the forenoon the French made the necessary preliminary movements. Conroux's division marched early from the Arga to the Ulzama valley about Sorauren. Gauthier's brigade (5 battalions) of Lamartinière's division occupied Zabaldica and the ground to the south of the village towards the foot of the Spaniards' Hill; the other brigade had the 119th to the north of the village and the 118th to the south of it in support of Gauthier, the 2nd Light remaining on the left bank of the river. One brigade of Maucune's division was on the crest of the mountain on the French side opposite the right of the 4th British division with the other brigade down the forward slope in front of the col.[1] Maucune was ordered to connect his right with Clausel's left division. A few howitzers were in action behind the walls of Zabaldica, where Reille himself remained. Clausel concentrated his wing in a ravine, lying to the east and rather to the north of Sorauren, which is formed by some under features thrown out on the southern slope of the main French hill. Conroux's division on the right had flanking parties out on to the hills on the right bank of the Ulzama.

There was no change made in the dispositions of the troops on the allied side. But soon after 11 a.m. the advanced guard of the 6th division appeared round the shoulder of the hill which borders the Ulzama valley south of Sorauren. Here the two British brigades formed up and then, covered by their Light troops and a squadron of cavalry, forded the

1. Colonel Michaud's report.

river above Oricain and formed in two lines across the valley. The Portuguese brigade had previously been detached by Wellington's order to hold the high ground on the right bank of the river.

A French look-out officer, posted on the high ground beyond the river, had between 10 and 11 a.m. sent information of the approach of the 6th division.[1] Its arrival behind the left flank of the allied first line was the cause of a departure from Soult's plan of a simultaneous attack by all his divisions on the allied advanced position at 1 p.m. For Clausel, seeing that this newly arrived reinforcement for the enemy was in a position to fall on the outer flank of the attack he was about to make, about noon sent Conroux's division from Sorauren down the valley to drive it back.[2] At the same time he advanced his other two divisions and formed them in line of brigade columns, Taupin's division on the right and Vandermaesen about 250 yards to his left, at the foot of the chapel height, their front being covered with skirmishers who pushed forward up the slopes.

With its front and flanks protected by light troops, Conroux's division in two lines of brigade masses moved down the valley. It first came under fire from the 7th Caçadores and the left wing of the 7th Fusiliers sent down from the left of Ross' brigade. Then Madden's Portuguese brigade of the 6th division appearing over the opposite hill, drove off the French flankers, and skirmishing down the hillside opened a heavy fire on the right flank of Conroux's column. But it pressed on till near a slight rise across the valley from behind which rose the leading British brigade of the 6th division, which, after pouring in a volley, with a loud cheer

1. Clausel's Report. He says Conroux advanced «tant pour les (the 6th division) éloigner de Sorauren, par ou il fallait nécessairement déboucher pour monter sur la montagne, que pour retarder la jonction des troupes ennemies.»
2. In his report on the action Clausel states the 6th division deployed at 1 p.m., and that "ses troupes étaient a portée de fusil de Sorauren." All the British accounts agree that Conroux moved about noon, and that he advanced a considerable distance (probably 1000 yards) in front of Sorauren before the 6th division attacked. Wyld's atlas of Peninsular battles shows the head of his column nearly three-quarters of a mile from Sorauren.

charged into the column. With its head overthrown and harassed by fire on all sides,[1] for by now more of Ross' and Campbell's men had lined the northern slopes of their hill, Conroux's division gave way and fighting hard commenced to retire slowly up the valley.

Seeing what had befallen Conroux, Clausel launched Taupin's and Vandermaeson's divisions against the allied left on the hill above, the din and smoke of the opposing skirmishers' fire filling the ravine below. A brigade of Taupin's division was the first to mount the slope; driving in the 7th Caçadores it reached the Chapel, when Ross' brigade charging down from above fell upon it and drove it down the hill. This was followed by attacks along the front of Ross' and Campbell's brigades, not simultaneous but in succession from right to left of the French, because as the crest trends backwards the left columns had further to move. As the French reached the crest, they were met by a volley from the British and Portuguese drawn up behind it, followed at once by a bayonet charge. It was everywhere a stern fight between worthy opponents, for the French infantry showed the greatest gallantry. But breathless from the ascent and broken by the fire they could seldom withstand the charge. At length, however, one of Vandermaesen's columns broke through the 10th Portuguese on Campbell's left, thus uncovering the right of Ross' brigade now engaged in front with Bechaud's brigade of Taupin; attacked in front and in flank the Fusilier brigade, fighting desperately, was forced down the backward slope, and the French proceeded to establish themselves on the hill.

But Wellington, having ordered Byng's reserve brigade to come up at the double, sent down the 27th and 48th

---

1. Sergeant Cooper, 7th Fusiliers, in *Seven Campaigns*, says, "Our fire was now redoubled. A Portuguese company of Caçadores that was joined to us, hearing the French calling out *'Española, Española,'* to make us think they were friends, cried out, *'No Española, mas fuego, mas fuego'* (more fire). We all did so, and the men fell fast on both sides."

regiments from Anson's brigade, "to charge that body of the enemy which had first established itself on the height and next those of the left of it."[1]

Right well did these regiments carry out their orders: thrice they charged the French masses and finally, aided by Ross' and Campbell's brigades, which had quickly rallied, drove them in disorder down the hill with heavy losses on both sides. Thus the allied line was re-established.

During this struggle on the hillside, the British brigades of the 6th division, with Cairne's brigade of artillery and the 13th Light Dragoons, continued to press Conroux's division up the valley.[2] By now they had come up level with Ross' left on the chapel height, up the slopes of which some of the regiments mounted.[3] The Portuguese brigade, keeping up its fire on the enemy's flank, had also worked up along the slopes beyond the river almost as far as Sorauren.

Whilst the battle was thus going on on the allied left, Reille had also attacked the right. His first effort was made with Gauthier's brigade of Lamartinière's division against the Spaniards' Hill. This was held by the 40th regiment, reduced by previous losses to little more than 400 strong, and two Spanish battalions, the 40th being in line across the hill about eighty yards from the crest,[4] with a Spanish regiment on each flank. About 1 p.m., Lamartinière gave the order to advance, and Gauthier moved forward in two columns in echelon, the 120th (8 battalions) on the right leading followed by the 122nd (2 battalions). The skirmishers of the 120th reached the crest but were driven off in disorder. The attacks of the two columns following them is thus described by an officer of the 40th:[5]

---

1. Wellington to Bathurst, San Estevan, August 1, 1818.
2. Barrett, *History of 13th Hussars*.
3. Blakeney, *A Boy in the Peninsular War*. Available in a Leonaur edition under the title *Light Bob*.
4. Col. Stretton, *With the 40th in the Pyrenees*.
5. Smythies, *History of the 40th Regiment*, Major Mills' letter.

The first column about 2,500 strong was somewhat in advance of the other: it moved up with the greatest gallantry and undeterred by the well directed missiles from the hill still preserved its steady form and solidity.[3] The Spaniards, the moment the French got half way up the ascent, ran away .... all attempts to rally them were ineffectual. We were drawn up in fine, a little retired from the brow of the hill, and were prepared for the worst. When the French gained the brow of the hill the order to charge was given, and with a threatening shout, vehement and prolonged, our battalion singly fell upon them with the bayonet, shivering their compact order and sweeping them some distance down the descent. Our men were hardly restrained from following too far and reluctantly obeyed orders to return to the hill, but a halt was made in time, and as expeditiously as possible the companies again formed up and quietly awaited the renewal of the attack. The second column of the French soon appeared, and ascending in precisely the same formation as the first advanced with great steadiness and spirit. It was, however, also driven from the edge and hurled down the hill. As in the former case our men pursued too far and the lapse of time enabled the enemy to reform their first column; which they did, and advanced a second time, but when it reached half way up the hill and within twenty-five yards of us, we charged again through fire and smoke and bayoneted all who stood in our way. After these *rencontres*, which assumed for a time the proportions of a desperate and prolonged struggle, we could see our fire was very destructive to the French, and they fell into utter confusion. One more effort was, however, made to rally, but without effect, and we could see the French officers at the head of their divisions trying to animate the soldiers by ges-

---

1. Col. Michaud says the 120th advanced rapidly but not in good order.

ture and example to renew the assault. The standards were even carried to the front and the drums beat the advance, but all to no purpose; there was no obedience to the summons, and our small cohort remained victorious on the heights. Lord Wellington was close at hand a witness of the whole, and sent the Prince of Orange to congratulate the regiment, and we were immediately reinforced by two regiments.

The French loss on and about the hill was 600, our loss only 100.

Whilst these attacks were going on, the 17th and 84th Light (3 battalions) of Maucune's division in two columns moving by the col which joins the Oricain hill to the main ridge attacked the remainder of Anson's brigade on the high ground above, but were repulsed with very heavy loss. The remaining regiment of the brigade, the 15th, was placed on the southern slope of the col to connect with Gauthier's brigade, which it was able to assist by taking the 40th in flank as it drove the French columns down the slope of the Spaniards' Hill.[1]

The French made no further attempts to renew the fight, and between 4 and 5 p.m. Soult ordered the troops to retire to their positions of the previous evening.

The demonstration by Foy led to nothing of importance. The French cavalry crossed the Egues stream and by carbine fire forced the 10th Hussars from some rocky ground on Picton's right. But the 18th Hussars, being better armed, drove the French from it and back over the stream. About 4 p.m. Foy,[1] by Soult's order, fell back again to Alzuza.

The casualties amongst the divisions of the allied army engaged amounted to 2,600, those of the French to over 3,000.

The crisis of the fight must have been over by 3.30 p.m., for at that hour Wellington sat down to resume his letter to Graham interrupted by the battle.

---

1. Michaud's report. Referring to Maucune's attack, he says, «*Les troupes furent reponssées sur tous les points et l'attaque manqua.*»

It is difficult to understand why Soult did not attack in force on the 27th; to grasp why he allowed all those precious hours of the morning to pass by is still more difficult. Granted that time was required for the preliminary movements of his army, his front, though on difficult ground, was quite a short one and the movements necessary could have been made the previous evening; or very early on that July morning, when sunrise is soon after 4.30 a.m., if he considered it inexpedient, on account of the fatigue of his men, to move during the night. It was perhaps his very last chance, and he failed to seize it. Soult did not possess that phase of moral courage "namely, the urgent desire to bring about a decision by battle"[1] characteristic of the greatest generals.

His plan of battle was, as we have seen, upset by the arrival of the 6th division which led to Clausel moving before the appointed time whereby the unity of his attack was ruined. The "gradually increasing pressure relentlessly applied to the enemy at all points," was absent. The attacks of the different portions of the French army, instead of being simultaneous, were made in succession and were defeated in succession. Wellington's estimate of Soult as a leader given years later seems a true one.

> Soult was not the ablest general opposed to me .... Soult did not quite understand a field of battle, he was an excellent *logician*,[2] knew very well how to bring his troops up to the field, but not so well how to use them when he had brought them up. On another occasion he said he was the best strategist of the French generals in Spain, but "very defective and irresolute in actual collision."[3]

---

1. Yorck, *Napoleon as a General*.
2. Stanhope, *Conversations with Duke of Wellington*. Logician is printed *tactician*—an obvious mistake. That part of staff duties dealing with the movement of troops was then known as logistics.
3. Ellesmere, *Personal Recollections of Duke of Wellington*. Napoleon's estimate of Soult was much the same, "an excellent War Minister or Chief of the Staff. He knows much better how to dispose an army than to act as Commander-in-Chief."—Colonel Picard, *Préceptes et Jugements de Napoléon*.

In his letter to Graham, Wellington concluded by saying "on the whole I never saw troops behave better." It was almost entirely an infantry fight, for there was little artillery up on the allied side and the French made little use of theirs. On both sides the ground was beyond the capability of movement of the artillery of that day—modern field artillery would now make light of the Oricain hill ground—so the allied infantry was deprived of that support which had been so splendidly given by the British gunners on the field of Vitoria. Hand to hand fighting and plenty of it had decided the day. How one must admire the grit and courage of officers and men, British, Portuguese and French, who fought that afternoon, many with tired limbs and but poorly filled stomachs. "I never saw such fighting as we have had," wrote Wellington; "the battle of the 28th was fair bludgeon work."[1]

Beyond the information already received that D'ErIon had moved on the 27th into the Baztan, no further news of him had as yet reached the allied headquarters. But now that the retirement of Hill and the 7th division to Lizaso had uncovered the passes from that valley, it was necessary to consider what his movements were likely to be. A direct advance down the Ulzama valley to join Soult would seem the most probable. It was possible, however, that D'ErIon might move off by Lizaso aiming at Wellington's left, or at Irurzun and the allies' communications if be found the Lizaso road open. There were available for manoeuvre against him, Hill's corps—2nd and Portuguese divisions—the 7th division, Long with one regiment of his brigade (14th Light Dragoons), and the 1st Hussars K.G.L.—During this part of the campaign the latter regiment seems to have been used as independent cavalry under Wellington's direct orders, as Murray constantly sends orders direct to Colonel Arentschild commanding it. The regiment had a high reputation throughout the army for outpost and reconnaissance duties.—On the Pamplona-Irurzun-Tolosa road the army was

---
1. Wellington to W. Bentinck, Lesaca, August 5, 1813.

much dependent for supplies and especially for ammunition, and along it the wounded were being evacuated. Wellington therefore could not permit it to be uncovered, and at 4 p.m. orders were sent to Hill that as " a precaution against any attempt the enemy may make to move a corps upon Irurzun," which he might do with the troops which may have followed either Dalhousie or Hill himself, the 7th division with the 14th Light Dragoons and the 1st Hussars were to be left about Lizaso; the cavalry being specially directed[1] to get early information of the enemy's movements and report them both to Hill and to general headquarters. Hill's own corps was to move towards Orcayen as previously ordered;[2] as, however, he might be required either to support the left of the troops then with Wellington (6th division) or the 7th division, he was requested to have the country to the east of his line of march reconnoitred, and though the head of his column was to be brought forward far enough to be able if necessary to rapidly support the 6th division, the rear of his column was not to be further south than Marcalain.

Murray also informed Hill of the result of the battle, and that Wellington would be found either on the heights in front of Villaba or in that village; also that the sick and wounded would be sent to Irurzun.[3]

In order to assist in the removal of the latter, Cotton was ordered to have D'Urban's brigade of Portuguese cavalry on the field at daylight on the 29th. Fane's cavalry brigade was also ordered to move up to Berrioplano.

Later on in the day, however, information appears to have

---

1. Murray had at 11.30 a.m. sent an order to Colonel Arentschild "to keep a good look-out towards the valley in which Lanz and Ostiz are situated to get information whether the enemy moves any troops from the Baztan by Lanz or from St. Estevan by Dona Maria." He was also directed to send a letter party to Irurzun.
2. Q.M.G. to Hill, near Orcayen, July 28, 3 p.m. Hill, unless he had received other orders direct from Wellington, was to move with as little delay as possible by route taken by 6th division towards Orcayen.
3. Q.M.G. to Hill, heights above Villaba, July 28, 1813, 4 p.m.

reached headquarters showing that the 7th division was in advance of Hill's corps. At 10 p.m., therefore, Murray again wrote to Hill as follows:[1]

> I wrote to you at four this afternoon about leaving the 7th division at Lizaso to oppose any attempt of the enemy upon Irurzun, supposing that the 7th would arrive later than you at Lizaso. If, however, the 7th division is so placed as to arrive to support the left of our position here before you, Lord Wellington desires the 7th division may come on and that you will remain in observation near Lizaso.

It is well this letter was sent, as the 7th division arrived at Lizaso at noon on 28th and Hill not until about two hours later. Having been rejoined by Barnes's brigade, Lord Dalhousie marched at 5 p.m. for Ollocarizqueta, in accordance with the orders he had already received, intending to reach that place by daybreak on 29th.[2] At 4 p.m., Hill wrote to the Quartermaster-General saying that he could not get further than Lizaso that day as the previous night had been so bad and dark and the roads very bad. If he received no other orders he would march at dawn on 29th for Ollocarizqueta.[3] During the night, Murray's letter of 10 p.m., 28th, reached him.

D'Erlon having ascertained on the morning of the 28th that the allied position above Irurita had been evacuated, marched with Darmagnac's and Abbé's divisions over the col de Velate and in the evening bivouacked on the plateau above Lanz. Maransin's division was left at Elizondo, but was ordered that evening to come on by the same route on the 29th. From the plateau the bivouac fires of Hill's troops were visible to the French. During a reconnaissance made towards Ostiz by the cavalry regiment with D'Erlon (22nd Chasseurs) other cavalry were sighted, but the latter, a reconnoitring patrol sent

---

1. Q.M.G. to Hill, heights above Villaba, July 28, 1813, 10 p.m.
2. Dalhousie to Q.M.G., Lizaso, July 28, 1813, 1.30 p.m.
3. Hill to Q.M.G., Lizaso, July 28, 1813, 4 p.m.

out from Ismert's brigade of Treilhard's division, retired, mistaking the 22nd for British cavalry. On their rejoining their brigade at nightfall, General Ismert wrote to D'Erlon informing him of the position of Soult's army and also reported the circumstance to the Marshal.

On the battlefield not a shot was fired after 7 p.m.

The light division halted during the 28th, on the Santa Cruz mountain above St. Estevan, not moving till about sunset, when the division began to descend towards Zubieta *en route* for Leiza and the Pamplona-Tolosa road. Why General Alten did not move earlier is not known. It seems probable that the order of the day for 27th failed to reach him[1] or else arrived very late, and that he did not move until he had ascertained that Hill had retired.

Villatte in considerable force attacked Longa near Vera and towards Salain on the evening of the 28th, but the latter maintained his ground and the French retired.[2]

---

1. Account by an officer of the division in Colbourn's *United Service Journal* for 1830 says, "We remained in position during whole of 28th, having completely lost trace of the army." See also Dalhousie to Q.M.G., 4 p.m., July 27.
2. Graham to Wellington, Oyarzun, July 30, 5 a.m.

CHAPTER 14

A Long Drawing of Breath

On the battlefield of Sorauren the opposing forces remained facing each other; and not a shot was fired during the day. The dead were buried, and in many parts of the field, a sort of mutual truce being established, the soldiers of both armies met amicably between the lines.[1]

No doubt both sides were exhausted by their efforts of the last four days. But the French were in the worst case. "The 29th passed on the French side in a sort of prostration succeeding their exertions of the preceding days. The soldiers had received no rations since leaving St. Jean Pied de Port. They were done up, however, rather than hungry. The regiments short of food sent fatigue parties into the neighbouring villages, but they brought back nothing, save a little wine."[2] The allies got their rations, and the cheers of the British troops which greeted an issue of rum—a custom which still survives—must have been heard with envy in the French lines.

On the evening of the 28th Hill had taken position on a high ridge on the right bank of one of the streams forming the head waters of the Ulzama about a mile and a half south-east of Lizaso. His left was towards the village of Be-

---

1. Notes by Capt. D. Mackenzie, 42nd Royal Highlanders (6th division): "As the forenoon advanced, the French came forward without their arms to a field of peace which lay between the armies. Our soldiers mixed with them in the most friendly manner, and the 29th was a day of idleness."
2. *Revue d'Histoire*, « La Bataille de Sorauren.»

unza and the right to the north of Arestegui. As D'Erlon's divisions had halted to the north of Lanz, where the road to Lizaso branches off, it appeared to Hill that they aimed at attacking him in the morning and in this sense he reported to general headquarters.

The 7th division having left Lizaso about 5 p.m. on the 28th, reached Marcalain (6 miles) that evening[1] and very early on the 29th was near the Oricain position. Hill's report being received during the night, the 7th division was ordered to move back to his support, and at 6.30 a.m. Murray wrote to Hill informing him of this and clearly laid down that the role of his corps for the present was to be as follows:[2]

> Your object must be to prevent the enemy moving towards Pamplona, by the direct road on Berrioplano from Lizaso, as also to prevent his moving, or sending detachments upon Irurzun.
>
> With the support of the 7th division you will probably be equal not only to secure the above objects, but even to act offensively, in case that should appear to be the most effectual means of preventing the enemy from moving upon Irurzun. But should you perceive that the enemy returns his force into the road of Olague and Ostiz, you will, of course, send back the 7th division to its destination on the left of this position. Be so good as to report if you have any information from the Light division and communicate with it by the party of the 1st Hussars stationed at Lecumberri. Major-General Fane's brigade of cavalry is on its way to Berrioplano.

Soult had with him a large force of cavalry, and Wellington at this moment was very anxious about Irurzun, not only on account of its strategic importance but also lest the French should make a raid on it, because the reserve of small arm ammunition with the army being almost exhausted, the ammu-

---

1. Wellington to Bathurst, San Estevan, August 1, 1813.
2. Q.M.G. to Hill, heights near Villaba, July 29, 1813, 6.30 a.m.

nition column mules had been sent there to take over a fresh supply, expected from Vitoria and Hernani.[1] To render the place secure, the following measures were taken. The Light division[2] was ordered into the Tolosa-Pamplona road and to advance along it towards Pamplona, but not to come beyond Irurzun without further orders. The officer commanding at Irurzun was directed to collect there all detachments on their way to join the army from Vitoria, and "in case any parties or patrols of the enemy should appear they are to be effectually resisted by the detachment."

General Fane was also ordered to move a squadron to Irurzun, the squadron commander being directed to send a patrol to gain communication with Sir R. Hill at Lizaso; he was also to communicate with the party of the 1st Hussars at Lecumberri. Fane was to put himself in communication with Hill and was asked to report when any reserve ammunition arrives at Irurzun.[3]

During the day Byng's brigade relieved Ross on the Chapel heights, and the 4th division was thus reunited towards the right of the position. Several guns were man-handled up on to the hill so as to form a battery on the left of the position commanding Sorauren and the mouth of the valley. Two were also placed on the highest point on the right. The guns were probably those of Brandeth's and Cairnes' brigades.[4] The 3rd division and the Spanish troops remained in their former positions.

During the night of July 28 Soult, having received General Ismert's report regarding D'Erlon's advance, sent orders to the latter to move to Ostiz behind the right of the army. But D'Erlon seems to have been in no hurry to advance,

---

1. Q.M.G. to Dickson, C.R.A., Lesaca, July 25, and heights before Villaba, July 29, 1813, 8 a.m.
2. Q.M.G. to C. Alten, near Villaba, July 29, 1813, 9.30 a.m.
3. Q.M.G. to Fane, position near Villaba, July 29,1813,10 a. m.
4. Dickson MSS., letter to Major-General McLeod, Passages, August 12, 1813, and Capt. Cairnes' letters of August 3 and September 3, 1813.

and it was noon before the divisions of Abbé and Darmagnac arrived at Ostiz after a march of little more than six miles. Maransin's division, less one battalion left at Elizondo to bring on an expected convoy of provisions, arrived at Lanz during the day.

Thus at last, and too late, D'Erlon's wing came into combination with the rest of the army. "It was in the destiny of their chief never to appear in time where his presence was necessary."[1]

It was now for Soult to decide what he would do. His supplies were practically exhausted, and facing him was the allied army whose strength he estimated at not less than 50,000 men. An army, too, commanded by Wellington, and of which a comparatively small portion only had on the 28th frustrated his attempt to reach Pamplona. Even with the addition of D'Erlon's troops, he judged it too hazardous to make another effort and attack again. To stay where he was was impossible, if only on account of lack of food and leaving out of consideration the menacing position the enemy was gradually assuming around him. To retreat was the only alternative left. And it seems practically certain that Soult had determined on this soon after it was evident what the result of the battle of the 28th was going to be. For on July 29 he sent off his chief supply officer to Bayonne to arrange for the despatch of supplies to the army, and the places he selected as refilling points become a key to the plan then forming in his mind. After having been reinforced by seventeen or eighteen thousand comparatively fresh troops, he could not face the ignominy of a direct retreat into France by the way he had come, for he was a brave and proud man. What would the Emperor think and say? Where would his reputation be, if an expedition intended to drive the allies beyond the Ebro and whose success was to be announced from Vitoria, should

---

1. *Revue d'Histoire*, «La bataille de Sorauren.» The wanderings of D'Erlon's corps on June 16, 1815, will be remembered.

flee back to the frontier foiled even before it reached Pamplona? No, retreat was inevitable, but it must be so masked as to appear a manoeuvre.

Soult had received no communication from Villatte since July 26. On the 28th D'Erlon had reported a rumour which had reached him in the Baztan that Villatte was about to cross the Bidassoa.[1] This rumour Soult seems to have seized on and transformed the crossing into an accomplished fact, with its corollary that Graham had retired from the river and that the road to San Sebastian was now open. D'Erlon's presence at Ostiz and Lanz gave him command, temporarily at least, of the Ulzama valley road to the Baztan and to France. Soult therefore determined to abandon his communication by Roncevaux with St Jean, to move to his right by the Ulzama valley, and concentrate his army about Lizaso, whence he could move towards Villatte either by the direct route towards the great road at Irurzun or gain it further north at Andoain or Hernani by the Dona Maria passes, and in the San Sebastian direction make another bid for success.

Which line he would take was to be decided on after the army had concentrated on July 31. Nor was the intention published; it was communicated to his lieutenant-generals only, and they were to treat it as confidential. As it would be difficult to move his artillery over the country he proposed to enter, and too many cavalry would be an encumbrance and add to supply difficulties, Soult determined to send all the artillery and some of the cavalry back to France. His instructions to his chief commissary,[2] already alluded to, were to send off all the supplies he could lay his hands on about Roncevaux so that they should arrive at Zabaldica before daylight on the 30th, or at Zubiri by mid-day. He was also to press on the evacuation of all the wounded and sick thence to St. Jean. From Bayonne, all

---

1. Soult to Minister of War, Zabaldica, July 29, 1813. D'Erlon received the information from General St. Paul, commanding one of the brigades of the Reserve division.
2. Soult to M. Favier, Zabaldica, July 29, 1813.

supplies he could find mule transport for were to be sent off so as to arrive at Lanz[1] by way of Elizondo not later than August 2, and a large convoy of food of all sorts was to be prepared and sent off in wheeled vehicles in two or three sections (accompanied by slaughter cattle) by the great road of Irun to the furthest point occupied by Villatte's reserve.

Early on the 29th the French artillery, escorted by part of the cavalry, commenced their march back into France by the Roncevaux road, and with them went all the wounded who could be moved. The remainder of the cavalry marching by Zubiri and Eugui crossed from the Arga into the Ulzama valley. To cover these movements and give the artillery time to get well away, the rest of the French army retained its strong position during the day. In a dispatch to the War Minister,[2] Soult thus vaguely expresses his future intentions.

> I have not received any report from General Villatte, but Count D'Erlon wrote on 28th saying he had heard from General St. Paul that the enemy's line had been withdrawn from the Bidassoa and that Villatte was about to cross; so I presume he is now at Ernani or Andoain, and that San Sebastian *est degagée*. If this result has been obtained my first plan of operation is completely fulfilled and I must now take steps to assure the success of the second. With this object I commence my movement tonight, but the line which the army holds before Pamplona will not be abandoned till after tomorrow. In my next report I shall have the honour of informing Your Excellency of my movements and their results. I am at my last day of supplies.

It is hardly surprising that the Minister replied that Soult's letters contained no information as to how he proposed to act so as to arrest the progress of the enemy before San Sebastian and Pamplona. Soult's real intention, then, seems to have been

---
1. Bayonne to Lanz, forty-two miles.
2. Soult to War Minister, Zabaldica, July 29, 1813.

to retire by his right, perhaps as far as the Baztan, pick up supplies there and then join Villatte.

His orders issued on the 29th prescribed how the manoeuvre was to be carried out on the 30th. D'Erlon's wing, forming the advanced guard of the army, was to move early from Ostiz to Lizaso picking up the cavalry *en route*. On arrival it was to hold the roads leading towards Pamplona "very strongly" and push reconnaissances towards the col of Dona Maria and towards Letassa and Irurzun. Clausel's divisions, which were holding the mouth of the Ulzama valley at Sorauren, the village and the high hill facing the allied position on the Oricain hill, were to be gradually relieved by those of Reille, who was to leave in the Arga valley only the 13th Chasseurs and one battalion of Lamartinière's division. On relief by Reille, Clausel's divisions were to move up the Ulzama valley towards Olague, but their march was to be so regulated that, if necessary, assistance could be given to disengage Reille if he was attacked.

Reille, who would thus become eventually responsible for the whole of the present front from Zabaldica to Sorauren, was to maintain his position till nightfall on the 30th and then in turn retire to Olague and Lanz, except the Arga valley detachment which was to move to Lanz by Zubiri and Urtazum.[1] The order also stated that from the 30th the line of communication by Roncevaux would be abandoned and that everything arriving at Zubiri from the rear after noon on that day was to be sent on to Lanz, where on the 30th headquarters would be established.[2]

Thus Soult's plan was based on nothing more than a rumour which had in fact no truth in it. But, greatest mistake of all, was to believe that he would be allowed to carry out the complicated and dangerous manoeuvre he proposed for the morning of the 30th, under the very eyes of a commander like Wellington, now ready to strike with all his strength.

1. In the Esteribar valley near Eugui.
2. Order of the day, Zabaldica, July 29, 1813.

During the afternoon, Wellington knew of the arrival of D'Erlon's troops at Ostiz. Colonel Sturgeon, who was observing them from the hills on the west of the valley, reported their strength at from eight to nine thousand men. Now that D'Erlon's position was known, the possibility of an attempt being made to turn the left of the allied position by the Lizaso road or of the movement of any large force towards Irurzun ceased for the moment; and Wellington was freed from the anxiety hitherto felt on this account. D'Erlon's advance to Ostiz seemed rather to indicate that Soult intended to attack again. The assumption of the offensive as soon as sufficient strength had been assembled, had always been Wellington's intention. Now that he had in hand over 40,000 men, excluding the blockading force, and Soult's whole force was in his front, the time for it had arrived. But Wellington was not going to parade his intention. The only movement ordered in the evening was that the 7th division was to close to its right so as to be ready to move on to the high ground above the right bank of the Ulzama held by the left of the 6th division. Wellington seems to have determined to make the time and manner of his offensive dependent on what the enemy did. His dispositions as they would stand in the morning were readily adaptable to the possibilities of the situation. If Soult attacked then, with Hill in his rear and the 7th division on his flank, a vigorous counterstroke driving him up the valley might well lead to his utter undoing. If he retreated, the allied troops were well placed to do him all the injury possible, as is proved by the events of the following day.

At 6.30 p.m. the following memorandum was sent to Sir R. Hill and Lord Dalhousie.[1]

> The force of the enemy which was approaching this from the side of Lanz is reported to have halted, and to have encamped in the vicinity of Ostiz.

---

1. Memorandum for Lord Dalhousie and Sir R. Hill, heights above Villaba, July 29, 1813, 6.30 p.m.

From the lateness of the hour it does not seem likely, therefore, that any serious attack can take place this evening.

Lord Dalhousie will be so good as to close his division towards its right that it may be in a situation whence it can with facility move to the ground on the wooded ridge, where Major-General Pack's left now is; and he will ascertain whether one of his brigades could be moved up to a high ridge which lies between the wooded ridge above mentioned and the great hill in its front.

Lord Dalhousie will be so good as to have it ascertained also whether (with the assistance of men) guns could be got up upon the ridge where the left of the 6th division now is.

Sir R. Hill's last report states his having sent the Conde d'Amaranthe's division to Marcalain.[1] This division should be left in a situation whence it may move to its right towards the 7th division, should such movement be required.

The remainder of the force under Sir R. Hill had better continue where it is. Sir R. Hill will be so good, however, to have the roads leading upon Ostiz ascertained and posts of infantry pushed forward in the direction of that place. The cavalry should also have posts as far forwards as possible towards Olague and Lanz. These measures will tend to keep the enemy jealous for his right and rear; and the line pointed out may become the direction also of an offensive movement against him should any circumstance occur to give a favourable opening for such a measure. Reports from Lieutenant-Colonel Sturgeon (on the great hill in Lord Dalhousie's front) state the enemy's force near Ostiz to appear to

---

1. The Portuguese division now consisted of one brigade only under Da Costa, as Campbell's brigade was with Wellington. It may have been sent to Marcalain during the day; but was certainly moved up again that evening or early on the 30th, as it was in Hill's line when he was attacked. Wyld's Atlas shows a brigade of the 7th division near Zildoz, watching the road from Ostiz to Marcalain on afternoon of 29th, and its advance from there on July 30.

him to be about 8,000 or 9,000 men. Posts of observation should be kept out on the most commanding hills all day, and should be again on the outlook as soon as there is light in the morning.

Whether Wellington gave verbal instructions for the next day to other divisional commanders is not known. From a letter addressed by Murray to Picton at 8 a.m. on the 30th, it seems possible he did.

The Light division reached Leiza on the 29th. From there mounted officers were sent out in various directions to get, if possible, tidings of the rest of the army. After a halt, the division marched again at 6 p.m. towards the great road.

As has been stated, it was Wellington's intention to make his attack depend on the enemy's movements. It may be thought he missed an excellent opportunity in not doing so on July 29. But there seem to be several reasons why it was judicious not to. First the shortage of ammunition; then the necessity of resting the men. An attack must only be the first act in a continuous series of operations whose end could not be exactly foreseen, but which must at the least consist in pushing the French over the frontier again. Once started they must be kept on the run and no halts to gain breath allowed. To give the army a day's rest after what the men had been through was therefore wise, and it would moreover enable the allied supply arrangements, thrown out of joint by the unexpected and rapid retreat, to be got into order again. Probably, too, Wellington was influenced by the strength of the ground held by the French. He afterwards said their position was "one of the strongest and most difficult of access that I have seen occupied by troops."[1] Now as always, he was anxious to avoid losses not absolutely necessary.

It is difficult to understand why Soult, having decided to retire by the Lanz valley, made the arrangement he did, whereby, as a preliminary, Reille's divisions from the Arga val-

---

1. Wellington to Bathurst, San Estevan, August 1, 1813.

ley were to move across and relieve those of Clausel about Sorauren and the centre of the position. This relief was bound to take time. Part of it at any rate could not fail to be observed from the enemy's position if carried out in daylight; it brought troops on to ground and into positions unfamiliar to them just at the time when an attack on them was not improbable. Reille's divisions might quite easily have been moved unseen into the Ostiz road over the hills close behind the French position. The procedure adopted was to say the least cumbersome, and to it may be attributed much of the loss sustained by the French the next day.

CHAPTER 15

Second Battle Of Sorauren

On the evening of July 29, the French army was posted as follows: on the right, Clausel's wing with Conroux's division in first line across the Ulzama valley and holding the village of Sorauren, with one regiment on the heights beyond the stream, and Taupin's and Vandermaesen's divisions on and behind the slopes of the hill above. Maucune's division of Reille's corps came next, holding the crest facing the 4th British division with Lamartinière's division on the eastern slopes and about the village of Zabaldica. Foy's division was on the high ground beyond the Arga river above Alzuza. In accordance with Soult's order of that day Reille's corps was on the morning of the 30th to take over the whole front, and the latter determined to effect the relief of Clausel's troops on the right by moving Maucune's division down into the Ulzama valley to take over the positions held by Conroux, replacing him on the high ground in the centre by Foy's division.

The morning of the 30th was bright and clear, and throughout the day the weather remained fine and exceedingly hot.[1]

Early in the morning, Foy's division, which had marched during the night to Iroz, ascended the slopes to relieve that of Maucune, which then moved down to take Conroux's place about Sorauren. For some reason Foy formed up his division on the southern slopes of the French hill opposite the right of the 4th division and within range of the British guns there,

---
1. Maxwell, *Sketches of the Peninsula*: "The day was broiling hot."

which now opened fire on him with considerable effect. Foy then moved up to the crest of the heights[1] and the artillery fire appears to have led the outposts and light troops on both sides to open fire along the whole front. The 3rd division with its artillery and two squadrons of cavalry also advanced towards the heights vacated by Foy. Meanwhile on the French right, Taupin's division had commenced to move up the valley towards Ostiz, and Maucune's troops to relieve those of Conroux. The movements here also drew the fire of the guns on the chapel height,[2] and there was sharp fighting between the hostile piquets and light troops in the valley below. Those of the allies obtained possession of Sorauren for a time but were driven out of it again.

In his dispatches on the operations Wellington thus states his plan of attack.

> I, however, determined to attack their position, and ordered Lieut.-General the Earl of Dalhousie to possess himself of the top of the mountain in his front, by which the enemy's right would be turned; and Lieut.-General Sir T. Picton to cross the heights on which the enemy's left had stood and to turn their left by the road to Roncesvalles. All the arrangements were made to attack the front of the enemy's position as the effect of those movements on their flanks should begin to appear.

But he was not yet sure whether the movements going on in the French position indicated a retreat or a massing on their right flank, and for the time held his hand. For at 8 a.m. Murray wrote to Picton,[3] who seems to have advanced further than Wellington wished, "to do no more in the first instance than put himself in a situation to advance by the Roncesvalles road; but will not move on by that road until it

---

1. *Revue d'Histoire,* quoting a letter from Foy, August 3, 1813.
2. Besides these guns, two had been also placed in position on the slopes of the hill on the right bank of the Ulzama.
1. Q.M.G. to Picton, July 30, 8 a.m.

is sufficiently ascertained that the enemy is not employed in any arrangement to enable him to act against our left flank."

Clausel's divisions, however, continued to retire along the Ostiz road. Though hidden from the allied position on the Oricain hill, this movement would be seen by Dalhousie's lookout parties, and the 7th division moved off along the hills on the opposite side of the valley. Seeing this movement Vandermaesen, whose division followed that of Taupin, sent two of his regiments up the hills to his left to reinforce the regiment Conroux had already placed there as a flank guard. When they reached the summit they found themselves face to face with Inglis' brigade of the 7th division, which charged and drove the whole down into the valley with heavy losses on both sides. Inglis, throwing his brigade into skirmishing order, pursued them down the hillside and opened fire on the flank of the column on the road. At this time the whole of Clausel's corps was in motion towards Ostiz, the Lieutenant-General himself being at its head, except the rear brigade of Conroux's division, which remained in position across the road about four hundred yards to the north of Sorauren in support of Maucune.

And now, there being no longer any doubt that a large portion of the French army was in full retreat, Wellington launched his attack on Reille's corps. It was probably about 9.15 a.m.[1] Under cover of the fire of the guns on the chapel height and those beyond the river, the leading British brigade of the 6th division—now commanded by the Adjutant-General (Pakenham) owing to Pack having been wounded on the 28th—pushed straight on against Sorauren and the valley gorge, while the Portuguese brigade advanced along the lower slopes beyond the river and Byng's brigade dashing down from the chapel hill assailed the village from the south-east.

The 4th division at the same time advanced against the formidable heights held by Foy with Anson's brigade and Stubb's Portuguese in front, each in two lines, the first being composed of the 40th, the 2nd provisional battalion (2nd Queens and 2/53rd),

---

1. The estimation of the times is based on Larpent's *Diary*.

the 7th Caçadores and 11th Portuguese, with Ross's brigade in reserve. On the right in the Arga valley the 3rd division with its light troops in front was advancing towards Zabaldica.

The guns on both flanks of the allied hill kept up a heavy fire on the French, and a stern fight raged in the valley below and on the opposite slopes. Taken in front and on both flanks by the 6th division and Byng, with their retreat up the valley cut off by the 7th division, Maucune's division and Conroux's rear brigade were in a trap. Reille recognized the danger and sent his chief staff officer to Maucune to convey his sanction to his withdrawing from the village and retiring up the valley to where Conroux's rear brigade was posted. Maucune heavily engaged, did not, however, consider it advisable to fall back. Then Reille himself ordered one brigade to retire up the valley, but on leaving the shelter of the village it came under so heavy a fire from the guns and the encircling infantry of the 6th division that it abandoned the road and mounted the slopes towards Foy.[1] Byng's brigade then rushed the village, and Reille seeing the hopelessness of the situation ordered Maucune to retire. But as he did so, the advance of the 4th division had reached the crest of the heights, and at about 10.30 a.m. "three-quarters of the circle round the basin of Sorauren was closed."[2] Scattering over the hills behind the village, the remnant of Maucune's division, mingled with parties from Conroux's and the other divisions of Clausel's corps, retired along the northern slopes of the divide between the valleys, while on the crest Foy was falling back before the 4th division. Seeing this confused mass of nearly 2,000 men moving back below him, Cole sent the 40th down from above to cut them off; rushing down with one company of the 53rd, this regiment charged the French just as they were checked by a ravine and took 700 of them prisoners, the remainder moving up the hill joined Foy.

Larpent thus describes the fighting on the French right.[3]

---

1. Reille's report.
2. *Revue d'Histoire*.
3. Larpent, *Diary*.

The firing began at daylight: at nine o'clock I determined to go and see what was going on, and mounting my black, proceeded up for the hills where the 6th and 7th divisions were on the opposite side of the valley from our grand position.[1] I met many wounded crawling back, and on the top found only the piquets left in the camp of the morning, and that the 7th division had just driven the French from the adjoining hill and were after them up the valley on the other side. I went to the point of the hill and saw the battle still raging strong, just opposite on the hills below on the other side of the valley opposite our position. The French, still steady and firing very briskly all round the side of one hill and in the village (Sorauren) below us, and our people creeping on by degrees under ridges towards the village and the hill and also advancing round the back of the hill. We had two mortars and a gun also[2] upon our position hill constantly at work playing on the French, and we saw the shells fall and burst close to the French line, whilst the wounded were carried off to the rear.

This went on for some time, above an hour after I came up, and we had men in reserve all round. I then saw our men in the village, and immediately under the French, and appearing at the top also. The French gave way, but went on firing all over the hill. In half an hour (say about 11 a.m.) I heard the loud huzzas of our soldiers, and saw no French left except on the next hills, where they seemed very numerous and strong but in confusion. The first huzzas were, I believe, for a body of about 1800 prisoners who were caught, being headed every way. There was soon a shout on our side close by our positions. It proved to be Lord Wellington and Marshal Beresford proceeding down to the village to water their horses and proceed on.

---

1. About four miles and a half from Berrioplano, whence he started at 9 a.m.
2. The French reports say there were seven or eight pieces. What Larpent took to be mortars were probably howitzers.

Lamartinière, on the French left in the Arga valley, seeing Foy falling back along the crest and his retreat threatened by Picton's advance over the hills on his left, realized that to avoid being cut off he must also take to the hill above. He therefore sent his first brigade to take position on the rocky crest about a mile behind Foy's original position.

On this brigade both Foy's division, with the stragglers and wounded of other divisions who had joined it, and Lamartinière's second brigade rallied, being closely pursued by the skirmishers of the 4th and 3rd divisions. Foy's rear-guard was here nearly cut off, but escaping, the whole continued to retreat along the crest of the ridge until about noon when Reille succeeded in concentrating his divisions, much reduced in numbers, in a position across the hills above Sarrisibar about two and a half miles in rear of the original French position.[1] With him were many men of Conroux's division, whose retreat up the valley had been cut off. Cole's advance had been slow owing to the difficult country and because he had been instructed to regulate his advance by that of the columns moving by the roads and not to press his attack against collected bodies of the enemy, but rather to wait for the effect on the enemy the allied advance by the valleys on either side was bound to have. Not a few exhausted and wounded prisoners fell into his hands.

From the Ostiz road, Clausel had been able to see much of what was happening to Reille's corps, and at about 11 a.m., recognizing that the latter was being driven from his position, he drew up the troops with him in a position just south of Ostiz commanding the road.

Clausel's corps had been followed up the valley by the 7th division; but Dalhousie did not attack, no support was as yet available from the rest of the army, and the French were in too great strength. After remaining about an hour in this position in order to give Reille's retreating troops on the hill time to get up level with him, Clausel retired to Etulain, about two miles beyond Ostiz, and there remained till about 4 p.m.

---

1. Colonel Michaud's report.

The retreat of a large portion of the French army up the Ulzama valley, menaced Hill in position south of Lizaso in proportion as the numbers retiring increased.

Therefore Wellington, as soon as the state of the fight permitted of his detaching troops from the field, had sent Campbell's brigade from the Oricain position and Morillo's division from San Miguel by the Oricain—Morcelain road to reinforce Hill. And, when the issue of the battle was no longer doubtful, made his dispositions for immediately following up the French. La Bispal was instructed to hand over the blockade of Pamplona to Don Carlos, making up his strength to 6000 infantry with all the artillery and the cavalry of the Andalusian reserve except one squadron; with the rest of his force la Bispal was to follow the column which moved up the Ostiz road.[1]

Before leaving the position the following instructions for the advance were issued by Murray:

> Position near Villaba, July 30, 1813,[2] arrangement for the advance of the army.
>
> The 3rd division, with two squadrons of light cavalry, will follow the enemy by the Roncesvalles road. Sir T. Picton will be hereafter informed what other troops will follow the 3rd division.
>
> The 4th division will for the present act along the hills that are between the Roncesvalles road and the Ostiz road. This division will connect the columns which advance by these two roads. Its own progress must, of course, be slow from the nature of the country; and Sir Lowry Cole is besides instructed not to press the enemy by any direct attack when he is strongly posted, but to wait a little in these cases for the cooperation of the columns moving by the roads, whose advance will, of course, alarm the enemy for his flanks.

---

1. Wellington to la Bispal, heights in front of Villaba, July 30.
2. Time of issue is not given.

The column moving by the Ostiz road will be composed as follows:

    Major-General Byng's brigade and one squadron 13th Light Dragoons.
    The 6th division.
    The remainder of the 13th Light Dragoons.
    The troops under the Conde de la Bispal.[1]

The 7th division will move by the hills on the left of the valley of the Ostiz; and Lord Dalhousie will regulate his advance in a manner similar to that ordered for the 4th division. He will communicate on his right with the column on the Ostiz road, and on the left with the troops under Sir R. Hill.

Sir Rowland Hill will be so good as to point his movements towards Lanz and towards Olague, regulating them according to those of the enemy, and communicating frequently to headquarters whatever he can ascertain respecting the enemy's march.[2]

Headquarters will be with the column on the Ostiz road. The 3rd division, 6th division and 2nd division will move with one brigade of artillery each. The remainder of the artillery is not to move for the present.

Major-General Long's brigade of cavalry will move with Sir R. Hill. Major-General Fane's brigade of cavalry will continue near Berrioplano. The remainder of the cavalry under Sir Stapleton Cotton will continue in the neighbourhood of Pamplona.

All the troops will send for their baggage.

    The Quartermaster-General had also written to Alten informing him that as the enemy had been withdrawing[3] all the morning, "though as yet it cannot be positively stated that their

---

1. A portion of these troops was subsequently ordered to move by Marcelain to reinforce Hill.
2. This instruction was issued before information had been received that D'Erlon had attacked Hill.
3. Q.M.G. to C. Alten, position near Villaba, July 30.

movement is a retreat by the roads of Roncesvalles and Lanz," the necessity of pressing the march of the Light Division towards Irurzun no longer existed, though the order to reach the great road at Lecumberri could not, he said, at the moment be cancelled, Alten was to do nothing to fatigue his troops.

There must needs have been some confusion and intermingling of units amongst the troops which had carried Sorauren and the valley mouth. When this had been put straight, the Ostiz road column commenced to march up the valley, probably about noon.

Reille with his divisions remained to the north of Sarrisibar till nearly 1 p.m., when, seeing that Clausel was abandoning his position near Ostiz and that the 4th division was approaching, he determined to continue his retreat in order to rejoin Soult. Owing, however, to the advance of the allied column by the valley road, he was still obliged to remain on the high ground and therefore ordered his divisional generals to march by Egoscue on Lanz distant about seven miles over the hills.[1]

Foy's division, which was on the left, was to form the rear and left flank guards. But after starting, the head of this division took a wrong path in the woods, and being obliged from time to time to ascend to the crest of the heights to stay the pursuit of the skirmishers of the 3rd and 4th divisions which clung to it, embarrassed moreover by the large mass of stragglers accompanying it, the division completely lost its way and found itself descending, not into the Ulzama, but into the Arga valley. "When the mistake was discovered, it was irreparable because it was then impossible to turn back the 7,000 to 8,000 stragglers who preceded, accompanied or followed the column." Foy with some difficulty got them assembled round the village of Iragui (about two and a half miles south west of Eugui) in order to prevent their fleeing to Zubiri, by which village they remembered they had come.[2] About seven o'clock, however, information reached Foy that Pic-

---

1. Reille's report of the right wing, August 12, 1813.
2. *Revue d'Histoire*, Foy to Soult, Cambo, August 10.

ton's division was approaching. It was then too late, he considered, to hope to reach Lanz before the enemy, and therefore determined to take the only line of escape into France now open to him, the track by Eugui, and the col of Urtiaga into the Aldudes, and sent a message to this effect to Reille. Leaving Iragui at 8 p.m. he reached the col of Urtiaga at 7 a.m. on 31st, and halted there till 8 p.m. in order to rally the stragglers. Having neither food to give them nor officers and non-commissioned officers to spare to get them into military formation again, he decided to send them off to find their own way to St. Jean Pied de Port, and wrote to the governor of the place to provide food for them and send them on to Espelette. Foy then moved to the col of Berdaritz in the hope of being able to rejoin the army by way of the Bastan. There he remained on the night of July 31, August 1, sending out a reconnaissance towards Elizondo.

Receiving information from his scouts that a strong allied column was entering the valley from Irurita, he determined to make for the col de Maya by that of Ispegui and Errazu and started off at 9 a.m. But the British cavalry were now advancing up the Bastan. Foy, therefore, seeing he could not hope to reach the col de Maya before them, relinquished the idea and moved down into the Baigorry valley, whence he marched to Cambo. But Foy's division, with the stragglers accompanying it, was not the only part of Reille's corps which went astray. General Gauthier of Lamartinière's division with part of his brigade had also lost his way with Foy. Instead, however, of retreating from Iragui towards the Aldudes, he made his way thence to Lanz during the night.

Lamartinière's flank guard of the 13th Chasseurs and one battalion of the 122nd was also cut off. Its orders were to fall back by Zubiri and Eugui to Lanz; on reaching Eugui, however, it became known that the road to Lanz via Olague was held by the enemy, the officer commanding, therefore determined to retreat to the Aldudes, which he did, about 500 to 600 stragglers accompanying the column. "Including the stragglers of all corps, a total amounting to the strength of two divisions had thus on this July 30 fallen out from Soult's command and the English had made not less than 3,000 prisoners."[1]

Early on the morning of July 30, Soult had left Zabaldica and crossed over the hill to Olabe, where he viewed the commencement of the retreat of Clausel's divisions. He then proceeded up the valley to join D'Erlon. Deserters, who had come in on the 29th, stated that Wellington intended to make an offensive movement in strength towards Lizaso on the 30th, and Soult was now led to believe the statements owing to reports which reached him during the morning that columns of the enemy had been observed descending from San Christoval and the Oricain heights. "The opportunity"—he reported to the War Minister[2]— "to defeat a detachment of the enemy appeared to me a good one, and I was all the more inclined to avail myself of it as it fitted in with my plan of action decided on the day before. I, therefore, proceeded towards D'Erlon and joined him beyond Olague on the heights on the Lizaso road." It would be interesting to know what passed between the Marshal and his Lieutenant-General at this their first meeting since the operations had commenced.

In front of D'Erlon's position stretched the little upland plateau of Lizaso, through which flow the Ulzama stream and its tributaries. About half a mile beyond the main channel of the river rises the crest of a long ridge running roughly east and west over depressions in which are carried the tracks towards Marcalain and Irurzun.

On this ridge Hill's troops had been in bivouac since the evening of the 28th. His right was across the Marcalain road, but his strength did not permit him to extend sufficiently far to the left towards Beunza to directly cover that to Irurzun.

The front of the position towards Lizaso is steep and much covered with wood, but the southern slopes are gen-

---

1. *Revue d'Histoire,* 144.
2. Soult to Clarke, bivouac on heights of Echalar, August 2, 1818.

tler. About half a mile behind Hill's right lay the village of Arestagui. The right was held by Ashworth and Da Costa's Portuguese brigades with two companies of the 28th regiment; from thence the line was carried on by the 1st British brigade of the 2nd division, now commanded by Lieut.-Colonel Fitzgerald of the 5/60th Rifles, as Cameron had been wounded at the Maya on the 25th. The lower edge of the wooded forward slopes all along the position was held by the light companies of the force and Pringle 's brigade was in reserve. There were advanced parties of cavalry out in front of the position, the greater part however of Long's brigade appears to have been in rear of it.[1] The artillery of the force was also behind the position, no guns were brought up on to the ridge. Early in the morning of the 80th, Sir Rowland Hill, having no expectation of being attacked and hearing the heavy firing towards Sorauren, had gone off to a hill some distance in rear of the right of his position in order to see if possible what was going on in that direction. It appears he had whilst there actually issued an order for his force to quit their position and retire in order to bring it nearer Wellington's left; when news reached him that the French were advancing the order was cancelled.[2]

On reaching Lizaso and seeing the ridge held by the enemy, Soult thought his opportunity had come and ordered D'Erlon to attack. The latter decided to contain the allies' right and front with Darmagnac's division, whilst Abbé, supported by Maransin, was to seize a height near Beunza which commanded the allied left, and then moving down from it sweep them off the ridge. Thus the soldiers who had so valiantly opposed each other on the Maya ridge on the 25th were this day again to cross bayonets.

Whilst Abbé commenced his turning movement, Darmagnac's division, in several columns, connected by regiments of

---

1. Wyld's plan of the action shows Long's cavalry brigade at Marcalain on night of July 29.
2. Henry, *Events of a Military Life*.

Treilhard's cavalry division, and covered by swarms of skirmishers, advanced against Hill's right and centre. Kept off for a time by the fire of the light companies, Darmagnac urgently pressed his attack, and driving in the allied skirmishers pushed up the steep and wooded slopes. But nowhere here could he gain a footing, for the light companies being reinforced from the battalion companies on the crest dashed at the French again and drove them down the hill. Henry, who was attending to the wounded on the hill, thus describes an incident he witnessed in the fight.

> At one point the light troops came running in, their faces begrimed with powder and sweat, quite close to the spot where Sir Rowland Hill and his staff were standing. I distinctly saw him turning back some men and heard his words addressing them: 'Go back my men, you must not let them up You shall be instantly supported. You must not let them up.' Back they went cheerfully and soon disappeared among the trees and with the aid of a couple of battalion companies, that dashed from the hill at double quick, soon beat down the enemy at this point.[1]

All along the rugged and wooded front of the position it was a fight of small bodies, "the regiments were all partially engaged, companies and even subdivisions all had their turn."[1] On the right, where the ground was more open, a strong French column had assailed the Portuguese, but Ashworth's brigade met it " with the greatest steadiness and drove the enemy before him at the point of the bayonet."[2]

All along the line D'Erlon had failed, for Darmagnac abandoning his role of holding the enemy engaged, had attempted to push his attacks home—all accounts agree that the French advanced with great dash and gallantry—and had been driven back before Abbé had really come into action.

The latter's column, aiming at the high ground on Hill's

---

1. Cadell, *History of 28th Regiment.*
2. Hill to Wellington, July 31, 1813.

left, when it arrived near the position moved to its right along the front seeking for the best place to ascend.[1] This being seen from above, the 1st British brigade, screened by the trees and brushwood, made a corresponding movement to its left. When the French, having reached an easier part of the ridge, began to ascend the 71st Highland Light Infantry extended in skirmishing order down the slope, the 50th formed line on the crest and the 92nd was formed in two bodies, one half-battalion being moved beyond the left of the 50th to watch for any turning movement on that flank and the other kept as a brigade reserve. All attempts of the French to gain the ridge here were repeatedly repulsed by the 1st brigade reinforced by the 34th regiment and 14th Portuguese, which Hill sent up from the general reserve.

But the rest of Abbé's division coming up followed by Maransin, they extended still further to their right, and there ascended. The first to reach the hill top was a strong grenadier battalion[1] which, issuing from a wood beyond the left of the 92nd wing with drums beating and shouts of *Vive l'Empereur*, advanced to the charge.

> The Highland skirmishers were at once called in. We had four small companies. Thinking it best to meet them half way Captain Seaton gave the command to charge. Our lads moved forward with great spirit to measure bayonets with their opponents, but from such an unequal trial of strength we were unexpectedly relieved by the 34th regiment, who coming in sight just as we were moving forward, gave us three hearty cheers and joined in our offensive.[1]

The French retired when the British arrived within thirty paces of them. Reinforced they again advanced, but the British held their ground. At length, however, the French massed in such strength on the ridge beyond the allied left, that Hill saw the position could no longer be held and about 3 p.m.[2]

---

1. Hope, *Military Memoirs of an Infantry Officer.*
2. Henry.

gave the order to retire to another line of heights running from north-east to south-west across the Marcalain road in front of the village of Eguaros.

The retirement commenced from the left and was "performed under Major-General Pringle with the greatest regularity and with small loss covered by a battalion of the 14th Portuguese."[1] Whilst it was being carried out Darmagnac again assailed the right, held to the last by a battalion of da Costa's brigade, but "were repulsed and finally driven down the ridge at the point of the bayonet by that battalion, part of Colonel Ashworth's brigade and a small detachment of the 28th regiment."[1] On reaching his second position, Hill, being now reinforced by Campbell's brigade and Morillo's division, whilst part of la Bispal's troops were also on their way to join him, again offered battle. But beyond demonstrating against Hill's right D'Erlon made no serious attack and the allied troops passed the night on the position they occupied. Their losses during the day were about 400.

Again had these men fought well and stoutly, whilst the skill and discipline of officers and men is shown in the admirable retreat they made. They had well earned Hill's praise thus expressed in his report to the Commander of the Forces: "The conduct of the officers and troops, British and Portuguese, was such as to entitle them to my entire approbation, and I could not have wished it to be better."[1]

It is the unexpected which happens in war, and this action also is an instance of the danger which may arise if a commander under such circumstances absents himself from his force. Had it not been that the allied troops were already practically in their fighting positions, a situation somewhat similar to that at the Maya might have been produced had the French attacked earlier whilst Hill and his staff were absent on the hill some three miles to the rear. His anxiety to get information about the fight at Sorauren can well be understood, but a staff officer, not the commander, should have gone to get it.

---

1. Hill's report to Wellington, July 31, 1813.

Had Darmagnac not pressed his attack too quickly, it seems clear Hill would have been forced to retire earlier than he did, and probably with heavier loss.

The road to Irurzun being now open, Soult considered he had gained his first object, and that he could now march towards San Sebastian by the Tolosa road, for he was yet in ignorance of all that had happened to Clausel and Reille. At 3 p.m. his chief of the staff wrote[1] to the latter informing him that D'Erlon had just beaten three British divisions and driven them back behind Ursun, that Clausel was ordered to protect his movement and when Reille no longer required Clausel's support the latter was to move to Lizaso, and Reille to take position behind Olague. But Reille, as we know, was then moving over the hills towards Lanz and Clausel was being driven up the road by Wellington's valley column.[2] By nightfall, however, Clausel had reached Lizaso and Reille "bivouacked between Olague and Lizaso." He had but "a handful of troops. Maueune's division, decimated at Sorauren and Lamartinière's in disorder and reduced to one brigade, were witnesses to defeat, and the absence of that of Foy presaged a disaster."[3]

During the night Foy's letter giving information of his movements and intended retreat to the Aldudes reached Reille.

Wellington and the valley column reached Olague about sunset. The 4th division was still on the hills to the right (east) above Barutain, the 3rd on the Roncesvalles road about Zubiri, the 7th on the hills to the left, Dalhousie having also moved towards Hill, and the latter on his position above Eguaros. Wellington had as yet no inkling of Soult's intention

---

1. Gazan to Reille, bivouac before Lizaso, July 31, 3 p.m.
2. Larpent, *Diary:* "We were again stopped a second time under some trees, for Lord Wellington had ordered the French to be moved from their position beyond Ostiz and driven to the vicinity of Lanz. In the villages and on the road, which was strewed with pouches, empty knapsacks, and broken muskets, we passed several bodies all stripped, and in some places could scarcely avoid treading on them."
3. *Revue d'Histoire.*

to move on Irurzun. He knew of D'Erlon's attack on Hill, and that the latter had been obliged to fall back. But this did not disturb the conclusion already arrived at that Soult with the larger portion of his force intended to retire by the col de Velate through the Baztan; because, as Hill's position flanked his line of retreat up the valley, it was necessary for Soult either to turn him out of it or contain him there. From the reports he had received Wellington judged that about three French divisions had retreated towards Roncevaux or the Aldudes. On this view of the situation, Murray issued the following instruction for the advance of the army on July 31:

> Ostiz, July 30, 1813. 9 p.m.
> Arrangement for the further advance of the army. The troops will continue to follow the enemy to-morrow morning at daybreak according to the following arrangement.
> The right column will continue to move by the Roncesvalles road, Sir T. Picton regulating its advance according to circumstances.
> The column on the Ostiz road will move forward in the same order as this day, subject, however, to the following arrangement on the march, viz.: At Olague the 6th division will move off to the right to Eugui, and the 13th Light Dragoons (except the squadron with the advanced guard) will move with the 6th division. The further destination of these troops is to march by Zilbeti to Linzoain and thence to join the 3rd division. They will not, however, leave Eugui till they are replaced there by other troops.
> Sir Lowry Cole will move the 4th division, when he can most conveniently do so, into the Ostiz and Lanz road, and will replace the 6th division in the column moving upon that road.
> Sir R. Hill will direct the movements of the troops under his orders towards Lanz, making his disposition so

as to turn always the right flank of any post taken up by the enemy and pressing him as much as circumstances will admit of. That part of the Conde de la Bispal's force which moved this afternoon to Marcalain is to support the troops under Sir R. Hill; Sir Rowland will therefore communicate the arrangement to the Conde de la Bispal, or the officer commanding these troops.

The ultimate destination of the 7th division is to move by the pass of Dona Maria. Lord Dalhousie will therefore give that direction to the division when he perceives it can be done without affecting the more immediate operations against the enemy; and Lord Dalhousie will concert with Sir R. Hill about the passing of the division to the left of Sir Rowland's troops, which latter are destined to return into the valley of the Baztan.

Sir R. Hill will direct the 1st Hussars to send one squadron with the 7th division by the route of Dona Maria.

Sir R. Hill will also make arrangements for the march of Brigadier-General Campbell's brigade of Portuguese infantry by Olague or from Lanz to Eugui. Its destination from thence is to move by the foundry of Eugui to the passes leading into the valley of les Aldudes.

The general officers commanding the several columns will be so good as to make the best arrangements they can for keeping up communication with each other; and they will communicate, either by that means, or by a more direct channel, as may be most convenient, with headquarters.

The artillery of the 3rd division will move as far forward on the Roncesvalles road as Sir T. Picton may deem expedient. The 6th division will not move any artillery towards Eugui. The artillery on the Lanz road will not proceed beyond Lanz without a special order.

If Sir R. Hill thinks Major-General Fane's brigade of cavalry may be of use to-morrow by moving by

Irurzun upon Lizaso, he will be so good as to send orders for that movement to Major-General Fane, either through a letter party which is at Berrioplano, or through the detachment of the brigade which is stationed at Irurzun.

Headquarters will move by the road of Lanz.

G. Murray

Q.M.G.

Murray also wrote to C. Alten telling him the situation of the army and its proposed movements, and ordering him "to put the light division in movement without delay towards Zubieta." But from a postscript to the message it appears[1] that it was not despatched till 11 a.m. on 31st from Lizaso.

The light division reached Lecumberri on the morning of the 30th, having "heard sounds like those of distant thunder on our left and we concluded the noise must be that of heavy musketry."[2] The division was still without any news of all that had happened.

Such were Wellington's orders for his further advance; it will be noticed that, with the substitution of the 6th for the 4th division, they provide for practically every part of the army moving in the direction of the position it occupied on July 25. It would seem as if Wellington considered he was unlikely to be able to bring the enemy again to battle before the frontier was reached. And beyond the frontier he would not at present go, being determined to first get possession of San Sebastian.

But Soult was really in worse case than Wellington imagined. After the disasters which had befallen Reille's divisions, there could no longer be any idea of moving towards Tolosa; and moreover Wellington's advanced guard at Olague was as near as he was to the road junction near Lanz by which he must gain the Velate pass, by far the best road into the Baztan

---

1. Q.M.G. to C. Alten, Ostiz, July 30, 1813, Suppy. Desp. VI.
2. *U.S. Journal*, 1830.

and towards France and by which he was expecting a supply convoy. He decided that D'Erlon's divisions were so far to the west as to render it unsafe to attempt to get his army on to the col de Velate road.[3] There remained only the Dona Maria passes leading to San Estevan and by these he determined to carry off his army.

The bubble had at last burst. The realization of failure and the fact that he must now go at top speed for France if he wished to save his army must have given Soult a bitter pang.

---

3. Soult to Clarke, bivouac on the heights of Echalar, August 2, 1813.

CHAPTER 16

The Retreat of the French

At 1 a.m. on July 31, the French army commenced its retreat from about Lizaso by the passes over the main range of the mountains towards San Estevan.[1] Maransin's division and the cavalry, accompanied by Soult, headed the column,[2] then came the baggage of the army, followed by the rest of the infantry, Reille's two divisions leading; then, according to the orders, were to come Clausel's three divisions, followed by those of Darmagnac and Abbé of D'Erlon's wing as rearguard. It was daylight before Reille's divisions moved from Lizaso. Clausel to save time led his divisions by a pass to the

---

1. Within a distance of about five miles to the west of the pass of Velate there are four other passes over the main range, viz. the pass of Sagre, quite close to that of Velate; the pass of Arraiz, towards which a track leads from the village of that name; the pass of Loyondi; and that of Eradi, by which the track from Lizaso by Larranizar, Auza and Urroz reaches San Estevan. The tracks crossing the last three passes join at Dona Maria, a village about a mile south of San Estevan, and it is difficult to say which of the passes is the one called Dona Maria in the orders and reports. Napier in his sketch of the operations shows Soult as crossing by the pass of Arraiz; but this pass is placed much further to the west than it really is. Clerc thinks the French crossed by those of Arraiz and Loyondi. It seems more probable, however, that Soult's main column went by the pass of Eradi, as D'Erlon's report on the action states that Abbé's division retired through Maransin's in position near the *venta* (inn) de Urroz, which would surely be on the road leading to that village.
2. Maransin's division was sent on to take position on the southern slopes leading to the passes of Eradi and Loyondi so as to cover the retreat of the army. Dumas: *Neuf mois de campagnes à la suite du Maréchal Soult.*

east, probably that of Loyondi, thus the army moved in two columns.

In accordance with the orders of the previous evening, both Hill and Dalhousie moved early towards Lizaso.

The morning was a splendid one.[1] It will be remembered that Hill, with the 2nd and Portuguese divisions, Morillo's division, and that portion of la Bispal's troops which had joined him the previous afternoon, had been ordered to move towards Lanz in order to march thence by the col de Velate road into the Baztan, whilst the 7th division, as soon as Hill's troops had cleared its front and "the immediate operations against the enemy permitted," was to move over the mountains by the pass of Dona Maria. But, as Wellington explained in a letter to la Bispal, written on the evening of August 1, when this order was given, the situation as regards the enemy was not at all what he thought it was.

During the 30th he had all along judged that Soult with the larger portion of his army was retiring towards the Baztan valley by the col de Velate. A very natural conclusion considering the losses the French had suffered on the morning of that day and the fact that this was the best and shortest route into France. He had then no suspicion that on that day Soult had intended to move towards Irurzun and Tolosa, and that therefore on the night of July 30-31 the greater portion of the French army lay between Hill and himself. Looking at the situation in this light, it had been his intention to halt the 4th division and la Bispal's Spaniards at Lanz until Hill came up, when, dropping Campbell's brigade, the 2nd and Portuguese divisions could lead the column and move straight away into the valley and resume possession of the col de Maya with Byng's brigade, which would be in front and belonged to the 2nd division, as advanced guard. "I did not know that Hill was always

---

1. Cadell, *Narrative of Campaigns of the 28th Regiment*: "The morning of the 31st broke with unusual splendour on the lofty Pyrenees."

encompassed by the enemy in superior force or that the latter was in such strength towards Dona Maria."[1]

Hill, of course, had a clearer idea of the situation. He knew that he had been attacked on the previous day by at least three infantry divisions accompanied by a numerous body of cavalry, and that in the evening this force had been still in his neighbourhood. Therefore when he approached Lizaso on the morning of the 31st and found that the French in strength were retiring towards the Dona Maria passes, he had no hesitation in departing from his instructions and ordering an immediate pursuit. The Quartermaster-General had joined Sir R. Hill[2] in the morning and seeing the real state of things arranged with him that the original orders were to remain in abeyance until the enemy had been attacked and driven over the mountains. Then the 7th division and a portion of Hill's troops, not less than a strong brigade, were to follow the French into the Baztan. Campbell's brigade was to move to Eugui, and Hill, with the rest of the corps, to Velate by the pass of Sagre, thus avoiding the detour of Lanz, and thence towards Almandoz and Berroeta.[3]

From Lizaso the summit of the main chain of the mountains lies between five and six miles to the north. From the crest numerous streams descend which form the head waters of the Ulzama river, their valleys being separated by long spurs which slope down into the little upland plain. Up these spurs, which are mostly wooded, run the tracks which cross the range. It was not till about 10 a.m. that Hill's advanced guard, composed of the 1st brigade of the 2nd division, commanded by Fitzgerald, and accompanied by General Stewart, who though not yet fully recovered from the wound received at Maya, had again taken

1. Wellington to la Bispal (in French), San Estevan, August 1, 9 p.m.
2. In his letter to la Bispal just quoted, Wellington expressed himself as follows with reference to Hill's decision: "The case was one of those in which it is obligatory on a general officer in his chief's confidence to depart from his orders."
3. Detail of the arrangement for the troops under Sir R. Hill, Lizaso, July 31, 1813, 11 a.m.

over command of the division¹ came up with the enemy at the foot of the hills which they were then ascending in great haste. The French had split into two columns,² for Clausel to gain time had led his divisions by a path to the right (east) of that by which the main column was ascending. The latter was covered by Abbé's division which lined the edge of a wood towards the foot of the spur. When Hill came up the 7th division on his right was closely pressing Clausel and he ordered the 2nd division "to ascend the hill by the road we were on."

The fighting on the hillside and at the crest is described by Lieut. Hope,³ and the main incidents tally exactly with Hill's official report.

> Hill immediately followed, the pursuit being led by the first brigade of 2nd division. We came up with the French rear-guard about noon,⁴ when serious skirmishing took place in the woods. The main body of D'Erlon's corps had by now gained the pass, the road to which leads up a steep rocky hill covered with trees and brushwood. On getting through the wood where they were first engaged, our troops found themselves within 300 yards of the enemy crowded together on the road. Now was the time for artillery, one gun and one howitzer were coming up, but the officer was at a loss for the road through the difficult ground, when Mr. Firth, the chaplain,⁵ who was as good

---

1. Stewart had been wounded in the leg and could only ride by having a pillow between his leg and the saddle.
2. Hill to Wellington, Elizondo, August 1, 1813.
3. Lieut. Hope, already quoted, paraphrased in Gardyne's *Life of a Regiment*.
4. Napier gives the time as 10 a.m.
5. This clergyman had been in the thick of the fighting at the Maya. "Being a strong man he carried down on his back, one after the other, three or four officers of our brigade who had been severely wounded, from the heights where the action was fought to the village of Maya, a distance of one mile and a half. During the whole Peninsular campaign this worthy clergyman was never seen to wear a cloak or greatcoat."—Narrative quoted in Cadell's *History of 28th Regiment*. Mr. Firth was a worthy predecessor of the late "Parson" Adams, the Indian chaplain who won his Victoria Cross in Afghanistan under Lord Roberts.

a soldier as a preacher, and who had been up with the leading troops, acted as guide to ground from which the guns could open on the enemy with effect. The first shell knocked down a number of men and almost every shot took effect, throwing the enemy's rear into confusion. The infantry were now called on. The 50th ascended the hill to the left of the road, the 71st in extended order skirmished with the French between the right of the 50th and the road, while the 92nd took the high road. The 2nd and 4th brigades 2nd division were in support and the 7th division moved by a parallel road on the right to attack the enemy's left. Their skirmishers being driven in, the main body several thousands strong faced about and made good a battle, the 92nd charged twice but were repulsed.

The French were so numerous and so strongly posted that Hill says in his report:[1]

> Lieutenant General Stewart was induced to withdraw them until the 7th division should be in closer co-operation with him. About this time the Lieutenant General was again wounded and the command devolved on Major General Pringle, who together with his own brigade renewed the attack on our side whilst the 7th division pressed them on the other and both divisions gained the summit about the same time, the enemy retiring after sustaining very considerable loss.
>
> The conduct of the officers and troops was conspicuously good, and I regret that the very thick fog prevented our taking that advantage of the situation of the enemy which it might otherwise have done. A part of each division pursued the enemy some distance down the hill and occasioned them considerable loss. Having thus far performed your Lordship's instructions,

---

1. Hill to Wellington, Elizondo, August 1, 1813.

I withdrew my column from the pass and moved it upon Almandoz.[1]

The 7th division, probably on account of the fog, remained about the pass and with it about 2,000 of la Bispal's men. Morillo's division proceeded by Wellington's order to rejoin Hill.[2] The remainder of la Bispal's force moved to Lanz, and marched next morning by the col de Velate to join Hill.[3]

At 11 a.m. from Lizaso, Murray sent a message to Wellington informing him of the real situation and of the orders he had consequently given. At the same hour he dispatched his instruction to Alten regarding the movement of the light division to Zubieta written at Ostiz the previous evening. It seems impossible to ascertain now why it was not sent off when written. But it must be remembered that then the real position of affairs was unknown at headquarters and that Wellington's object in ordering the move was probably to get the division back as quickly as possible to a position where it could, if necessary, support Longa on the Bidassoa. From Graham's letters Wellington knew the Spanish commanders had been all along anxious regarding their flank about Lesaca; Giron, also, had written to him on the subject. Though he does not seem to have shared their anxiety, Wellington appears to have desired to quiet their fears by further support as soon as he could give it, and that the moves of both Light and 7th divisions ordered on the 30th had this object in view.[4] It was not till Soult's real line of retreat on San Estevan was known that either he or Murray recognized the decisive role which

---

1. Hope says, "At the close of this engagement I could only muster thirteen privates out of the eighty-two non-commissioned officers and privates which I carried into action six days before."
2. Wellington to Q.M.G., Irurita, July 81, 1813, 3 p.m.
3. They were originally intended for the valley column, but eventually the whole of la Bispal's command was ordered on 30th to move round by Marcalain and join Hill.
4. Wellington to Graham, heights before Villaba, July 30, 1813: "The Light division will probably be this day at Lecumberri; they shall move forward tomorrow towards Zubieta and Sumbilla to communicate with your right."

could be given to the Light division. The delay in dispatching the order was, as we shall see, most unfortunate. It' was, however, one of those chances of war of which these operations furnish not a few instances. The Quartermaster-General also wrote to Graham telling him how matters stood, that Hill was "going to act immediately against a French column retiring by the Dona Maria road" and that orders were going to the Light division to move towards Zubieta.[1]

The valley column was early on the march and Byng's brigade, which with the 13th Light Dragoons formed the advanced guard and with which Wellington moved, passed Lanz by 7 a.m.[2] At noon Wellington was at Almandoz. After passing Lanz no traces of the enemy had been found on the road, but he soon had information of the real state of affairs about Lizaso, and then wrote as follows to Alten:

> Near Almandoz, July 31, noon.
>
> I sent to you yesterday[3] to desire you would return to Zubieta; but it is just possible you may not have received the order or that you may have been disturbed from the station at which I thought you in consequence of hearing from Colonel Rooke that General Hill was pressed by the enemy in the afternoon.
>
> If you should have arrived at Zubieta, I give you notice that a large body of the enemy are moving upon Dona Maria and it is very desirable you should head them at San Estevan. If you find you cannot head them there, you might at Sumbilla, or you might cut in upon their line of march. They are in the greatest disorder. The head of our troops is here and others are following the enemy by Dona Maria. Communicate this to Sir Thomas Graham.

---

1. Q.M.G. to Graham, Lizaso, July 31, 1813, 11 a.m.
2. By the order of the 31st the 13th Light Dragoons was to accompany 6th division. Apparently this was altered, as the regiment was in the Baztan on August 5.
3. Q.M.G. to Alten, before mentioned.

This order was sent in triplicate Wellington also sent a message to Longa informing him of the French retreat.[1]

From Almandoz, Wellington and the advanced guard moved on towards Irurita. At 3 p.m. Byng's brigade was in Hill's old position on the heights above the village with the 4th division coming up. During the march information had come in either from the cavalry or from inhabitants that there was a convoy of provisions for the French at Elizondo. "Lord Wellington ordered the 57th regiment to throw off their packs and make a dash for it."[2] The order created great enthusiasm in the regiment, which started off at the double; on reaching Elizondo the French escort—a battalion of the 28th Light left there by Maransin—was vigorously attacked and the whole convoy of 150 mules and several carts captured and many prisoners taken.

Wellington determined to halt and rest the troops at Irurita—the 4th division would then have marched over twenty miles—and at 3 p.m. he wrote to Murray[3] approving the arrangements the latter had made at Lizaso in the morning and added, "I have Byng's brigade up, and the 4th division following. I shall make the troops dine and see what is to be done in the evening. I have sent a patrol towards San Estevan. I have written to order the Light division at Zubieta to act on the enemy's rear at San Estevan if possible, if not at Sumbilla."

Murray and the headquarter establishment remained for the night at Lanz.[4] Hill reached Almandoz, the 7th division remained on the crest of the mountains and Wellington and the troops with him retained their position above Irurita.

It was not until 10 p.m. that the last regiments of D'Erlon's corps reached San Estevan. Meanwhile Soult had been greatly alarmed by the news which reached him of the arrival of al-

---

1. Wellington to la Bispal, Irurita, August 1, 6 a.m.
2. Woollright, *History of 57th Regiment*. Larpent: "I hear we took thirty cars of bread and brandy and some baggage also."
3. Wellington to Q.M.G., heights of Irurita, July 31, 1818, 3 p.m.
4. Larpent, *Diary*: "Thus we remained (at Lanz) loaded until 4 o'clock. Lord Wellington then sent on (back) for fresh horses and his light canteens. At last General Murray came in .... we were all to go to our old quarters."

lied troops in the Baztan at Irurita and of the capture of his convoy at Elizondo. And indeed he had ample cause, for now he was cut off from the road to France by Elizondo and the col de Maya, and there remained to him but the indifferent road by Sumbilla along the deep and narrow valley in which the Bidassoa river flows towards Vera and the sea; the only alternative being to take to the hills above San Estevan in order to strike the *chemin des Anglais* on the Achiola mountain and thus reach Zugarramurdi or Urdax; a track fit for infantry only, impracticable for his wounded, the cavalry and the baggage of the army, and liable to be blocked moreover near the pass of Maya should the enemy push on there.

Nor could Soult afford to lose any time. Behind him were the strong forces of the enemy which had driven his rear-guard from the passes during the forenoon and whose further pursuit had been stayed only on account of the dense fog. They might be even now advancing, for it was impossible for Soult to know that Hill had moved to the Velate road. A few miles to the east, along a good road, was another body of the enemy, who might at any moment come down on his flank. An early retreat was thus inevitable and Soult commenced his preparations for it as soon as it was dark by sending the cavalry, the wounded and the train of army to Sumbilla, where they were to be joined by Reille's infantry as soon as they could be relieved. The column under command of Reille was to march before daylight for Echalar. D'Erlon was to move from Sumbilla by a track which led across the hills to the same place. Clausel's three divisions were to close the column and cover the retreat. Meanwhile the French army, as its units arrived from the mountains, was being concentrated around San Estevan protected towards the east by Reille's two divisions which Soult had posted across the valley beyond the village.

Such then were the positions of the opposing forces on the evening of July 31. The story,[1] so dramatically told by

---

1. It was a current one in the camps of the army at the time (see Larpent).

Napier, of Wellington on this afternoon watching the French from behind some rocks on a commanding position whilst three marauding British soldiers entered the valley and were seized by Soult's *gens-d'armes*, whereby the Marshal become aware of the presence of the enemy at Irurita, and half an hour later commenced his retreat, thus foiling Wellington's combinations and saving himself from surrender or annihilation, seems really to have little foundation, at any rate so far as the inferences drawn from what probably were facts are concerned. Soult appears to have known perfectly well that an allied column was moving by the col de Velate road—indeed it had been seen by one of Reille's staff officers before that general's infantry had left Lizaso—and the first thing he did as soon as Reille's infantry began to arrive at San Estevan was to send them along the Elizondo road to cover his flank. Later on his scouts informed him of the arrival of allied troops about Irurita and of the capture of the envoy at Elizondo. Soult was, of course, unaware of the position of the Light division and that there was danger ahead of him to the west as well as to the east. But with all his experience of war he had quite sufficient knowledge of his enemy's movements to convince him that no time was to be lost if he was to get himself out of the difficult position he was in.

That Wellington had any deep-laid plan of surrounding the French army about San Estevan is sufficiently disproved by the narrative of the events of this day and the 30th. He started on the pursuit very far from expecting events would take the course they did. As has been already stated, his main idea seems to have been to get the army back as soon as possible into the positions occupied on July 25, doing the enemy as much damage as possible en route. It was not till Soult went over the Dona Maria passes that he recognized what an effective instrument for this he had in the Light division if he could get it up in time. There seems little doubt his combination against Soult would have been stronger had Murray not felt bound by his chief's instructions to order

Hill to move to the col de Velate road from the Dona Maria pass. This, however, will be further mentioned when considering the events of August 1. If the fog had not come down on the passes when it did the course of events would probably have been considerably changed, for it is unlikely Hill would have stayed his pursuit.

The orders sent by Murray or Wellington for the march of the Light division to Zubieta reached Alten at Lecumberri during the evening and the division started soon afterwards.

CHAPTER 17

The Retreat of the French

Near San Estevan the river Bidassoa, running east to west from Elizondo, bends sharply to the right, and, with many bends in its course, flows nearly due north to Vera, and thence towards the sea. The rift through the hills in which it flows can hardly be termed a valley, the slopes on either side descend to the water's edge, never at the road level more than a few hundred yards apart; and in places the valley narrows till the river and the road are almost in a gorge. The hills above the river are at their highest about Sumbilla, the Mendaur or Santa Cruz mountain to the west of that village rising to about 3,700 feet; thence the general fall of the ground is towards the north, and the difference of level between the river and the heights above gradually diminishes. The slopes down to the river are steep, in some places almost precipitous, and north of Sumbilla are on both banks covered with forest and brushwood. The road, now a fairly good one, then probably narrower and not so well graded, is cut out of the slopes on the right bank and follows quite closely the windings of the river.

About seven miles by road to the north of Sumbilla, the Sari stream joins the Bidassoa from the east, the road is carried across this tributary by a masonry bridge just beyond which a road branches off to the right and leads to the village of Echalar, about two miles up the Sari valley. About a mile south of this road junction a track to the village of

Yanci is carried over the Bidassoa by a masonry bridge; and at about the same distance to the north of it the road to Lezaca crosses by another bridge, both villages being to the west of the river.

At 2.30 a.m. on August 1, Reille's column commenced its march from Sumbilla to Echalar by the river road. The order of march was as follows: The 118th regiment of Lamartinière's division headed the column as advanced guard, then came the Treilhard's dragoon division, followed by the remainder of Lamartinière's division, in rear of this were the wounded, carried in litters, and on the horses of a dragoon regiment, they were followed by the baggage and vehicles and behind them came all that was left of Maucune's division. A battalion of Lamartinière's division was detailed to move along the heights above the road as a right flank guard, but as in the darkness the battalion could make little progress over the steep slopes, it came back into the road. No troops were sent across the river and the left flank of the column was thus unprotected.

Since the departure of the Light division from Santa Barbara and Lezaca on July 27, Longa's Spanish division had continued to hold the heights on the left bank of the Bidassoa, his right being at Yanci and left at the ford of Enderlaza—about two and a half miles northwest of Vera[1]—and he had been ordered to hold the bridges of Yanci and Lezaca with strong posts. On Longa's left was the corps of Giron holding the San Marcial heights and the left bank of the river towards the sea with the 1st British division in support of it. On the evening of July 28, Villatte had demonstrated against Longa's front about Vera and Salain, and as both Graham[2] and Giron thought a more serious attack might follow, the latter reinforced Longa by a brigade from his own corps, and Graham ordered up a British brigade from the 5th division, which, however, was sent back later.

---

1. Q.M.G.'s instructions of July 25 and 27.
2. Graham to Wellington, Oyarzun, July 30, 1813, 5 a.m.

Murray's message to Graham dispatched from Lizaso at 11 a.m. on July 31, reached the latter "in the middle of last night,"[1] (July 31 August 1). Graham realized the necessity of stopping the retreat of the French up the Bidassoa valley; but he was at this time anxious for his own front about Irun, for he thought it likely that Villatte might be reinforced from Soult's army and that he would be attacked.[2] Graham felt therefore that "all that could be attempted to interrupt the enemy's retreat was to reinforce Longa, and to desire him to endeavour to hold the bridge of Yanci with a greater force"; a brigade from Barcena's division was sent to join Longa,[3] who, on the morning of August 1, had troops in Yanci and two companies holding the bridge.

According to Soult's order D'Erlon's divisions were to follow Reille's column as far as Sumbilla, from which place they were to ascend the hills and follow a track leading direct to Echalar. Owing to some mistake, however, the head of his column turned into the river road, and before the corps was clear of the village, Clausel's leading division, which came up by a parallel track along the hillside, also arrived, with the result that there was a block and considerable confusion.[4] Subsequently however, Maransin's division moved off the road on to the heights above.

It is now, however, time to turn to the movements of the main allied army. An interesting letter written by Wellington to la Bispal, early on the morning of the 1st explains the view he then took of the situation, and the measures proposed to meet it.

---

1 Graham to Q.M.G., Oyarzun, August 1, 1813, 7 p.m.
2. Graham to Wellington, Oyarzun, July 30, 7 a.m.: "The enemy has so short a line and so good a road from St. Jean Pied de Port to Urrugue that it is not improbable he may reinforce his right so as to make some attempt on this flank of the army."
3. It seems uncertain whether this brigade was the one sent to reinforce Longa after the action on evening of 28th and had remained with him, or whether the brigade first sent had been withdrawn previously to August 1, and Barcena's brigade sent on that morning.
4. Soult to Clarke, bivouac heights of Echalar, August 2, 1813.

Ikubita, August 1, 6 a.m.
I have just received your note of half past nine last night. As far as I can judge the enemy have six divisions between Dona Maria and San Estevan. They were still quiet at twelve last night. There are three divisions certainly about Eugui and Roncesvalles. I have here the 4th division and General Byng. I have sent the 4th division upon San Estevan with the intention of aiding Dalhousie's advance and to endeavour to cut some off. Byng's brigade shall wait here till a later hour in the day, when I shall know better how things are situated and how far Sir Rowland Hill has advanced. I am only afraid Dalhousie will be too weak in the enemy's front. I sent in triplicate to the Light division at Zubieta yesterday, to desire that General Alten would move towards San Estevan and at all events get hold of Sumbilla if he could. I have heard nothing of him. I likewise sent to Longa to apprise him of the enemy's retreat by San Estevan.

This letter was sent under cover to the Quartermaster-General, whom it reached at Velate at 9.45 a.m. Murray sent it on to la Bispal with an endorsement requesting him to move with his force and follow the 2,000 of his men (then with the 7th division), who had been already ordered to march by the passes "in order that there may be a sufficient force at hand should it be required."

About 7 a.m. the 4th division approached San Estevan to the east of which Vandermaesen's division, the rearguard of Clausel's corps, was drawn up facing east across the valley with its left on the slopes above it with Taupin's division in support.[1] Cole, seeking to turn the enemy's left flank and cut him off from Sumbilla, sent his skirmishers up the heights to his right. Vandermaesen seeing this also moved to his left up the hill; but the 4th division men gained the heights first. Then Vandermaesen, under fire from the crest above and pressed by

---

1. Clausel's Report.

the rest of the 4th division, fearing too lest he should be intercepted before reaching Sumbilla, fell back with heavy loss towards the village, to the south of which two regiments of Taupin's division had taken position across the road and along the slopes to cover his retreat. Thus all three of Clausel's divisions were now crowded up in the narrow valley in and about Sumbilla, whilst Darmagnac's division was not yet clear of it. The 4th division was pressing on, and already its skirmishers were working round on the slopes to the north of the village. Soult, rightly judging the best way out of the dilemma, was to get Clausel's troops off the road on to the hills, ordered him to take the path leading direct to Echalar. Then the French succeeded in forming a line of defence across the hills, above the village, and for an hour a musketry fight went on, for the 7th division was not yet up, and the 4th division, unsupported, was not strong enough to come to grips with so large a French force. Under cover of this fight Clausel gradually withdrew his divisions and moved by the Echalar track, across which Maransin's division of D'Erlon's corps was already in position.[1] The 4th division pursued the French column on the road; Clausel, with Maransin, retired towards Echalar and in the evening bivouacked about a mile and a half south of the village. Meanwhile Wellington had reached San Estevan, and from there sent the following instruction to the Quarter-Master-General:

> San Estevan, August 1, 9.15 a.m.
> The enemy have fled from hence by the road of Sumbilla, 80,000 have passed through this town since yesterday at twelve o'clock.
> The 4th division are following upon Sumbilla and they shall be pushed on if possible to Lesaca where I shall stay this night, but my station will be known at Sumbilla.
> The 7th division are ordered to follow the 4th; I will order the Light upon Yanci and Lesaca from Zubieta.

---

1. Soult moved with this column.

Upon seeing this order Major General Byng must move his brigade from Irurita by Elizondo, and if possible get possession of the *puerto* de Maya, throwing his piquets into Urdax. Sir R. Hill will support Byng by occupying Elizondo, and if possible Ariscun, with those troops of the column under him which first come up. If Sir R. Hill's troops have not made a long march it is desirable they should occupy the *puerto* de Maya this day, and in that case Byng should take possession of the position of Ainhoa to be supported in the morning by the whole of Sir R. Hill's corps. Sir R. Hill to report by a staff officer where his troops, including Byng, will be this afternoon. Morillo might halt this day at Legasa. I have no knowledge of what is passing on the right so as to give orders for the 3rd or 6th divisions. But the 6th at least ought to be placed this day so as to be able to support the right of the troops taking the position of Ainhoa in the morning. Let the baggage of 4th division be ordered to follow it to Sumbilla and thence to Lesaca. Let headquarters come up to Irurita or Berroeta. My light baggage to follow 4th division. I have just received your letter of half-past six a.m. Let headquarters come to San Estevan from Berroeta. I have heard from the Light division near Zubieta, and they will follow the disposition above pointed out. I have not heard from Dalhousie.

Wellington

To be shown to General Byng, Sir R. Hill, the officer in charge of baggage 4th division, my servants and Sir W. Beresford's at Irurita.

From the above it is clear that the 7th division had not then arrived and must have been late starting from the Dona Maria Pass, the distance thence to San Estevan being under six miles downhill. No orders appear to have been sent to Dalhousie on the evening of July 31, but he knew the situation and had received those issued at Ostiz at 9 p.m. on

30th, as well as a copy of the instruction given to Hill by the Quartermaster-General at Lizaso at 11 a.m. on 31st. Probably the 7th division did not move till after the firing about San Estevan was heard.

The Light division had, as we have seen, started from Lecumberri on the evening of the 31st, and marched to Leiza where it halted during the night. "Pretty early"[1] on the morning of August 1, the march was resumed over the *puerto de Leiza* into the Ezcurra valley and, passing through Saldias and Zubieta, the division about midday reached a deep valley between Ituren and Elgorriaga, where it was formed up and halted for an hour,[2] patrols being sent out towards San Estevan. The day was exceedingly hot and the division had then marched about seventeen miles from Leiza, over a bad stony track. From the halting-place it moved to its left and climbed up the slopes of the Mendaur mountain. Whilst the combat, which has been described, was in progress between the 4th division and the rear of the French column, a series of accidents began to happen to its head. About a mile south of the bridge of Yanci a party of Longa 's men from the village above had concealed themselves amongst the brushwood on the left bank of the river. When the 118th at the head of Reille's column approached, the Spaniards opened fire on it; the regiment halted and commenced to return the fire. Whilst this was going on the leading squadrons of Treilhard's dragoons also halted and, getting down to the river, commenced to water their horses. As the command to "halt" was passing down the cavalry column on the winding road, it was somewhere changed to "retire," and the rear regiments, seized with a panic, probably on account of the firing in front, turned about and at a gallop dashed down on to Lamartinière's division at the head of which Reille was riding. With difficulty they were prevented riding over the

---

1. Quartermaster Surtees, *Twenty-five Years in the Rifle Brigade*. This book is available in a Leonaur edition under the title *Surtees of the 95th (Rifles)*.
2. *U.S. Journal* 1830.

general and the infantry; no one could give any reason for the rush except that the command to retire had come down from the front. At length some sort of order being restored, Reille sent the 2nd Light infantry to the front through the cavalry and himself followed.[1]

Meanwhile the Spaniards, less than a hundred in number, had been driven off by the fire of the 118th, and the 2nd Light coming up the march was resumed. No flank guard was, however, sent across the river. Reille seeing this when he came up, left a staff officer at the spot with orders to send the first battalion which arrived across the river to hold the spur where the Spanish ambuscade had been placed and then returned towards Lamartinière's division.

The Spaniards had retired over the crest of the hill; later on being reinforced they again descended and opened fire on the French column at a point about three quarters of a mile above the bridge. Some companies of the 120th, which were moving along the river, engaged them whilst the rest of the infantry pressed on. Meanwhile after a fight the 118th drove away the two Spanish companies defending the bridge and, after placing a battalion to hold the high ground immediately beyond it, the column continued its march and commenced to move up the road leading to Echalar, whither Reille, who thought the way for his troops was now open, himself proceeded. But the cavalry division and some of the baggage had alone passed, when the Spaniards, reinforced by the rest of the battalion, again attacked, drove the French flank guard from the hill and again obtained possession of the bridge. Thus passage along the road was again closed. What followed is thus described in the letter sent by Graham to the Quartermaster-General at 7 p.m. that evening.

> However, the enemy got there (the bridge) when he had only two companies, which were driven from it; they (the French) passed it and occupied a strong

---

1. Reille's report and that of Colonel Michaud.

height on this side of it, from which Longa, reinforced by a light battalion of Barcena's brigade (one of Giron's sent in support), drove the enemy. It held the bridge for some hours against the attacks of a much superior force. De Lancey[1] who had gone that way, left them about three this afternoon, when the enemy's fire had slackened and he was in hopes that they would hold it. But Lieutenant-Colonel Bouverie, who stayed later, and is but just returned, tells me that the enemy having got a good many men up the hill unperceived, gained the summit and so turned this battalion, which was obliged to give way.

The enemy had a quantity of baggage and were in great confusion, and numbers of men were scrambling over the mountain on the other side trying to escape without fighting. I do not suppose the Spaniards would attempt to retake the bridge, the road will therefore be open for the enemy to pass on, unless this delay should have given the Light division time to come up from Zubieta, where, I understand, it would arrive about ten this morning. Had it been possible for it to get to Zubieta yesterday, as I hoped from your letter, this column of the enemy must have suffered great loss. Both de Lancey and Bouverie speak highly of the behaviour of this light battalion of Barcena's brigade.

The French having regained the hill commanding the bridge, the way past it was again open and the remainder of the column commenced to move on. But now a danger greater than any the head of the harassed column had yet experienced was at hand, for the Light division was approaching.[2] Having halted for about an

---

1. Colonel W. de Lancey, the Deputy Quartermaster-General, who was detached with Graham.
2. D'Erlon states in his report that "when the English troops arrived in the evening Darmagnac's division had entirely passed (the bridge), except some baggage." This left only Abbé's division still to pass.

hour near Ituren, the division climbed up the southern slopes of the Mendaur mountain. The summit, some 8,500 feet above the road, was reached about 3 p.m. and, passing by their old camp of July 26, the division moved on along the ridge towards Aranaz. Here the 2nd brigade, which had been in rear during the march and suffered much from checks and stoppages, had to be halted, for the men were utterly exhausted, some had died of fatigue and of the heat, which was very great, and not a few others had been driven by fatigue to quit the ranks, and "leaning on the muzzles of their firelocks, looking pictures of despair, muttered in disconsolate accents that they had never fallen out before."[1] But the 1st brigade, composed of the 43rd regiment, the 1st and 3rd battalions of the 95th rifles, and the 17th Portuguese, moved on along the ridge towards the river and here they came in view of the enemy's column moving along the Bidassoa.

This gave our men new life. My battalion, the first and the 43rd continued to move on and as they approached the enemy seemed to acquire fresh vigour. At length we reached the point of attack, the bridge of Yanci, and here the 1st battalion, turning downwards towards the river, at once left the wood and ground above the bridge to be occupied by us. The enemy sent a pretty strong corps of light troops across the river which got engaged with our people, but we soon drove them down through the wood again towards the bridge. At length we got two companies posted just over the bridge in front of which all the rear of the French column had to pass. Poor creatures, they became so alarmed, they instantly began to cut away and cast off all the loads of baggage and both cavalry and infantry to make the best of their way away But the mountain on the right was inaccessible, consequently they had all, as it were, to run the gauntlet Great

---

1. *U.S. Journal* 1830.

was the execution done at the bridge, and many were the schemes they had to avoid passing. At length they got a battalion up behind a stone wall above the road on the opposite side from whose fire we received some damage and consequently these poor people were not so much exposed.¹

Holding some houses near the bridge and extended amongst the brushwood on the slopes above the river, the brigade as long as daylight remained poured a heavy fire at short range on the French as they passed along the road below.² The enemy lost heavily, and much baggage with many prisoners thus fell in to the hands of the 4th division advanced guard which was following them up.

On the evening of August 1, the French army was assembled round Echalar, Reille's divisions between the village and the heights to the north, those of d'Erlon to the north-west across the track leading towards Vera with Clausel's corps to the south, both holding the spurs leading down to the Bidassoa. But how different was their state now to what it had been eight days before. A French writer³ thus describes it:

> Those troops were without food, without ammunition, without discipline, without confidence. All the generals have stated that the troops had no longer any wish to fight. Entire regiments were disorganized. Maucune's division had not a thousand men in the ranks; the 1st of the Line, which had had but 4 officers and 193 of other ranks killed or wounded, could put into line only twenty seven men at Echalar. In Clausel's divisions the higher command no longer existed, two divisional generals out of three and four brigade commanders out of six were *hors-de-combat*.

---

1. Surtees.
1. Leach, *Rough Sketches*: "Our fire threw them into great confusion, which was increased by their being aware the advanced guard of the 4th division was following them." This book is available in a Leonaur edition under the title *Captain of the 95th (Rifles)*.
2. Capt. Vidal de la Blache, *Revue d'Histoire*, «La bataille de Sorauren.»

In the evening the allied army was distributed as follows: Headquarters at San Estevan. Byng's brigade at the col de Maya, 2nd division, beyond Elizondo, 4th division between Sumbilla and the bridge of Yanci, 7th division between San Estevan and Sumbilla. Light division about the bridge and village of Yanci. 3rd division moving towards Roncevaux and the 6th towards the Aldudes.

During the day the French had lost heavily both in men and *moral*. They had escaped, however, the disaster which might well have befallen them. Wellington was ill-satisfied with the results obtained. Writing to Graham[1] a few days later, he said: "Many events turned out unfortunately for us on the 1st instant, each of which ought to have been in our favour; and we should have done the enemy a great deal more mischief than we did in his passage down the valley." He does not specify the particular events referred to, but they seem fairly apparent from the narrative. No explanation is forthcoming of the tardy arrival of the 7th division. It was the fault perhaps of the divisional commander. If, however, no instructions were sent him on the evening of July 31, some blame attaches to headquarters. It would seem as if Wellington was somewhat anxious about this division.[2] In front of it lay the larger portion of the French army and the only support immediately available for it was the 4th division at Irurita. Ignorant, as Wellington says he was, of what was happening on his right, on which side he estimated the enemy's strength at three divisions, he was obliged to leave Byng's brigade to guard the road over the pass of Velate by which the trains of his army were advancing. Later on, Hill and the Light division would also be available, but the exact position of neither was known to Wellington. In fact, owing to the events of the 31st, and the difficult nature of the country, the allied army was not sufficiently concentrated to be able to take full advantage of the opportunity offered it on the morning of August 1.

---

1. Wellington to Graham, Lesaca, August 4, 1813.
2. Wellington to la Bispal, Irurita, August 1, 1813, 6 a.m.

The reason why the Light division did not receive the order to move to Zubieta earlier has already been discussed. Soon after its receipt on the evening of the 31st, the division marched to Leiza, seven miles—and there encamped for the night. But, as Surtees says,[1] "certainly we might have marched during the night as far as Saldias (about eight miles beyond Leiza) if absolutely necessary." It may have been that Alten wished to cross the pass of Leiza in daylight. But the division had been over the road before; it had been resting during the 31st, and by moving during the night the men would have a shorter distance to march in the heat of the next day. But to decide how far Alten was justified in halting for the night, it is necessary to know how far he was then acquainted with the general situation. If Alten marched, having received the Quartermaster-General's message only—and it was almost bound to reach him first, having a start of an hour in time of dispatch, and about ten miles in distance—all he knew was that the army was "following the enemy in the direction of the passes," one column moving by Dona Maria and that he was to move without delay towards Zubieta. In this case, the halt at Leiza can perhaps be justified. But it cannot if he had received Wellington's message sent from Almandoz at noon that day. The available evidence on the point is conflicting. Surtees relates that an aide-de-camp of Lord Wellington arrived at Lecumberri "more dead than alive in the evening with orders to retrace our steps and again advance." This was the substance of Murray's letter and Surtees, who was quartermaster of the 3rd battalion 95th Rifles, might easily have been mistaken about the staff officer. It would look as if he was, because further on he mentions:

> It was reported that another dispatch had been received during the night directing us to proceed with all haste as the enemy was retreating by San Estevan, and we were to attack him wherever found.

---

3. Surtees.

Cooke[1] says "on the evening of 31st, we received orders to, if possible, overtake the enemy and attack him wherever found." His account was published after that of Surtees. Perhaps as good evidence as any that Wellington's order had not been received is that given by G. Simmons' journal[2] in which he says: I lost this little affair by being ordered to remain at Loyza a sufficient time to try by Court Martial, Sergeant Hayes." It is little likely the officer commanding the battalion would have left three officers, witnesses and prisoner behind if he had known that it was probable the battalion might be engaged early in the day. It seems likely Wellington's order arrived either during the night or on the morning of August 1, and that the message Wellington received from Alten at San Estevan about 9.15 a.m. on the 1st was an acknowledgment on the receipt of the order.

Napier criticizes Alten's move down the Lerins valley as far as Elgorriaga before turning off to his left and ascending the hills. His argument being that if the division had turned off close to Zubieta by the track it had used descending on July 27, it would have reached the bridge of Yanci much earlier than it did. As a matter of fact, the division, when it halted between Ituren and Elgorriaga was, including the distance marched from Zubieta to the halting-place, at least a mile nearer the summit of the Mendaur mountain, an obligatory point in both routes towards the bridge. From where the division halted, it was, of course, considerably nearer Sumbilla, to reach which place it could move over the long spur running south-east from the summit of the mountain near which it would then be unnecessary to go. No doubt the ascent from Zubieta to the Mendaur mountain, though longer, was a less severe climb than that the division made; but it is incorrect to say that by taking it the Light division would have arrived *much earlier*. It must be remembered too that when the decision to pass Zubieta was

---

1. *U.S. Journal* 1830.
2. Verner, *A British Rifleman*.

taken Alten could not have known what the exact situation about San Estevan was. He probably wished to get nearer to find out how matters stood—he would be likely to do so before and during the halt—and yet be able to cut in on the French at Sumbilla if an opportunity offered.

Alten is also censured for not having crossed one brigade over the Bidassoa near the bridge of Yanci, whilst the other lined the left bank of the river. From all accounts of the march, it appears that it was absolutely necessary to halt the 2nd brigade near Aranaz; the men could not go on without a rest and, as it was, the 1st brigade only arrived near the bridge about sunset. Napier has hardly treated Alten fairly—it is well known he was no admirer of his divisional commander.— His criticisms would carry more weight had he been an eyewitness of the events of the day. He was not, however, then present with his regiment.

Both Graham and Longa "took counsel of their fears." Neither did all they might have done. Since the departure of the Light division and especially since he had been attacked on the evening of the 28th, Longa had been in a state of anxiety about the defence of the line allotted to him. Graham writing to Wellington on July 30 says:

> Longa has been asking for reinforcements .... your Lordship will see by the style of his letter, which I enclose, that it is not improbable he will retire on the heights and pass of Arrichusiguri (Maya mountain).

There was indeed cause for him to be anxious on August 1, for on that day Villatte, knowing as he did of Soult's retreat along the Bidassoa, should undoubtedly have vigorously attacked Longa in order to prevent his taking any measures to block the valley road. All he did was to make a feeble demonstration against the allied front towards Irun. Graham, with a river in his front and strong ground already entrenched on his bank, had ample strength to meet any attack Villatte, even if reinforced, could make. Knowing Longa's state of mind, as well as the little dependence ever to be placed on Spanish leaders in combined operations, Graham would have done well to have reinforced him, as he originally intended, with a British as well as a Spanish brigade.

It is perhaps permissible to think that had Wellington been present with Hill at Lizaso on July 31, he would at once have cancelled the order Hill had received to move to the Velate road, an order the execution of which Murray in Wellington's absence only felt justified in postponing. For then a disposition of the allied army would have been produced which would have left Soult little chance of escape. Every available man could then have been directed on the main objective, that portion of the French army then with Soult. With Hill's corps and the 7th division descending in the early morning on to San Estevan and the valley to the east of it, the 4th division and la Bispal's Spaniards could have sent at once up the hills on the right bank of the Bidassoa from the road below Irurita and they would have been on the top of the ridge before Clausel's divisions moved up there from Sumbilla. Hill's corps would have been ample to deal with the French rearguard, the 7th division could also have ascended as the 4th actually did, and the allied force on the hills would have prevented Clausel making good the heights and driven him down again into the congested valley road. Then the 7th division could have harried the march from the hills above; whilst the 4th division and the Spaniards moved on to block the Echalar road or even that along the river near the bridge of Yanci.

CHAPTER 18

Soult's Failure

Near Echalar, the French frontier, following the crest of the high ground from the Rhune mountain by the Ibantelly peak to that of the Atchuria, juts out into a large salient enclosing the valleys of the streams forming the head waters of the Lourgorrieta river, a tributary of the Nivelle. From Echalar a track leads over the hills by the pass of Echalar and joins the Sare-Ainhoa road close to the former village. Other tracks also cross the frontier on both sides of the pass, the most northerly that from Vera by the pass of that name to Sare.

In an order issued on the evening of August 1, Soult directed that the French army was "to reunite tomorrow morning on the col between Echalar and Sare." Accordingly early on the morning of the 2nd, the divisions moved on to and over the hills to the north-east of Echalar and took up positions as follows: Clausel's divisions were in the centre and in first line, Vandermaesen held a height between Echalar and the pass *("le premier plateau en arrière de Echalar ")* across the track and had a company in Echalar, Conroux was on the frontier line holding the pass and heights on each side of it with Taupin in support in rear.[1] Reille held the Ibantelly peak with one brigade of Maucune's division, from there Lamartinière's division prolonged the line as far as the Palombiere heights about a mile behind the frontier line. The other brigade of Maucune's division was on the extreme right holding the road from

---
1. Clausel's report on operations of the left wing.

Vera to Sare and connecting with Villatte's reserve division which had troops on the Rhune mountain.² D'Erlon's divisions formed the left of the second line, his right, Maransin's division, connecting with Lamartinière at the Palombiere, and his left "prolonged in the direction of the col de Maya and Zugarramurdi."²

Soult occupied this position "whilst he could reconnoitre the country and the movements of the enemy,"³ but Wellington "would not suffer the affront."

As will have been inferred from Wellington's instructions to the Quartermaster-General sent from San Estevan on the morning of the 1st, the commander in chief had in his mind at this time not to stay his advance on the positions previously occupied on July 25, but to push forward into France. Hill's reoccupation on August 2, of the Maya ridge, with Byng as advanced guard at Urdax, was the first step and secured possession of this gate into France. On the previous evening Graham had been desired to get up his pontoons, artillery and cavalry, and to make all arrangements for crossing the Bidassoa with part of his force, whilst the rest maintained the blockade of San Sebastian.⁴ For Wellington and Hill, advancing by Sare and Ainhoa, would turn the Rhune mountain together with all the strong ground which stretches from it along the right bank of the river towards the sea, and threaten Villatte's line of retreat. But Soult, holding the pass of Echalar and the hills about it, for the present barred the way to the troops now with Wellington.

A thick fog hung over the mountain tops during the morning, and prevented any reconnaissance of Soult's position; it does not appear to have cleared off till after midday, and for a few hours only. Wellington having then recon-

---

1. Reille's report.
2. D'Erlon's report.
3. Soult to Clarke, bivouac heights of Echalar, August 2, 1813.
4. Wellington to Graham, San Estevan, August 1, 1813, 8 p.m.: "I hope tomorrow to be beyond the frontier."

noitred towards Echalar, during which he narrowly escaped capture, determined to dislodge the French from the pass by a combined movement and attack of the three divisions he had available,[1] which, meanwhile, were moving up. The 1st brigade of the Light division held the Echalar road till relieved by the 4th division and then marched towards Vera by the river road. Just as the brigade was passing near the Sari bridge, Wellington and his staff rode up from San Estevan. Ever a man of few words he said nothing, but "seeing how we had handled the enemy the evening before," smiled and nodded approvingly to the regiments, "which much pleased the soldiers"[2] who, tired and still without food, went on happy at the sign of their chief's approval. At the bridge of Lesaca the 2nd brigade from Yanci joined the column and the division moved on and took up its former positions on the Sta. Barbara heights. The 7th division marched to Sumbilla and there ascending the heights to the right, moved with Barnes' brigade—1-6th, 3rd provisional battalion (2-24th and 2-58th) and the Brunswick Oels—as advanced guard towards Echalar.

Wellington's plan was that the 4th division from Echalar was to assail the French front at the pass, the Light their right at the Ibantelly peak, which sheer and rocky rises from the eastern end of the Sta. Barbara heights, whilst the 7th division from Sumbilla was to attack the heights to the allied right of the Echalar pass.

But Barnes' brigade approached the village some distance ahead of the rest of the division and before either the 4th or Light were in their preparatory positions, Dalhousie, who was up, rightly judging the temper both of his men and of the enemy, let Barnes go in unsupported. Forming for attack, the brigade moved up the slopes from the village and falling on Vandermaesen's division swept it from its position and back up the hill, and despite the fire from Conroux's division car-

---

1. Wellington to Bathurst, Lesaca, August 4, 1813.
2. Surtees, also Cope, *History of the Rifle Brigade*.

ried the pass.[1] Then the remainder of the division coming up the heights about it were carried and held. And now the mist descended again. In a letter written next day, Lord Dalhousie thus describes Barnes' attack.[2]

> We have been licking and kicking the fellows along every day since we saw you. Yesterday the 7th division—Barnes' brigade only—had a proper thump at them on these heights here, we caught them cooking above and plundering below in the village. I thought it best to be at them instantly and I really believe Barnes was among them before their packs were well on. Their whole force was on the upper ridge and two divisions as a rear-guard below. Barnes drove them back and back up the hill until they all opened on him, and I really believe had not a thick fog come on they would have destroyed him, as it is he has lost 200 men. You may judge his resolute impetuosity when eight or ten thousand over him retired up a ridge before Barnes with a thousand. Fortunately Lord Wellington saw it all, and was so delighted that he desired me to issue an order to the brigade to say that their attack was the most gallant, the finest thing he had ever seen.

Magnificent but perhaps not war some may say, yet who shall blame the gallant leaders?

It is true the 4th division arrived before the end of the action, that the French had fulfilled their mission as a rear-guard, that they were worn with fatigue and ill provided with ammunition, but the real cause of their inferiority belongs to the highest part of war. The British soldiers, their natural fierceness stimulated by the remarkable personal daring of their general, Barnes, were

---

1. Clausel in his report says, "The resistance ought to have been greater, and in the ordinary state of the army the enemy could never have established himself on the principal chain of the Pyrenees."
2. Dalhousie to Capt. Cairnes, Echalar, August 3, 1813, in Dickson MSS.

excited by the pride of success; and the French divisions were those which had failed in the attack on the 28th, which had been utterly defeated on the 80th, and which had suffered so severely the day before at Sumbilla. Such then is the preponderance of moral power.[1]

Having lost the pass, Clausel withdrew down the slopes on the French side connecting his right with Lamartinière's division on the Lassarrieta hill. But this position was only tenable as long as the Ibantelly remained in possession of the French, and it was now about to be assailed. For the 1st brigade of the Light division had been ordered to drive the enemy from it. "Fortunately an excellent commissary overtook the division and rations were served out, which the men devoured in the act of priming and loading for the attack,"[2] with the 1st and 3rd battalions 95th in first line in extended order, followed by the 43rd and 17th Portuguese, the brigade advanced against the hill. The 3rd Rifles moved up the face of the hill while the 1st battalion on its right worked up the southern slopes. It was a hard climb up "craggy, steep, almost perpendicular"; but the riflemen pressed on. Simmons, who was with the first battalion thus describes the close of the fight.

> The enemy opened fire on us, Captain Pemberton, who was with my brother and myself, received a severe wound, several men were knocked over as we gradually approached the top. The enemy made a charge but were soon stopped and a fog coming on and we still advancing and firing upon them, they gave up the hill without fiercely contending for it. Our 1st and 3rd battalions were the only ones in the fight, and what pleased our fellows most, was beating the enemy over their own boundaries and letting the French peasantry see their soldiers run away.

---

1. Napier, *History of Peninsular War*.
2. Levinge, *History of the 43rd Light Infantry*.

Henceforth the peak was known as Barnard's hill by the riflemen, after Lieutenant-Colonel Barnard of the 1st battalion who led it that day.

Hearing the firing on the Ibantelly, Reille sent a brigade of Lamartinière's division to support Montfort, and went himself in that direction. But before the reinforcement could reach the hill, the shouts of the British riflemen rose from the summit, and the defenders came rushing down. Then Reille, fearing his flank would be turned by a British advance from the hill, ordered his divisions to retire in succession; but an order from Soult stopped the movement before the lower slopes of the hill were evacuated and the 1st brigade of the Light division did not advance beyond the summit. Meanwhile Clausel's divisions had commenced to retreat. Conroux reached Sare at 4.30 p.m. and was followed by Vandermaesen's and Taupin's divisions. Later Reille's troops also reached Sare where the five divisions passed the night."A supply depot which General Lhuillier by a happy inspiration had formed close by without doubt contributed to keep these demoralized troops there."[1] D'Erlon's corps was not engaged during the day; at 4 p.m. in accordance with an order from Soult, he commenced his retreat on Ainhoa, meeting on his way only a reconnoitring party sent out by Hill, which retired towards the col de Maya. In the evening his divisions bivouacked, Darmagnac and Maransinto the north of Ainhoa and Abbé between that village and Urdax with one regiment about Zugarramurdi, the only unit of the army, which had accompanied Soult, to spend the night in Spanish territory.

The effect of the fog, which prevailed for so large a part of the day, had been to delay operations and prevent any strong pursuit of the French. And now Wellington decided to postpone for a few days any advance into France. His reasons were partly purely military, partly political. A discussion of them lies outside the scope of this summary; it will suffice perhaps to state in his own words those of a military nature which

---

1. Vidal de la Blache, *la bataille de Sorauren*.

weighed with him. "The troops are, of course, a good deal fatigued, and we have suffered very considerably, particularly the English troops in the 2nd division, in the affair in the Puerto de Maya, which, with the existing want of shoes and of musket ammunition, induces me to delay for a day or two any forward movement, and to doubt the expediency of making one at all."[1] In accordance with this decision headquarters were again established at Lesaca on the evening of August 2, and the army distributed as follows:

Hills' Corps—the 2nd and Portuguese divisions, less Campbell's brigade, Morillo's division and Long's cavalry brigade, on the Maya ridge and in the upper Baztan.

3rd division, near Roncevaux.

4th division, Echalar.

6th division, with Campbell's brigade, in the

Aldudes. 7th division, Echalar pass and heights. Light division, heights of Sta. Barbara, with the

17th Portuguese holding the Ibantelly peak. La Bispal's corps, Sumbilla and San Estevan, moved on August 3, to Yanci.

Graham's corps and Giron's 4th Spanish army, less Mendizabel's division about Santona, retained their former positions.

The cavalry in the neighbourhood of Pamplona, which was blockaded by Don Carlos' Spanish division.

The artillery of the 2nd, 3rd and Portuguese divisions with their divisions, the batteries of the 4th, 6th, 7th and Light divisions were in the Baztan and Lanz valleys.

Thus, as we have seen, after nine days of almost continuous fighting, Soult's expedition which was to drive the allies beyond the Ebro had ended in failure and the allies again held nearly the same positions as on July 25. Though it was scattered, the French had still an army; nevertheless King Joseph's prediction[2] that any attempt to re-enter Spain with the then existing means and numbers might cause the loss of the army had well-nigh come true. The army had been saved, but the

---
1. Wellington to Graham, Lesaca, August 4, 1813
2. Joseph to Clarke, Bayonne, July 5, 1813.

nine days campaign had cost it 13,163 officers and men killed, wounded and prisoners and its *moral* was gone. The troops had no longer confidence in their leader or in themselves. Major Baltazar writing to the War Minister said:

> I cannot conceal from your Excellency that the result of this unfortunate expedition has had a most mischievous effect on the spirit of the army in general, the state of affairs has become even more unfortunate than after the retreat in June.

Soult, seeking to explain his failure, was very ungenerous to his troops. "I was strangely deceived," he wrote to the minister,[1] "when I informed your Excellency that the *moral* of the troops was excellent and that they would do their duty, they have shown only *un premier movement d'impulsion et point de constance*," a singularly unjust estimate of the fighting value of those men who had fought with such courage and ardour at the Maya, Sorauren and elsewhere.

No, it was not the soldiers' fault that the expedition had failed. The causes of failure must be sought elsewhere and perhaps it has been shown in these pages that chief amongst them were rashness in starting with an insufficiently thought out plan and with insufficient means, indifferent leading by the commander and some of his highest officers, and an underrating of the enemy's general and his troops.

Several of the points of interest which arose during the operations have already been touched on; it may, however, not be out of place in concluding our survey of them to comment again on some of the broader aspects of the campaign.

The possession of the initiative gave Soult the choice of the line on which he would operate. As regards time he had not so free a hand as the Emperor's instructions and the Minister of War's urgings, which he had not strength enough to resist, tied him to almost immediate action. His choice of line was sound, as Wellington would require longer time to con-

---

1. Soult to Clarke, bivouac on heights of Echalar, August 2, 1813.

centrate towards the right of his extended front than on either his centre or left. St. Jean-Pied-de-Port which became the French advanced base was a fortress and connected by a good road with Bayonne.

Soult was able to deceive Wellington, and the audacity of his plan was the chief cause of the latter being deceived. The initial success was with Soult. On the pedestal of the statue of Danton in Paris is inscribed the following extract from one of his speeches in the legislative assembly in 1792. *"Pour vaincre les ennemis de la patrie, il nous faut l'audace, encore l'audace et toujours l'audace."* All war has proved the truth of the saying. Soult opened with *l'audace*, but it seems to have been a characteristic of the man at this time that once up against British troops his confidence failed him. To push on towards Pamplona, as quickly as he possibly could and at almost any cost, was essential if he was to forestall the concentration of force Wellington would assuredly put in motion to block his way towards the fortress. Yet he hesitated in front of Byng's small force on July 25, and lost valuable time by neglecting to use adequate force against him. It was the same against Cole on the afternoon of the 26th and yet again on the 27th, when he had his fairest chance of at least a partial success. On the morning of the 28th the precious hours during which the 6th division was marching from Lizaso were also wasted. That luck was on the side of the allies must be admitted. The fogs on the 25th and morning of the 26th had stood them in good stead. But above all else perhaps was the indecision displayed by D'Erlon after the fight at the Maya ridge. With one practically intact division in hand at the end of the fight, he allowed the two British brigades of the 2nd division to slip through his fingers, gave Hill the command of the col de Velate road—which from Hill's position involved that also of the Dona Maria passes—and feared to attack him again as long as he held the position about Irurita. D'Erlon's hesitations and delays, attributed by himself to his fears for his flanks and an exaggerated estimate of the enemy's strength, can perhaps only be explained, as we have said, by the fact that although his troops had gained possession of the Maya ridge on July 25, he himself had been morally defeated.

Soult crossed the mountains in two main columns; D'Erlon on the right at the Maya, Reille and Clausel on the left about Roncevaux. That the generally safer plan of passing at one point only was not adopted was probably due to two main causes, the necessity of covering the road into France by the col de Maya, and the need to reduce the length of the column, especially in such country, where deployment for action was a more lengthy and difficult business than it usually is.

It seems, however, a question whether it would not have been sounder to have taken the risks of an advance on one line looking to the difficulty of maintaining co-ordination between columns separated by difficult country with the then existing means of communication. Moreover, the large mass of cavalry and artillery, which Soult took with his main column, could be no use till the open country was gained, and the greater part of it might have been left to move as a separate echelon well in rear.

But perhaps it would have been better still had D'Erlon moved, as Napier suggests, by the Baigorry valley, the pass of Urtiaga and Eugui into the Lanz valley road leaving one of his divisions to contain Hill at the Maya. This would equally have obliged Hill to evacuate the Baztan and would have better assured D'Erlon's junction with Soult, for Campbell with his brigade could not have made any effectual resistance. Once near the Lanz valley road, D'Erlon would have forced the allies to abandon its use and thus caused further delay in their concentration.

The French were fairly beaten on July 28; their supplies were practically exhausted, ammunition was running short and retreat was inevitable. Soult, however, desirous to make one more effort for success, planned his attempt to gain the great road and San Sebastian. The attempt, as we have seen, had to be hastily abandoned and the whole army directed on San Estevan, whereby it was nearly lost. Audacity often wins, but not a blind stroke like this, which was based on no sure information and involved a flank march across the front of an army already victorious and of practically equal strength, commanded too by a general so little likely to fail to take full advantage of so signal an opportunity. It had no reasonable chance of success and gravely imperilled the cause Soult had been sent to safeguard, for his army was the sole barrier to an invasion of southern France. The attempt was not "the conception of a great commander";[1] it has been condemned by French soldier writers both of that period and of to-day, and we can hardly fail to agree with them.

Retreat being inevitable, Soult could not have regained France without suffering loss had he gone by the ways he had come or, as suggested by Colonel Michaud in his report,[2] Clausel by Roncevaux, D'Erlon and Reille by the Velate and Dona Maria passes, but it would probably not have been so great as actually experienced and the army would not have been so utterly shaken as it was.

To turn now to the allied side. Though Soult's choice of line took Wellington by surprise, he met the situation with great coolness. The necessary preliminary movements to meet it were promptly taken on the night of July 25-26. He was determined not to commit himself till he had more complete information and this cautious resolution cannot but be admired, and the more so the intricate and difficult nature of the country is considered. A weaker man would perhaps have acted with greater haste and so might have played into the enemy's hands. That he acted as deliberately as he did was because he had thoroughly thought out the possibilities of the situation both as regards the enemy and his own army,—that this was so is proved amongst other things by his secret communication to Hill of how

---

1. Napier.
2. Written in May 1814. Col. Michaud was chief engineer of Reille's corps.

he intended to act, "in case things did not go well in front of Pamplona"[1]—because he knew his opponent, had complete confidence in himself and in the fighting power of his troops, and because he never for a moment lost sight of the resumption of the offensive on the earliest opportunity. The quick resolution taken on the bridge of Sorauren shows the skilled and practised leader perfectly accustomed to handling troops.

Cole's failure to keep Wellington informed of his movements and Picton's decision to retire on the night of July 26 well-nigh upset their chief's arrangements. As Wellington in a conversation with Larpent said not long afterwards,[2] "Had I been as regularly informed of how matters stood on the 26th and 27th as I was of what passed on the 25th, that need not have happened; but General Cole never told me exactly how far he found it necessary to give way, or let me know by what a superior force he was pressed and that he intended giving way; and the French might have been stopped sooner than they were. In truth, I suspected that all Soult's plan was merely by manoeuvres to get me out of the hills, and to relieve one or both of the besieged places, as things should turn up and succeed for him, and I expected him to turn short round towards San Sebastian accordingly. I had then no notion that with an army so lately beaten he had serious thoughts, as I am now sure he had, of driving us behind the Ebro. The consequence was the 2nd division halted a day and a half at Trinita and Berroeta, on the 26th, and till three on the 27th; and the 7th division only took a short march to San Estevan, as I was unwilling to lose a bit more of the mountains than was absolutely necessary from the probable loss of men in recovering such ground. On the night before we marched, or at three in the morning of the 26th, I knew all that had

---

1. See chapter 12.
2. Larpent, *Diary*: "I then observed that the only time I felt uneasy was when we were stopped at Lanz and sent across to Lizaso, for all faces seemed very long, and the removal of the wounded was very much pressed."

passed on the first attack and acted accordingly. Had I been as well informed, and had everything been communicated to me as punctually on the next evening, the march of Several divisions would have been different. I should and could have pressed them more on the 27th."[1]

If we consider the nature of the country and of its communications, and that messengers on foot or on horseback were the only means available for the transmission of reports and orders, it will, I think, be admitted that the concentration of the six divisions of the allied army by July 28 was a fine piece of staff work and it seems to have been uniformly good throughout the operations. Doubtless there were mistakes here and there but there could hardly be a higher test than was applied during these stirring anxious nine days.

From what one not infrequently hears and reads nowadays it would almost seem as if it was thought that knowledge of the duties of the general staff, after having been made in Germany, first came to the British army about the time of the Franco-German War of 1870-71. It was not so; during long years of peace much of the knowledge disappeared and the Crimean War proved that the practical skill had been lost. It would, however, be quite a mistake to suppose that during the later years of the Peninsular War the staff officers of that army as a whole were other than skilled and competent men at their work. Sufficient credit has never been given to Sir George Murray, the Quartermaster-General and chief of the staff. Napier was no friend of his. To represent him, as has been done, as little more than a zealous and competent chief clerk, is entirely wrong. Wellington, too, was fortunate in having the assistance of two such able officers as Sir J. Kennedy, the commissary general, and Dr. (afterwards Sir James) McGrigor, his principal medical officer. To illustrate headquarter methods must be the excuse for quoting Larpent once more.[2]

---

1. Larpent, *Diary*. Lesaca, August 24, 1813.
2. He is writing respecting an unnamed individual with the army "who plays the great man well and has a taste for humbug."

From Lord Wellington downwards there is mighty little. Everyone works hard and does his business. The substance and not the form is attended to; in dress, and many other respects I think, almost too little so. The maxim, however, of our chief is 'Let every one do his duty well, and never let me hear of any difficulties about anything,' and that is all he cares about.

That Wellington's arrangements worked as well as they did is largely due to the care taken in the organization of the service of intercommunication throughout the army. The point is constantly insisted upon in Wellington's instructions, and there is hardly a published operation order which does not contain directions as to how communication was to be secured and its channels. A modern army has at its disposal all sorts of improved means of communication undreamt of a hundred years ago. How these would have facilitated the tasks of both commanders will be at once appreciated. Instead of being for many hours in complete ignorance of all that was happening along his extended front, with but a short delay Wellington would have had full information, and the power of personal communication with his subordinate commanders, and measures to meet any situation could have been taken at once. Soult, too, would have been in communication with his lieutenant-generals, and we may assume that Reille would have been kept to his orders on the 26th, and D'Erlon stirred out of his inaction on the same day. On the whole it will probably be considered that in the given situation the possession of these means would have been of the greater advantage to the allies. But, however, up-to-date the means of communication—and it must not be forgotten that they are not infallible even to-day—breakdowns do occur, and however well organized the service is, co-operation cannot be secured unless subordinate commanders keep their superiors and neighbouring commanders regularly informed of what is going on. The consequences of the failures of Cole, Picton and Alten (their staffs are of course included) to keep up regular communication with headquarters are just as much warnings to present time soldiers as they were to the men of those days. For without regular and constant intercommunication strategical combinations cannot be co-ordinated or co-operation and mutual support obtained on the battle-field.

Napoleon said that in war "the man is everything, men are nothing"; in other words, however good the troops may be, victory cannot be assured unless a real leader is there to command them. In Wellington the allied army had the man. On the other hand, however able the commander, success will not be his unless his troops are brave, staunch and skilful. So what of the men of "that army which recovered the character of the nations of Europe, broke the spell, and induced others to believe they might be successful, establishing an imperishable reputation"?[1] For the most part uneducated as we reckon it nowadays, bound in the iron discipline of the lash and the provost-marshal; yet they were not the ruffianly crew we are sometimes given to suppose they were. Blackguards there were amongst them, and small wonder when some of the means taken to fill the ranks are remembered.

To learn what they were read what some of them say of themselves and what the regimental officers who led them say of them. In these narratives, which do not gloss over failings, you will find touching tributes to their skill as soldiers, their bravery and endurance, their devotion to their officers, kindnesses to each other and to wounded friends and foes. For the most part good honest countrymen, English, Scots and Irish, strong and of great endurance—for the weakly soon fell by the way—they were fashioned by regimental discipline and much experience of war into soldiers very formidable, staunch and of great spirit. To quote Rifleman Harris:

---

1. Sir A. Leith-Hay, *A Narrative of the Peninsular War.*

The men seemed invincible, nothing I thought could have beaten them. There was perhaps as intelligent and talented a set of men amongst us as ever carried a weapon in any country. They seemed at times to need but a glance at what was going on to know all about its why and wherefore.[1]

There seems to have been a feeling amongst some of the officers at this time that perhaps our men might meet the French at a disadvantage when fighting in the hills, "for which the lightness and activity of the latter peculiarly fitted them, and in which they had hitherto been considered unrivalled."[2] How little the apprehension was justified the narrative has shown. The allied army never fought better or with greater skill than in these operations. Their previous successes over the French had given the men perfect confidence in themselves, their officers and their leader. They knew they could beat the French in anything like equal numbers whenever they met them, whether on the hillside or elsewhere. In short they had that *moral* which is the surest guarantee of success. The times were rougher than they are now, and so were the soldiers; not all heroes by any means, but men of many failings no doubt who fought for their country with all their might, and whose courage, constancy and spirit no one, least of all their foes in the field, has ever questioned. With them must ever be associated the remembrance of those Portuguese, brave companions in arms, who stood shoulder to shoulder with them in all their fights, Nor must the dashing ardour and courage of their opponents, foemen worthy of their steel, be forgotten. It does but add to their glory. Enemies on the field they were, but there was no enmity between the British and French armies; when not fighting great good will existed between them.

---

1. Benjamin Harris, *The Compleat Rifleman Harris: the adventures of a soldier of the 95th (Rifles) during the Peninsular Campaign of the Napoleonic Wars*, Leonaur, 2006.
2. Capt. Hamilton, *Annals of the Peninsular Campaigns*.

"What Alexander's Macedonians were at Arbela, Hannibal's Africans at Cannae, Caesar's Romans at Pharsalia, Napoleon's guards at Austerlitz, such were Wellington's British soldiers at this period. Six years of uninterrupted war had engrafted on their natural strength and fierceness a confidence which rendered them invincible," so says Napier, the sharer and chronicler of their deeds, and what more is necessary?

They and their great captain have long since passed away and the times have changed. Many of them lie in nameless graves on the ridges and in the glens of the mountains, and before their task was ended many more were yet to fall in that far corner of fair France whose soil has been so richly watered by the blood of brave men. Around and above them rise the Pyrenees *monumentum cere perennius.*

Though gone, they have left a bright example of constancy, of hardihood and of bravery, not only to those who follow in their footsteps and serve their king and country, but to all succeeding generations of their countrymen. Well will it be with us if, when our next hour of trial comes, as come it assuredly will, the British Empire has to fight for her such a leader and such soldiers as those of the old Peninsular Army.

Appendices

Appendix A

ANGLO-PORTUGUESE ARMY AND SPANISH TROOPS UNDER THE COMMAND OF FIELD-MARSHAL THE MARQUIS OF WELLINGTON

ANGLO-PORTUGUESE ARMY

Staff

Commanding the Forces : Field-Marshal the Marquis of Wellington, K.G., K.B.
Military Secretary : Lieut.-Colonel Lord Fitzroy Somerset.
Quartermaster-General : Major-General Sir George Murray, K.B.
Adjutant-General : Major-General Hon. E. Pakenham.

Major-General Pakenham took over temporary command of 6th Division when Major-General Pack was wounded on July 28, and the duties of A.G. were carried on by Lieut.-Colonel Waters, A.A.G.

Civil Staff

Commissary-General : Sir R. Kennedy.
Principal Medical Officer : Inspector-General Dr. McGrigor.
Purveyor-General : Mr. James.
Judge Advocate : Mr. F. Larpent, Barrister-at-Law.

Commanding Royal Artillery : Lieut.-Colonel A. Dickson.
Chief Engineer : Lieut.-Colonel Sir R. Fletcher, Bart.

Composition of Divisions and Brigades on July 25, 1813

Cavalry : Lieut.-General Sir Stapleton Cotton, K.B., commanding.

Brigades:

Lieut.-Colonel Sir Robert Hill (Household Brigade)	1st L. Guards 2nd ,, ,, R. Horse Guards	} 2 squadrons of each.
Major-General Ponsonby	5th Dragoon Guards 3rd Dragoons 4th ,,	
Major-General Vandeleur	12th Lt. Dragoons 16th ,, ,,	
Major-General Long	13th Lt. Dragoons 14th ,, ,,	
Major-General Baron Victor Alten	18th Hussars 1st Hussars, K.G.L.	
Major-General Bock	1st Dragoons, K.G.L. 2nd ,, ,,	
Major-General Fane	3rd Dragoon Guards 1st (Royal) Dragoons	
Major-General Lord E. Somerset (Hussar Brigade)	10th R. Hussars 15th Hussars	
Brigadier-General D'Urban	1st Portuguese Cavalry 6th ,, ,, 11th ,, ,, 12th ,, ,,	
Colonel Campbell	4th Portuguese Cavalry (not brigaded)	

ARTILLERY

Commanded by Lieut.-Colonel A. Dickson

There were 96 field guns and 6 heavy 18-pounders with the Army in the field, 18 of the field guns being Portuguese. The field guns were at this time distributed as follows:

With Cavalry Brigades	{ Capt. Bean's troop Horse Artillery
	  Major Gardiner's troop Horse Artillery
	  Capt. N. Ramsay's ,, ,, ,,

1st Division	{ Capt. Du Bordieu's brigade Field Artillery, 9-pounders

2nd and Portuguese Divisions	Capt. Maxwell's brigade Field Artillery, 9-pounders Major Cunha's brigade Portuguese Artillery, 6-pounders Capt. Michell's brigade Portuguese Artillery, 9-pounders
3rd Division	Capt. Douglas's brigade, 9-pounders
4th Division	Major Sympher's brigade, 9-pounders, King's German Legion
5th Division	Major Lawson's brigade, 6-pounders (heavy)
6th Division	Capt. Brandreth's brigade, 6-pounders (heavy)
7th Division	Capt. Cairnes' brigade, 9-pounders
Light Division	Major Ross's troop Horse Artillery (The Chestnut Troop), 6-pounders
Reserve Artillery (with Graham's corps)	Lieut.-Colonel Hartmann, K.G.L., Commanding Capt. Webber-Smith's troop Horse Artillery, 9-pounders Capt. Parker's brigade, 9-pounders Major Arriage's brigade (Portuguese), 9-pounders.

With the 18-pounders were two companies of Artillery, Capt. Morrison's and Capt. Glubb's. There were also four other Companies not attached to brigades of guns, one of which was in charge of the reserve ammunition of the Army.

Each troop and brigade had five guns, 9 or 6 pounders, and one $5\frac{1}{2}$-inch howitzer. The 6-pounders were either "heavy" or "light." The Horse Artillery troops had generally one or two "heavy," and the remaining guns "light" 6-pounders, and their establishment of horses, draft and riding, was from 175 to 188.*

ENGINEERS

Commanded by Lieut.-Colonel Sir R. Fletcher

5th, 6th, 7th, and 8th Companies 2nd Battalion Royal Sappers and Miners.

---

* Dickson MSS., Series C, chap. vii., edited by Major J. H. Leslie.

INFANTRY DIVISIONS

First Division

Lieut.-General Sir Thomas Graham, K.B. (commanding a Corps)
Major-General Howard, Commanding

Brigades:

Major-General Hon. E. Stopford
- 1st Coldstream Guards
- 1/3 Guards
- 1 Company 5/60th Rifles

Colonel Halkett
- 1st Line Batt. King's German Legion
- 2nd Line Batt. King's German Legion
- 5th Line Batt. King's German Legion
- 1st Light Batt. King's German Legion
- 2nd Light Batt. King's German Legion

General Howard's brigade—1/1st and 3/1st Guards—temporarily commanded by Colonel P. Maitland, owing to much sickness had been unable to take the field when the campaign opened. The brigade left Oporto on June 29 and rejoined the Division at Oyarzun on August 18, 1813.

2nd Division

Lieut.-General Sir Rowland Hill, K.B. (commanding a Corps)
Lieut.-General Hon. W. Stewart

Brigades:

Lieut.-Colonel Cameron, 92nd, wounded at Maya 25/7/13; then Lieut.-Colonel Fitzgerald, 5/60th (taken prisoner of war, 31/7/13)
- 1/50th Foot
- 1/71st Highland L.I.
- 1/92nd Highlanders
- 1 Company 5/60th Rifles

Major-General Byng
- 1/3rd Foot (Buffs)
- 1/57th Foot
- 1st Provisional Battn. { 2/31st Foot, 2/66th Foot }
- 1 Company 5/60th Rifles

Major-General Pringle
{ 1/28th Foot
2/34th ,,
1/39th ,,
1 Company 5/60th Rifles

Colonel Ashworth
{ 6th Portuguese
18th ,,
6th Caçadores

Portuguese Division : Silveira, Conde de Amaranthe

Brigadier-Gen. Da Costa
{ 2nd Portuguese
14th ,,

Brigadier-General A. Campbell
{ 4th Portuguese
10th ,,
10th Caçadores

3rd Division
Lieut.-General Sir Thomas Picton, K.B.

Brigades :

Major-General Brisbane
{ 1/45th Foot
74th Highlanders
1/88th Connaught Rangers
Headquarters and 3 Cos. 5/60th

Major-General Hon. C. Colville
{ 1/5th Fusiliers
2/83rd Foot
2/87th
94th

Major-General Power
{ 9th Portuguese
21st ,,
11th Caçadores

4th Division
Lieut.-General Hon. Sir G. Lowry Cole, K.B.

Brigades :

Major-General W. Anson
{ 3/27th (Inniskillings)
1/40th Foot
1/48th ,,
2nd Provisional } 2nd Queen's
Battn.   } 2/53rd Foot

Major-General Ross
- 1/7th R. Fusiliers
- 20th Foot
- 1/23rd R. Welsh Fusiliers
- 1 Company Brunswick Oels

Colonel Stubbs
- 11th Portuguese
- 23rd   ,,
- 7th Caçadores

5th Division
Major-General Oswald

Brigades:

Major-General Hay
- 3/1st Royals
- 1/9th Foot
- 1/38th ,,
- 1 Company Brunswick Oels

Major-General Robinson
- 1/4th Foot
- 2/47th ,,
- 2/59th ,,
- 1 Company Brunswick Oels

Major-General Spry
- 3rd Portuguese
- 15th ,,
- 8th Caçadores

6th Division
Major-General D. Pack, wounded July 28, 1813, when Major-General Hon. E. Pakenham assumed temporary command

Brigades:

Major-General Stirling
- 1/42nd Black Watch
- 1/79th Highlanders
- 1/91st Highlanders
- 1 Company 5/60th

Major-General Lambert
- 1/11th Foot
- 1/32nd ,,
- 1/36th ,,
- 1/61st ,,

Brigadier-General Madden
- 8th Portuguese
- 12th ,,
- 9th Caçadores

7th Division
Lieut.-General Earl of Dalhousie, K.B.

Brigades :

Major-General Barnes
- 1/6th Foot
- 3rd Provisional Battn. { 2/24th Foot, 2/58th Foot }
- 9 Companies Brunswick Oels

Major-General Inglis
- 51st Foot
- 68th ,,
- 1/82nd Foot
- Chasseurs Britanniques

Major-General Le Cor
- 7th Portuguese
- 19th ,,
- 2nd Caçadores

Light Division
Major-General Baron Charles Alten

Brigades :

Major-General Kempt
- 1/43rd Light Infantry
- 1/95th Rifles
- 3/95th ,,
- 1st Caçadores

Major-General Skerrett
- 1/52nd Light Infantry
- 2/95th Rifles
- 3rd Caçadores
- 17th Portuguese

Unattached Portuguese Brigades :

Major-General Bradford
- 13th Portuguese
- 24th ,,
- 5th Caçadores

Brigadier-General Wilson
- 1st Portuguese
- 16th ,,
- 4th Caçadores

Royal Staff Corps

Corps of Guides

On July 16, 1813, the strength present under arms (British, Germans, and Portuguese) of the Divisions of the Anglo-Portuguese Army was as follows:

	Officers.	Sergeants.*	Trumpeters and Drummers.*	Rank and File.	Total.
Cavalry Division	410	540	129	7,074	8,153
1st Infantry Division	172	276	96	3,945	4,489†
2nd ,, ,,	389	488	203	7,873	8,953
Portuguese Division	222	216	72	4,274	4,784
3rd Division	260	318	182	4,160	4,920‡
4th ,,	350	319	145	5,781	6,595‡
5th ,,	286	329	133	4,731	5,479
6th ,,	337	365	146	5,924	6,772‡
7th ,,	319	312	129	4,694	5,454
Light ,,	242	279	122	4,096	4,739
Bradford's Portuguese Brigade	126	110	33	1,599	1,868
Wilson's ,, ,,	79	128	61	1,726	1,994
	3,192	3,680	1,451	55,877	64,200

```
Total of all ranks     . . . .    64,200
Add for Artillery and Sappers and Miners, say  4,000
                                              ──────
                                              68,200
In addition to the above there were on this date:
  Sick and wounded     . . . .    20,705
  On command           . . . .     6,528
  Missing and prisoners of war still on
    strength of units  . . . .     2,342
                                              ──────
      Total strength   . . . .    97,775
```

* Except in the Rifle battalions the sergeants and drummers and buglers carried no firearms; the strength of the rank and file therefore practically gives the number of rifles and muskets which could be brought into action.

† Does not include 1st Guards brigade not present in the field.

‡ State on July 14.

Spanish Troops

On September, 22, 1812, Wellington had been appointed by the Cortes Generalissimo of the Spanish Armies.

On July 25, 1813, the following Spanish troops were serving under his immediate command.

4th Spanish Army
Commanded by General Don P. Giron

1st Division		General Don P. Morillo—about Roncevaux
2nd	,,	General Don Carlos de Espana—marching from Burgos towards Pamplona, where it arrived on July 27
3rd	,,	General Don D. del Barco—with Sir T. Graham's Corps, holding line of Bidassoa
4th	,,	General Don P. de la Barcena—with Sir T. Graham's Corps, holding line of Bidassoa
5th	,,	General Don J. Portier—with Sir T. Graham's Corps, holding line of Bidassoa
6th	,,	General Don F. Longa—about Lesaca
7th	,,	General Don G. Mendizabel—part with Sir T. Graham's Corps, remainder with blockade of Santona
8th	,,	General Don E. Mina—about Zaragoza

Excluding Mina and part of Mendizabel's division at Santona effective strength probably about 25,000.

Reserve Army of Andalusia
General the Conde de la Bispal

1st Division		General Don Virues ⎫ blockading Pamplona
2nd	,,	General Don A. Latone ⎭

Strength about 11,000

Cavalry

About 2000 men under Villemar and Julian Sanchez, the latter being with Mina

Appendix B

EFFECTIVE STRENGTH OF FRENCH ARMY, JULY 16, 1813

Strength present under arms of the Army of Spain on July 16, 1813, from reorganization statement sent by Soult to Minister of War (*Armée d'Espagne, Correspondance Militaire, juillet, 1813*).[1]

Division.	Commander.	Brigadiers.	Number of Battalions.	Officers.	Other Ranks.	Officers.	Other Ranks.
	General of Division.	*Right Wing*—LIEUT.-GENERAL COUNT REILLE					
1st	Foy	Fririon / Berlier	9	179	5,228		
7th	Maucune	Pinautau / Montfort	8	140	3,885		
9th	Lamartinière	Gauthier / Menne	12	126	5,926	445	15,039
		Centre—LIEUT.-GENERAL COUNT D'ERLON					
2nd	Darmagnac	Chassé / Gruardet	8	165	6,602		
3rd	Abbé	Rignoux / Remond	8	179	7,348		
6th	Maransin[2]	Baron St. Pol / Moguery	8	132	5,641	476	19,591

4th	Conroux	Rey Schwiter	9	128	6,645		
5th	Vandermaesen	Barbot Rouget	6	119	3,931		
8th	Taupin	Starin de Grave Lecamur	10	163	5,346		
				Total Infantry		410	15,922
						1,331	50,552
1st Cavalry Division	Baron P. Soult			325	3,746		
2nd Cavalry Division	Treilhard			98	1,932		
				Total Cavalry		423	5,678
				Grand Total		1,754	56,230

Reserve Division—GENERAL OF DIVISION, VILLATTE

Thauvenot, French Brigade
Henstein, German " } total Infantry officers and troops 11,654
St. Paul, Italian "
Casapalonist, Spanish "

Certain light cavalry regiments and also artillery (32 guns) were attached to the Reserve Division. With these and sappers, &c., its strength probably was about 15,000.

Garrisons. S. Sebastian, 3,086; Pamplona, 3,124; Santona, 1,674; Bayonne, about 2,000.

The artillery of the Army amounted to 140 guns, 122 field and 18 mountain. In the organization table each division is shown as having a company of foot artillery and one of the train of the artillery for a battery of 8 guns. Cavalry divisions 6 guns. But Soult only took into the field, 66 field and 8 mountain guns.[3] The 13th Chasseurs were attached to the right wing, the 22nd to the centre and 15th to the left wing *pour la service de la ligne et de l'ordonnance*. The transport allowed for each battalion was four bât mules or horses and one for each squadron, and an order was issued that general and other mounted officers were not to take a greater number of horses than allowed by regulation.

[1] In his forwarding letter, Soult says the numbers are to be taken as approximate only.
[2] Maransin commanded in place of Darricau on sick leave.
[3] Baltazar to War Minister. Bayonne July 19, 1813. On the 23rd he wrote, *J'ai vu presque toute l'armée, il est difficile d'imaginer de plus belles troupes.*

Appendix C

ORDER BY MARSHAL SOULT JULY 23, 1813

Olhonce, in front of St. Jean-Pied-de-Port:
23rd July, 1813

Part 1: During the 23rd and 24th an issue of four days' rations in advance will be made to all the troops, and the generals will assure themselves that all ball ammunition which may have been damaged by the recent rain is replaced.

During the afternoon of the 24th Lieut.-Generals Reille and Clausel, also the general commanding the artillery, will make all the necessary preliminary arrangements for the movements which will take place on the morning of the 25th. For this purpose General Reille will assemble the three divisions of the right wing (Foy, Maucune, and Lamartinière) behind the rock of Adarca (or Airóla), placing them so that they cannot be seen by the enemy. He will relieve the troops of General Conroux's division on this rock or in advance of it, also the posts found by this division in the valley of St. Etienne-de-Baigorry; these posts will then be taken up by the national guards of the valley. The eight mountain guns with their personnel and train, which are now with the divisions of the left wing, will be formed into one battery under command of a captain and are placed at General Reille's disposal.

The G.O.C. artillery will send with the right wing column a reserve of sixty thousand rounds of ammunition on mules.

General Clausel will concentrate the division Conroux as soon as it has been relieved by the right wing at the rock of Airóla and in the valley of St. Etienne-de-Baigorry, and will form up the divisions of the left wing on the plateau of the *venta* d'Orizon and on the heights to the left of Arnégui where the division Taupin now is.

He will also tell off a detachment which during the day and the morning of the 25th will move by Beherobie towards the plateau of Iropil to threaten the enemy's right.

During the 24th, General Tirlet will commence to move the artillery on to the plateau in front of the *venta* d'Orizon. Some guns are to be placed in preparatory positions and the rest parked. He will employ for this purpose the teams of oxen which have been placed at his disposal; but will see that the horses follow and that each carriage is accompanied by gunners with tools and drag-ropes to assist in the passage of bad places on the road. The horse artillery batteries which have marched with the divisions of the right wing will be attached to this artillery and are placed at General Tirlet's disposal.

The commandant of the national guards in the Baigorry valley and of that part of the Aldudes we occupy will be ordered to hold himself in readiness with all his available men to move during the night 24th–25th, and seize the mountain called Hausa between the passes of Ispeguy and Berdaritz.

The commandant of the national guards of the valleys of St. Michel, of Lauribar, and of the other valleys on the left will concentrate his men secretly in the most favourable spot to avoid being seen between Beherobie and the plateau of Iropil so as to be ready to advance as soon as ordered to do so.

The detachment sent by General Clausel to manœuvre on our left will join these guards and a good officer is to be appointed to command it.

Lieut.-General D'Erlon will during the 24th make all arrangements so as to be ready to attack the enemy on the 25th, to seize the pass of Maya, and to pursue the enemy as soon as he retreats.

General Villatte will be warned that the army will attack the enemy on the morning of the 25th and that he is to conform in accordance with the instructions I have forwarded to him direct.

Part II: At 4 a.m. on the 25th movement will be general and spontaneous along the whole line. General Reille, with the three divisions of the right wing and the light mountain guns, will advance on Linduz, where he will take up a position, sending immediately advance guards *(têtes de colonne)* in the directions of Ibaneta, Roncevaux and Espinal, also towards the passes of Atalosti and Sahorgain, to seize them or at least to forbid their use to the enemy. He is also to threaten the passes of Urtiaga, Ernazabel, and Velate.

During this movement General Reille's column is to always follow the crest of the mountains, and he will drive back all the enemy's troops opposing him. On arriving at the Linduz he will dispose his troops so as to resist every effort the enemy may make against him. During his march he will take care to watch all the movements of the enemy's troops in the Val Carlos and in the Aldudes, as well as of any which may come from the lake of Ispeguy or from the Baztan Valley and, if occasion arises, threaten their retreat.

He will order the national guards of the valleys of St. Etienne-de-Baigorry and of the Aldudes to seize the Hausa mountain before daylight on the 25th, to extend as much as possible along that mountain, and to light many fires—but not before five o'clock in the morning—and make a great show of movement along the mountain so as to induce the enemy to believe a large number of troops *(immensément de troupes)* are assembled there. These national guards will keep a good look-out towards the pass of Ispeguy, manoeuvring at the same time towards that of Berdaritz in order to gain possession of the pass, or at all events to prevent the enemy using it. As soon as the enemy's retreat permits of their advance, they will push forward always along the crest of the mountains towards the pass of Velate and seize it; thus obliging the enemy's troops in the Baztan valley to retreat by their left and abandon all their *materiel*. The national guards will take all possible measures to harass the enemy and take prisoners. When they see that a division of the centre commanded by General D'Erlon crosses the pass of Maya and moves towards Arizcun and Elisondo, they will send a detachment to meet it, give information, and provide guides. General Clausel will move forward the divisions of the left wing towards the plateau in front of Château-Pignon, where he will form for attack on the position of Alto-Biscar. This position will probably not be strongly defended when the enemy sees he is being turned by the advance of the right wing on the Linduz and also on his right by the movements of the left flank detachment and the national guards, which is to be in the direction of Orbaizeta. General Clausel will vigorously press his attack in order to prevent any reconnaissance by the enemy or any detachments being sent out and to enable prisoners to be made. He will send a detachment into the Val Carlos to push back the enemy's troops now there. The movements of this detachment are to be directed towards the pass of Ibaneta and it is to take all military precautions.

He will order the detachment and the national guards working on his left to concentrate before daylight on the 25th on the plateau of Iropil, where they will light large fires and make demonstrations so as to make the enemy believe a large number of troops are assembled there. He will direct this column to then move on Orbaizeta so as to cause the enemy to believe his right is seriously threatened and that his retreat on Berguete will be cut off unless he promptly abandons the Alto-Biscar position.

When General Clausel has gained possession of Alto-Biscar he will pursue the enemy vigorously, moving by Ibaneta and Roncevaux on Burguete, where he will await further orders. Advanced guards are to be pushed out in all directions and communication with General Reille opened as soon as possible in order that co-operation between the two columns may be assured as soon as they arrive on the same alignment.

Part III: General Tirlet, commanding the artillery, will cause it to follow the movement, and will be prepared to bring as large a number of guns as possible into action as soon as the attack commences.

The general commanding the engineers will send a detachment of fifty sappers with tools with General

Reille's column to be employed in repairing the track in the direction which the column will advance. The remainder of the engineers are to march in front of the artillery and are to be employed unceasingly in repairing the roads.

The Lieutenant-Generals will dispose of the light cavalry regiments under their orders in such manner as they consider best for the service.

Generals Soult and Treilhard will concentrate their cavalry divisions in rear of St. Jean-Pied-de-Port by the morning of the 25th, where they will hold themselves in readiness to advance as soon as ordered. Whilst waiting horses are to be fed, and the generals will arrange that every trooper carries with him at least two days' forage.

As soon as General Soult arrives at St. Jean-Pied-de-Port he will send a detachment into the valley of St. Etienne-de-Baigorry and towards the pass of Ispeguy to watch all that takes place in that direction and to keep up communication with General D'Erlon. As soon as the divisions of the centre debouch frequent reports are to be sent by the officer commanding this detachment.

Part IV: The object of these movements is to force the right of the enemy's line, to seize the position of Alto-Biscar, and to give us command of the principal routes leading towards Pamplona as well as of those passes by which the enemy's troops in the Baztan could retire in that direction.

When these results have been obtained, the divisions of the right and left wings will manœuvre in the direction of Zubiri.

It is to be expected that the enemy's troops now in the Baztan valley, in the Aldudes, and at the passes of

Ispeguy and Maya will either retreat as soon as they obtain information of our movements or that they will manoeuvre as soon as the positions they defend are turned.

General D'Erlon will seize this moment to vigorously attack and carry the pass of Maya; whence he will move by Ariscun on Elizondo and then on the pass of Velate or that of Urtiaga by Berdaritz, according to the direction of the enemy's retreat. *But he will never lose sight of the fact that he is to endeavour to join the rest of the army as soon as possible in the directions already named* and that he is to open communication with General Reille. He will send frequent reports to the Marshal commanding-in-chief, especially by the passes of Ispeguy and Berdaritz as soon as these passes are open.

The Marshal commanding-in-chief will be with the left attack commanded by General Clausel, where all reports are to be sent.

Le Maréchal de L'empire,

Lieutenant-General de l'Empereur,

(Signed) *M^{al}- Duc de Dalmatie*

Appendix D

ANGLO-PORTUGUESE ARMY: STATEMENT OF LOSSES DURING THE OPERATIONS, JULY 25 TO AUGUST 2, 1813

Place, Date and Corps	Killed in action			Wounded			Missing			Total
	Officers	Other Ranks	Total	Officers	Other Ranks	Total	Officers	Other Ranks	Total	
Maya July 25, 1813										
General Staff	—	—	—	2	—	—	—	—	—	2
1/28th Foot	1	8	9	6	112	118	1	31	32	159
2/34th ,,	1	21	22	4	54	58	6	82	88	168
1/39th ,,	2	10	11	7	111	118	2	53	55	186
1/50th ,,	3	21	24	10	158	168	2	55	57	249
1/71st ,,	2	16	18	4	120	124	1	53	54	196
1/92nd ,,	—	34	34	19	268	287	—	22	22	343
1/82nd ,,	—	8	8	4	67	71	—	—	—	79
1/6th ,,	—	2	2	2	17	19	—	—	—	21
B. Oels	—	8	8	3	15	18	—	15	15	41
5/60th Foot	2	5	7	—	11	11	1	25	26	44
Total loss at Maya	11	132	143	61	931	992	13	336	349	1484

The greater part of the missing were killed or so badly wounded that they fell into the hands of the French during the retreat along the ridge. On July 27 Major Balkazar reported to the Minister of War that 100 prisoners from the col de Maya arrived at Bayonne on the afternoon of the 26th.

Place, Date and Corps	Killed in action			Wounded			Missing			Total
	Officers	Other Ranks	Total	Officers	Other Ranks	Total	Officers	Other Ranks	Total	
ALTO-BISCAR AND LINDUZ, *July 25*										
1/7th Foot	1	6	7	—	24	24	—	—	—	31
1/20th ,,	1	14	15	8	105	113	—	11	11	139
1/23rd ,,	—	6	6	4	32	36	—	—	—	42
Portuguese	—	3	3	—	20	20	—	6	6	29
	2	29	31	12	181	193	—	17	17	241[1]
July 26, 1813										
3/27th Foot	—	6	6	2	19	21	—	15	15	42
1/40th ,,	1	3	4	5	84	89	—	—	—	93
1/48th ,,	—	1	1	2	2	4	—	2	2	7
2/53rd ,,	—	—	—	1	14	15	—	—	—	15
5/60th ,,	—	—	—	1	1	2	—	—	—	2
Portuguese	—	1	1	—	3	3	—	—	—	4
Total, July 26	1	11	12	11	123	134	—	17	17	163
SORAUREN, *July 27*										
1/40th Foot	—	—	—	—	8	8	—	—	—	8
2/53rd ,,	—	—	—	—	3	3	—	4	4	7

										Total
5/60th Foot	—	—	—	—	—	—	—	—	—	1
Royal Artillery	—	—	—	—	—	—	—	—	—	1
Total, July 27	2	—	—	—	—	13	18	—	—	17
SORAUREN, *July 28*										
General Staff	—	—	—	2	—	—	—	4	4	4
Royal Artillery	—	1	—	—	6	6	—	—	—	6
2nd Queen's	1	—	1	1	9	10	—	—	—	11
3/3rd Buffs	—	—	—	—	2	2	—	—	—	2
1/7th Foot	1	46	47	10	159	169	1	—	—	217
1/11th „	—	5	5	4	42	46	—	—	—	51
1/20th „	1	23	24	5	79	84	—	—	—	108
1/23rd „	2	16	18	4	59	63	—	—	—	81
3/27th „	2	41	43	9	195	204	7	7	7	254
2/31st „	—	—	—	1	4	5	—	—	—	5
1/32nd „	—	—	—	1	23	24	—	—	—	24
1/36th „	—	—	—	2	16	18	—	—	—	18
1/40th „	1	19	20	4	105	109	—	—	—	129
1/42nd „	—	8	3	—	19	19	—	—	—	22
1/48th „	2	10	12	8	104	112	11	11	11	185
2/53rd „	—	—	—	—	9	9	—	—	—	9
1/57th „	—	2	2	2	59	61	—	—	—	68
5/60th „	—	1	1	—	4	4	—	—	—	5

[1] Casualty Lists do not give returns for other Corps.

Place, Date and Corps	Killed in action			Wounded			Missing			Total
	Officers	Other Ranks	Total	Officers	Other Ranks	Total	Officers	Other Ranks	Total	
SORAUREN *July 28, 1818 (con.)*										
1/61st Foot	—	2	2	2	58	60	—	—	—	62
1/79th ,,	—	4	4	1	30	31	—	—	—	35
1/91st ,,	—	12	12	6	92	98	—	2	2	112
B. Oels	—	1	1	—	3	3	—	1	1	5
Total British	11	186	197	62	1077	1139	1	21	22	1358
Total Portuguese	3	160	163	45	850	895	—	44	44	1102
Total loss July 28	14	346	360	107	1927	2034	1	65	66	2460[1]
July 29 . .	—	—	—	—	—	—	—	—	—	—
SORAUREN AND BEUNZA *July 30, 1813*										
General Staff	—	—	—	1	—	—	—	—	—	1
14th L. Dragoons	—	—	—	—	—	—	—	1	1	1
1st Hussars K.G.L.	—	1	1	1	2	3	—	1	1	4
Royal Artillery	1	3	4	—	8	8	—	—	—	9
3/3rd Foot	—	—	—	1	25	26	—	—	—	30
1/6th Foot	—	—	—	—	5	6	—	1	1	7
1/11th ,,	—	2	2	—	20	20	—	1	1	23
2/24th ,,	—	—	—	—	1	1	—	—	—	1
2/31st ,,	—	2	2	2	23	25	—	—	—	—

Regiment	Killed Off.	Killed Men	Killed Total	Wounded Off.	Wounded Men	Wounded Total	Missing Off.	Missing Men	Missing Total	Grand Total
1/32nd Foot	—	3	3	2	28	30	—	—	—	33
2/34th "	1	5	6	1	15	16	—	9	9	31
1/36th "	—	6	6	1	19	20	—	—	—	26
1/39th "	—	—	—	—	3	3	—	—	—	3
1/40th "	—	—	—	1	6	7	—	—	—	7
1/42nd "	—	1	1	—	7	7	—	—	—	8
1/45th "	—	3	3	1	7	8	—	—	—	8
1/50th "	—	2	2	2	14	16	—	11	11	30
51st "	—	—	—	—	22	22	—	—	—	24
2/53rd "	—	—	—	—	6	6	—	—	—	6
1/57th "	—	2	2	2	33	35	—	—	—	37
2/58th "	—	1	1	—	1	1	—	—	—	2
5/60th Rifles	—	2	2	1	28	29	—	—	—	31
1/61st Foot	—	1	1	2	10	12	—	—	—	13
2/66th "	—	—	—	4	19	23	—	—	—	28
68th "	1	3	4	3	16	19	—	—	—	23
1/71st "	—	8	8	1	28	29	—	13	13	50
74th "	1	6	7	4	38	42	—	—	—	49
1/79th "	—	1	1	—	17	17	—	—	—	18
1/82nd "	—	9	9	7	76	83	—	—	—	92
1/88th "	—	—	—	—	1	1	—	—	—	1
1/91st "	—	1	1	—	7	8	—	—	—	9
1/92nd "	—	9	9	1	26	27	—	1	1	37
Chasseurs Britanniques	1	12	13	1	19	28	—	4	4	45
Brunswick Oels	—	2	2	9	1	1	—	14	14	17
Portuguese	5	89	94	47	544	591	—	57	59	744
	4	138	142	44	799	843	—	185	185	1120
Total July 30th	9	227	236	91	1843	1434	2	192	194	1864

[1] Spanish loss was 192 officers and men.

Place, Date and Corps	Killed in action			Wounded			Missing			Total
	Officers	Other Ranks	Total	Officers	Other Ranks	Total	Officers	Other Ranks	Total	
July 31, 1813										
General Staff	—	—	—	1	—	—	—	—	—	1
1/28th Foot	—	1	1	—	1	1	—	—	—	2
2/34th ,,	—	1	1	—	13	13	—	2	2	16
1/39th ,,	—	—	—	—	4	4	—	—	—	4
1/50th ,,	—	6	6	—	26	26	—	14	14	46
51st ,,	—	5	5	—	40	40	—	6	6	51
1/57th ,,	—	1	1	—	1	1	—	—	—	2
5/60th ,,	—	—	—	—	2	2	1	—	1	3
68th ,,	—	5	5	—	25	25	—	—	—	30
1/71st ,,	—	2	2	1	34	35	—	—	—	37
1/82nd ,,	—	—	—	—	3	3	—	—	—	3
1/92nd ,,	—	12	12	6	69	75	—	4	4	91
Chasseurs Britanniques	—	9	9	1	15	16	—	8	8	33
	—	42	42	9	233	242	1	34	35	319
Portuguese	1	11	12	4	36	40	—	16	16	68
Total July 31	1	53	54	13	269	282	1	50	51	387
August 1										
1/20th Foot	—	1	1	1	5	6	—	—	—	7
1/23rd ,,	—	1	1	—	4	4	—	—	—	5
3/27th ,,	—	1	1	1	14	15	—	—	—	16

	Officers Killed	Sergeants Killed	R&F Killed	Officers Wounded	Sergeants Wounded	R&F Wounded	Officers Missing	Sergeants Missing	R&F Missing	Total
1/40th Foot	—	—	—	—	2	2	—	—	—	2
1/43rd "	—	1	1	—	3	3	—	—	—	4
5/60th Rifles	—	—	—	1	7	8	—	—	—	8
1/88th Foot	—	—	—	—	3	3	—	—	—	3
1/95th Rifles	—	—	—	—	2	2	—	—	—	2
3/95th "	—	3	3	1	5	6	—	1	1	10
Portuguese	—	7	7	4	45	49	—	1	1	57
	—	—	—	—	8	8	—	—	—	8
Total August 1	—	7	7	4	53	57	—	1	1	65
August 2										
General Staff	—	—	1	1	—	1	—	—	—	1
1/6th Foot	1	12	18	3	119	122	—	3	3	138
1/7th "	—	—	—	—	4	4	—	—	—	4
1/20th "	1	—	1	3	26	29	—	—	—	30
1/23rd "	—	—	—	—	3	3	—	1	1	3
2/24th "	—	6	6	3	55	58	—	—	—	65
1/43rd "	—	—	—	—	1	1	—	1	1	1
2/58th "	—	9	9	6	60	66	—	—	—	76
1/95th Rifles	—	1	1	1	10	11	—	—	—	12
3/95th "	—	1	1	—	13	13	—	2	2	14
B. Oels	—	1	1	4	7	11	—	—	—	14
Portuguese	2	30	32	21	298	319	—	7	7	358
	—	1	1	1	7	8	—	—	—	9
Total August 2	2	31	33	22	305	327	—	7	7	367

Total casualties, British and Portuguese, July 25 to August 2, 1813, inclusive.

Place, Date and Corps	Killed in action			Wounded			Missing			Total
	Officers	Other Ranks	Total	Officers	Other Ranks	Total	Officers	Other Ranks	Total	
British	32	522	554	227	3422	3647	17	488	505	4708
Portuguese	8	314	322	94	1725	1817	—	201	201	2340
Total	40	836	876	321	5147	5464	17	689	706	7048

Total casualties in the French army during the same period.

| 101 | 1807 | 1908 | 277 | 8268 | 8545 | 45[1] | 2665[1] | 2710[1] | 13,163 |

Eight per cent. of the Officers of the French Divisions were killed in action and 22½ per cent. of the remainder wounded. In a letter to the Minister of War, September 1, 1813, Soult attributes this heavy loss to the superior marksmanship of the allied Light troops.

[1] Prisoners of War.

Maps

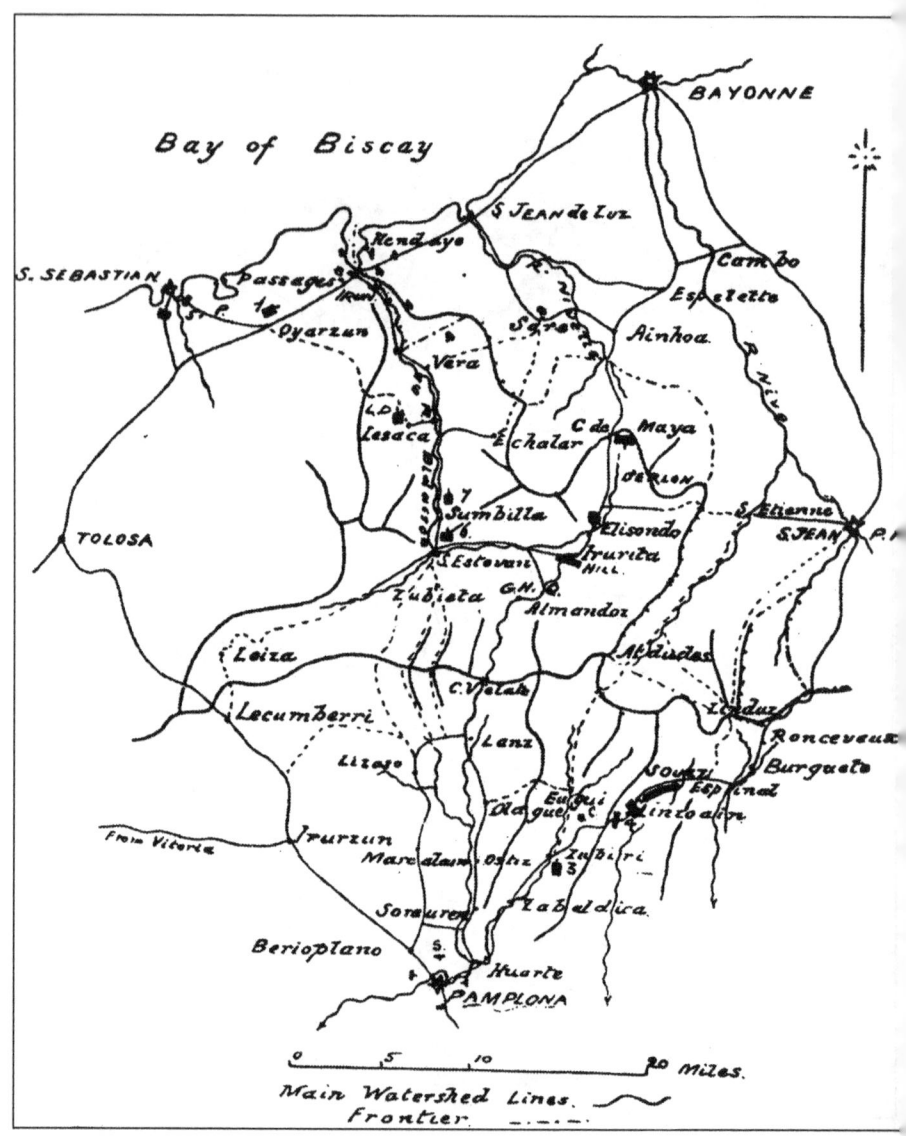

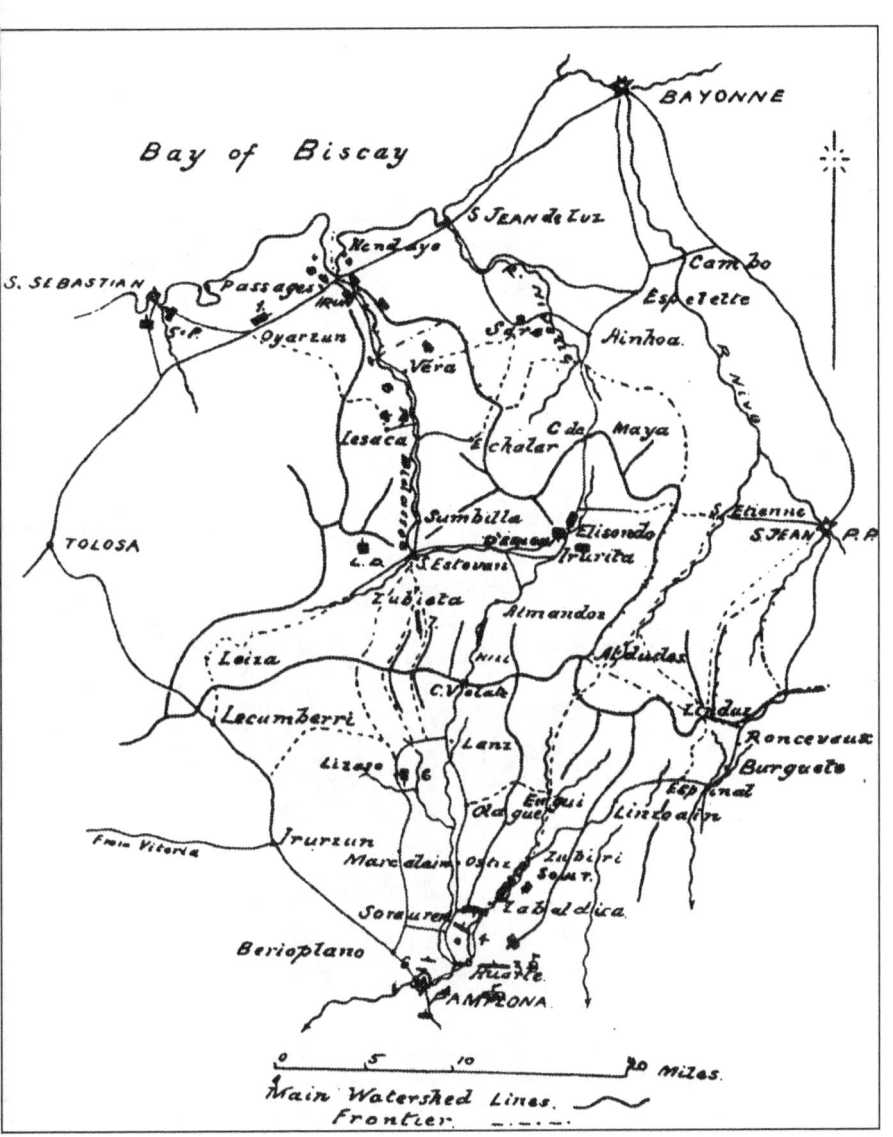

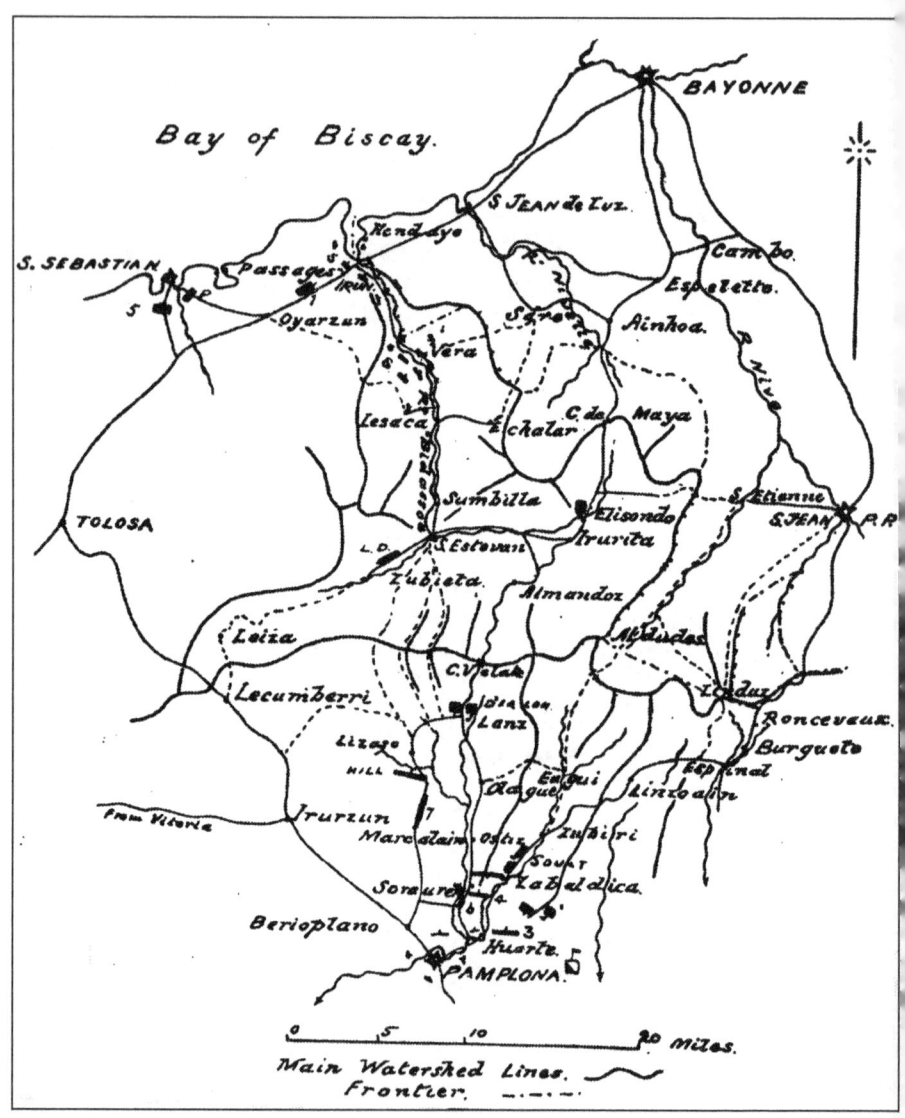

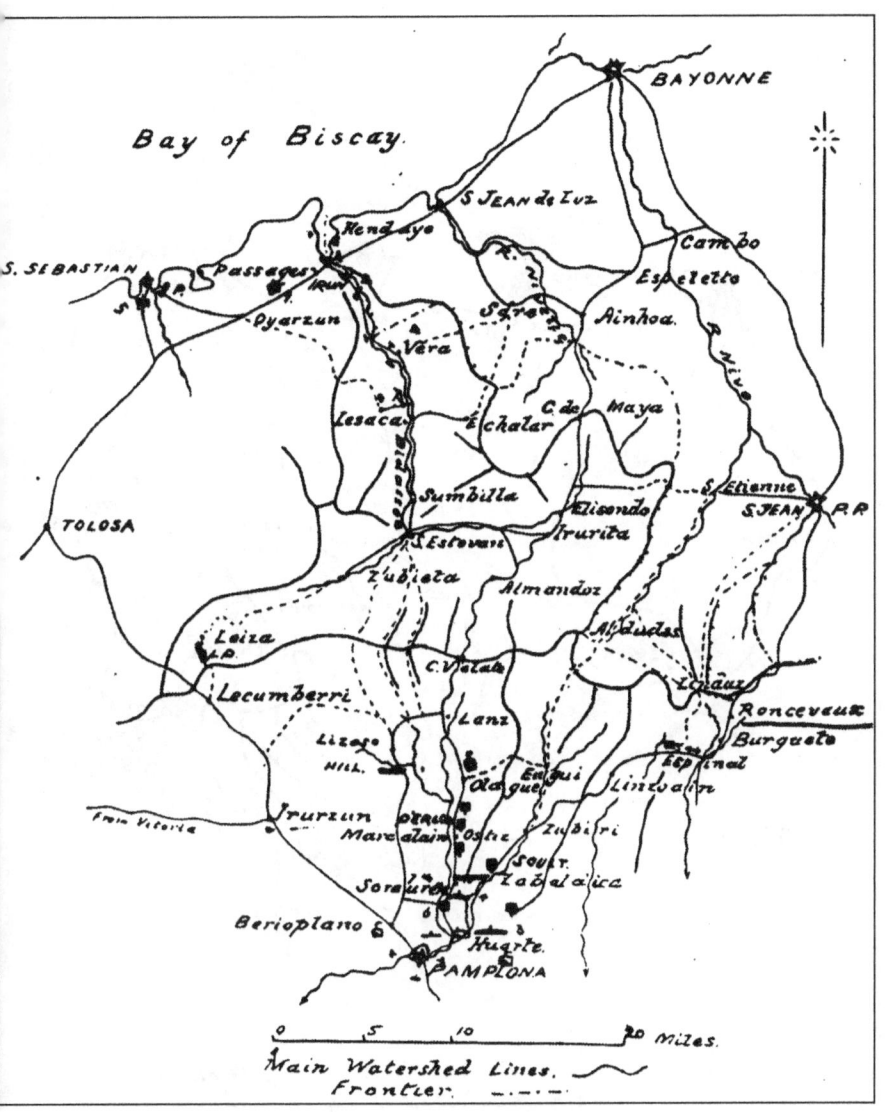

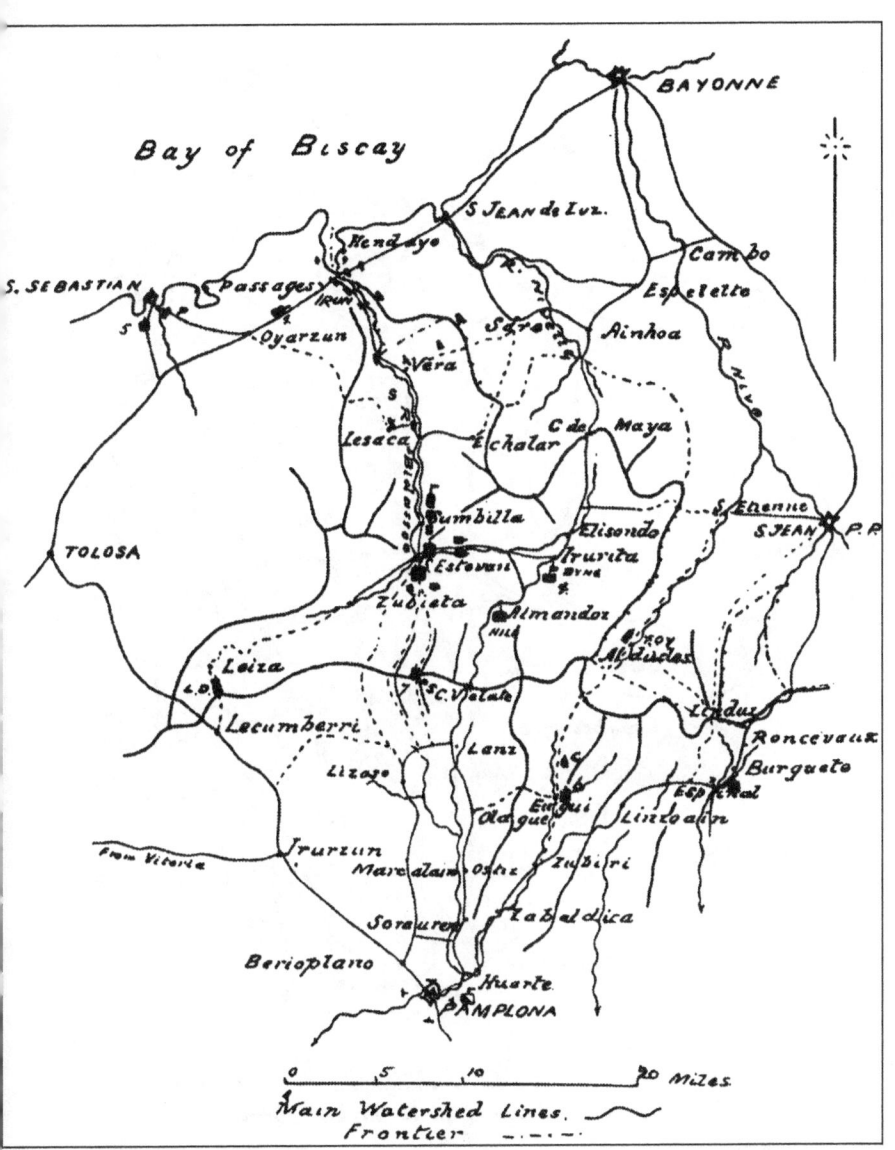

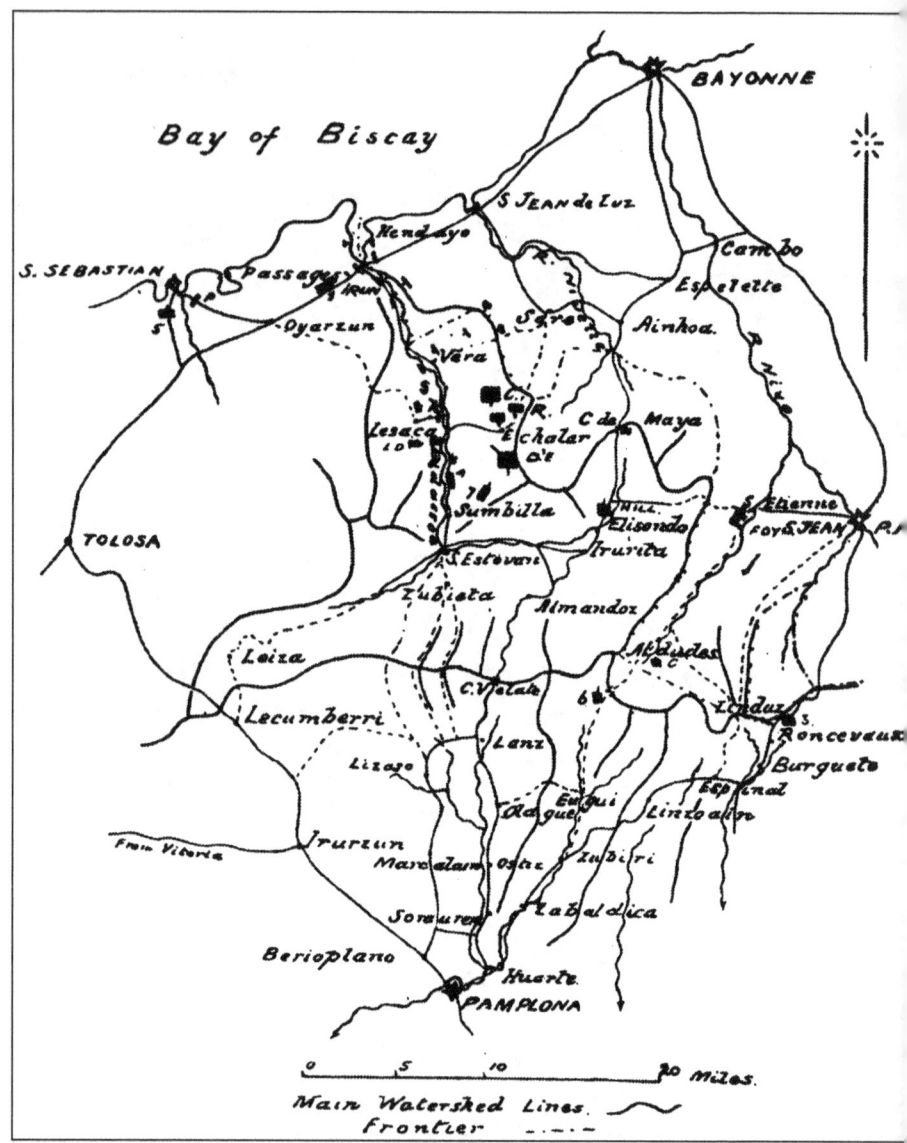

ALSO FROM LEONAUR
AVAILABLE IN SOFTCOVER OR HARDCOVER WITH DUST JACKET

CAPTAIN OF THE 95th (Rifles) *by Jonathan Leach*—An officer of Wellington's Sharpshooters during the Peninsular, South of France and Waterloo Campaigns of the Napoleonic Wars.

THE KHAKEE RESSALAH *by Robert Henry Wallace Dunlop*—Service & adventure with the Meerut volunteer horse during the Indian mutiny 1857-1858

BUGLER AND OFFICER OF THE RIFLES *by William Green & Harry Smith* With the 95th (Rifles) during the Peninsular & Waterloo Campaigns of the Napoleonic Wars

BAYONETS, BUGLES AND BONNETS *by James 'Thomas' Todd*—Experiences of hard soldiering with the 71st Foot - the Highland Light Infantry - through many battles of the Napoleonic wars including the Peninsular & Waterloo Campaigns

A NORFOLK SOLDIER IN THE FIRST SIKH WAR *by J W Baldwin*—Experiences of a private of H.M. 9th Regiment of Foot in the battles for the Punjab, India 1845-46

A CAVALRY OFFICER DURING THE SEPOY REVOLT *by A.R.D. Mackenzie*—Experiences with the 3rd Bengal Light Cavalry, the Guides and Sikh Irregular Cavalry from the outbreak to Delhi and Lucknow

THE ADVENTURES OF A LIGHT DRAGOON *by George Farmer & G.R. Gleig*—A cavalryman during the Peninsular & Waterloo Campaigns, in captivity & at the siege of Bhurtpore, India

THE COMPLEAT RIFLEMAN HARRIS *by Benjamin Harris as told to & transcribed by Captain Henry Curling*—The adventures of a soldier of the 95th (Rifles) during the Peninsular Campaign of the Napoleonic Wars

THE RED DRAGOON *by W.J. Adams*—With the 7th Dragoon Guards in the Cape of Good Hope against the Boers & the Kaffir tribes during the 'war of the axe' 1843-48

THE LIFE OF THE REAL BRIGADIER GERARD - Volume 1 - THE YOUNG HUSSAR 1782 - 1807 *by Jean-Baptiste De Marbot*—A French Cavalryman Of the Napoleonic Wars at Marengo, Austerlitz, Jena, Eylau & Friedland

THE LIFE OF THE REAL BRIGADIER GERARD Volume 2 IMPERIAL AIDE-DE-CAMP 1807 - 1811 *by Jean-Baptiste De Marbot*—A French Cavalryman of the Napoleonic Wars at Saragossa, Landshut, Eckmuhl, Ratisbon, Aspern-Essling, Wagram, Busaco & Torres Vedras

AVAILABLE ONLINE AT
www.leonaur.com
AND OTHER GOOD BOOK STORES

ALSO FROM LEONAUR
AVAILABLE IN SOFTCOVER OR HARDCOVER WITH DUST JACKET

THE COMPLEAT RIFLEMAN HARRIS by *Benjamin Harris as told to & transcribed by Captain Henry Curling*—The adventures of a soldier of the 95th (Rifles) during the Peninsular Campaign of the Napoleonic Wars

WITH WELLINGTON'S LIGHT CAVALRY by *William Tomkinson*—The Experiences of an officer of the 16th Light Dragoons in the Peninsular and Waterloo campaigns of the Napoleonic Wars.

SERGEANT BOURGOGNE by *Adrien Bourgogne*—With Napoleon's Imperial Guard in the Russian Campaign and on the Retreat from Moscow 1812 - 13.

SWORDS OF HONOUR by *Henry Newbolt & Stanley L. Wood*—The Careers of Six Outstanding Officers from the Napoleonic Wars, the Wars for India and the American Civil War, with dozens of illustrations by Stanley L. Wood.

SURTEES OF THE RIFLES by *William Surtees*—A Soldier of the 95th (Rifles) in the Peninsular campaign of the Napoleonic Wars.

ENSIGN BELL IN THE PENINSULAR WAR by *George Bell*—The Experiences of a young British Soldier of the 34th Regiment 'The Cumberland Gentlemen' in the Napoleonic wars.

HUSSAR IN WINTER by *Alexander Gordon*—A British Cavalry Officer during the retreat to Corunna in the Peninsular campaign of the Napoleonic Wars.

NAPOLEONIC WAR STORIES by *Sir Arthur Quiller-Couch*—Tales of soldiers, spies, battles & sieges from the Peninsular & Waterloo campaingns.

JOURNALS OF ROBERT ROGERS OF THE RANGERS by *Robert Rogers*—The exploits of Rogers & the Rangers in his own words during 1755-1761 in the French & Indian War.

KERSHAW'S BRIGADE VOLUME 1 by *D. Augustus Dickert*—Manassas, Seven Pines, Sharpsburg (Antietam), Fredricksburg, Chancellorsville, Gettysburg, Chickamauga, Chattanooga, Fort Sanders & Bean Station..

KERSHAW'S BRIGADE VOLUME 2 by *D. Augustus Dickert*—At the wilderness, Cold Harbour, Petersburg, The Shenandoah Valley and Cedar Creek.

A TIGER ON HORSEBACK by *L. March Phillips*—The Experiences of a Trooper & Officer of Rimington's Guides - The Tigers - during the Anglo-Boer war 1899 - 1902.

AVAILABLE ONLINE AT
www.leonaur.com
AND OTHER GOOD BOOK STORES

ALSO FROM LEONAUR
AVAILABLE IN SOFTCOVER OR HARDCOVER WITH DUST JACKET

SEPOYS, SIEGE & STORM *by Charles John Griffiths*—The Experiences of a young officer of H.M.'s 61st Regiment at Ferozepore, Delhi ridge and at the fall of Delhi during the Indian mutiny 1857.

CAMPAIGNING IN ZULULAND *by W. E. Montague*—Experiences on campaign during the Zulu war of 1879 with the 94th Regiment.

THE STORY OF THE GUIDES *by G. J. Younghusband*—The Exploits of the Soldiers of the famous Indian Army Regiment from the northwest frontier 1847 - 1900..

ZULU: 1879 *by D.C.F. Moodie & the Leonaur Editors*—The Anglo-Zulu War of 1879 from contemporary sources: First Hand Accounts, Interviews, Dispatches, Official Documents & Newspaper Reports.

THE RECOLLECTIONS OF SKINNER OF SKINNER'S HORSE *by James Skinner*—James Skinner and his 'Yellow Boys' Irregular cavalry in the wars of India between the British, Mahratta, Rajput, Mogul, Sikh & Pindarree Forces.

TOMMY ATKINS' WAR STORIES 14 FIRST HAND ACCOUNTS—Fourteen first hand accounts from the ranks of the British Army during Queen Victoria's Empire Original & True Battle Stories Recollections of the Indian Mutiny With the 49th in the Crimea With the Guards in Egypt The Charge of the Six Hundred With Wolseley in Ashanti Alma, Inkermann and Magdala With the Gunners at Tel-el-Kebir Russian Guns and Indian Rebels Rough Work in the Crimea In the Maori Rising Facing the Zulus From Sebastopol to Lucknow Sent to Save Gordon On the March to Chitral Tommy by Rudyard Kipling

CHASSEUR OF 1914 *by Marcel Dupont*—Experiences of the twilight of the French Light Cavalry by a young officer during the early battles of the great war in Europe.

TROOP HORSE & TRENCH *by R. A. Lloyd*—The experiences of a British Lifeguardsman of the household cavalry fighting on the western front during the First World War 1914-18.

THE EAST AFRICAN MOUNTED RIFLES *by C. J. Wilson*—Experiences of the campaign in the East African bush during the First World War.

THE FIGHTING CAMELIERS *by Frank Reid*—The exploits of the Imperial Camel Corps in the desert and Palestine campaigns of the First World War.

AVAILABLE ONLINE AT
www.leonaur.com
AND OTHER GOOD BOOK STORES

ALSO FROM LEONAUR
AVAILABLE IN SOFTCOVER OR HARDCOVER WITH DUST JACKET

EW2 EYEWITNESS TO WAR SERIES
CAPTAIN OF THE 95th (Rifles) *by Jonathan Leach*

An officer of Wellington's Sharpshooters during the Peninsular, South of France and Waterloo Campaigns of the Napoleonic Wars.

SOFTCOVER : **ISBN 1-84677-001-7**
HARDCOVER : **ISBN 1-84677-016-5**

WF1 THE WARFARE FICTION SERIES
NAPOLEONIC WAR STORIES
by Sir Arthur Quiller-Couch

Tales of soldiers, spies, battles & Sieges from the Peninsular & Waterloo campaigns

SOFTCOVER : **ISBN 1-84677-003-3**
HARDCOVER : **ISBN 1-84677-014-9**

EW1 EYEWITNESS TO WAR SERIES
RIFLEMAN COSTELLO *by Edward Costello*

The adventures of a soldier of the 95th (Rifles) in the Peninsular & Waterloo Campaigns of the Napoleonic wars.

SOFTCOVER : **ISBN 1-84677-000-9**
HARDCOVER : **ISBN 1-84677-018-1**

MC1 THE MILITARY COMMANDERS SERIES
JOURNALS OF ROBERT ROGERS OF THE RANGERS *by Robert Rogers*

The exploits of Rogers & the Rangers in his own words during 1755-1761 in the French & Indian War.

SOFTCOVER : **ISBN 1-84677-002-5**
HARDCOVER : **ISBN 1-84677-010-6**

AVAILABLE ONLINE AT
www.leonaur.com
AND OTHER GOOD BOOK STORES

www.ingramcontent.com/pod-product-compliance
Lightning Source LLC
Chambersburg PA
CBHW031624160426
43196CB00006B/272